Additional Praise for
It's More Than Money—It's Your Life!

"Finally we have a manual that spells it out and tells it like it is for women and money. Any woman over 21 who cares about her financial health, well-being, and future must read this book."

—Cherie Carter-Scott, Ph.D.
author of *If Success Is a Game, These Are the Rules: 10 Rules for a Fulfilling Life*

"Money Clubs are a great place for women to get inspiration and take action toward financial security. In this entertaining and easy-to-read guide, Candace and Ginita make dealing with money fun and rewarding."

—Jennifer Openshaw
CEO, Family Financial Network, Founder, Women's Financial Network, and Host, Public Television's *What's Your Net Worth?*

"Finally—a money book you want to read! No stuffy abstract theories here. Instead, lots of specific, concrete ideas on real money issues real women encounter every day. *It's More Than Money* is a breeze to read, with friendly, encouraging language, and lots of laugh-out-loud humor. The book shows you how to save money, make money, and make money your friend. Don't wait another minute—you'll want to get started today!"

—Martha Barletta
author of *Marketing to Women: How to Understand, Reach, and Increase Your Share of the World's Largest Market Segment*

"If you have ever let fear or lack of information keep you from achieving your financial goals, you must read this book today. Candace Bahr and Ginita Wall have written an engaging, user-friendly guide chock full of expert advice, easy-to-use worksheets, and personal stories that will help any woman take small but critical steps to master her finances and become a money star. *It's More Than Money* is a must-read for women who are ready to change their financial lives and anyone who wants to get the most out of their money."

—Derek T. Dingle
Vice President and Executive Editor, *Black Enterprise* magazine

"This book is a 'must-read' for anyone serious about their money. The stories will inspire you, and the step-by-step expert advice makes financial success achievable. Read it and share it with friends. Candace and Ginita have created a wonderfully warm and dynamic book that can make a difference in your life!"

—Victoria Collins, Ph.D., CFP®
coauthor of *Best Intentions: Ensuring Your Estate
Plan Delivers Both Wealth and Wisdom*

"Candace Bahr and Ginita Wall have successfully guided women to financial security for 25 years. Now, through the Money Clubs, they've provided a roadmap and a toolkit for all to reach that destination. Stop struggling with money on your own, join friends to share the wealth of your growing knowledge, and celebrate the new, more financially confident you."

—Ann Perry
author of *The Wise Inheritor: A Guide to Managing,
Investing, and Enjoying Your Inheritance*

"The concept of a Money Club resonates with women because it is a safe and supportive environment to learn how to make, manage, and invest your money. Candace and Ginita do a great job helping women understand their economic life. Get your friends together and start a Money Club right now!"

—Nancy Dailey, Ph.D.
author of *When Baby Boom Women Retire*

IT'S MORE THAN MONEY— IT'S YOUR LIFE!

The New Money Club for Women

CANDACE BAHR, CEA, CDS
GINITA WALL, CPA, CFP®, CDS

WILEY

John Wiley & Sons, Inc.

Published by John Wiley & Sons, Inc., Hoboken, New Jersey.
Published simultaneously in Canada.

For general information on our other products and services, or technical support, please contact our Customer Care Department within the United States at 800-762-2974, outside the United States at 317-572-3993 or fax 317-572-4002.

Wiley also publishes its books in a variety of electronic formats. Some content that appears in print may not be available in electronic books.

For more information about Wiley products, visit our web site at www.wiley.com.

Library of Congress Cataloging-in-Publication Data:

Bahr, Candace.
    It's more than money—it's your life: the new money club for women/ Candace Bahr and Ginita Wall.
        p. cm.
Includes index.
    ISBN 0-471-44974-1 (CLOTH)
    1. Women—Finance, Personal. I. Wall, Ginita. II. Title.
    HG179.B267 2004
    332.024'0082—dc22

                                                                2003018291

Printed in the United States of America

10 9 8 7 6 5 4 3 2 1

We dedicate this book to our parents,
Howard and Beatrice Bahr, and Theodore and Gina Allen.
They gave us encouragement to pursue our dreams,
and the belief we were capable of accomplishing anything.
These are gifts above all monetary riches.

To women everywhere, these things we wish for you:
To prosper through giving, to grow as you inspire.
To accept the abundance that good friends offer.
To create enduring worth for the world.

Acknowledgments

No book is ever the result of the authors' efforts alone. We have been fortunate to have many people around to encourage and support us through the process.

We couldn't have written this book without the diligent efforts of Leslie Rosenberg, who helped us crystallize our ideas and capture them on paper. Thanks also to Jessica Richman who lent her creative wit to this project at a time when we needed her most. WIFE.org and the Money Clubs have benefited greatly from the talents of our web master extraordinaire, David Barnett. Karla Swatek, book publicist and ever-supportive friend, continues to be invaluable in helping us get the word out. And special thanks to Maru Corrada, who started the very first Money Club, and now volunteers her time to help others start clubs of their own.

We are indebted to those close to us who not only listened but gave us sage advice and pitched in when we needed them: Terri Bernhardt, Brian Crogan, Denise Raines, and Kay Weston. Candace is especially grateful for the support and encouragement of her husband, John, who held down the fort at home and at the office and still managed time to read page after page of manuscript, and for the inspiration and insights of her wonderful daughter Carrie, who has wisdom beyond her years.

Thanks to Candace's sisters, Beatrice Mann and Merry Hirons, who were there to help out and serve as willing sounding boards, and to her sisters-in-law Marilyn Kemp, Joanne Goetzinger, and Carol Drosdeck, who always offer support. Special thanks to Mary Baranowski, the perfect model of what every mother-in-law should be. And thanks also to Al and Lillian Rosenfeld, and their daughter, Shana, who provided us shelter, sustenance, and wonderful hospitality on our trips to New York.

We extend our gratitude to those wonderful women who helped test Money Club materials and concepts in focus groups—we had such fun those evenings, and we learned a lot about ourselves and each other. Thank you, Lerena Barbe, Valerie Brown, Sharon Dodson, Edith Fine, Nancy Gordon, Linda Howard, Rhonda Jimerson, Julie Johnson, Maria Katona, Marianne Kripps, Michele Larez, Connie Leigh, Felicia Lewis, Joy Martin, Mary Ann Neis, Ann Perry, Claire Plotner, Rory Powell, Suzi Resnik, Lesley Seaton, Alice Solovay, Viki Turnipseed, and Megan Wilfong. For their constant enthusiasm, thanks to Virginia Ann Hodge and Kelly Ferrin.

For their passion, vision, and unfailing support, we thank Rosetta Jones and Randa Ghnaim of VISA; Deb Sandgren, Tom Topinka, and Janice Luvera of General Electric; Meggan Lennon and the gang at Peppercom.

Thanks to those who encouraged us as we incubated and hatched the Money Club concept: our agents Mike Larsen and Elizabeth Pomada, our editor Debra Englander, Col. Marcus Beauregard, Cynthia Silbert, and the folks at America Saves. Judy Chapa, while at the U.S. Treasury, saw the powerful potential in Money Clubs and helped us connect the dots.

Most of all, we thank our loyal clients as well as the members of WIFE. We learned so much from all of you. Your stories have provided wonderful insights for this book and the Money Clubs.

To all of you, our heartfelt thanks.

Contents

PART ONE

Money Truths
and Dreams

CHAPTER 1

How to Become a Money Star

> *Dear WIFE,*
>
> *Help! I just opened my retirement statement and it hit me: It's not going to be enough. I can't seem to get ahead. My friends are in the same boat. We aren't experts at money management, so how can we encourage and support each other to get a grip on our financial lives? We've helped each other through relationships, raising children, and career problems, but when it comes to financial matters, we just don't know where to start.*
>
> *Seeking Guidance in St. Louis*
>
> *Dear Seeking,*
>
> *Welcome to the Club! One of the incredible strengths of women is our ability to support each other and learn from each other. You don't need a financial guru to tell you what to do. As you read on, you will learn how you and your friends can use your combined strengths to realize your financial dreams. The power is already in your hands. Read on, and amazing things will happen!*

Every Woman Needs a Wife

We've answered many letters like this over the years. In 1988, when we founded the nonprofit Women's Institute for Financial Education, we chose the acronym WIFE intentionally. Isn't it often the wife who counsels and empowers, listens and advises? That is our mission, to empower you to succeed and prosper. We are here as your support and guides. You've got a WIFE.

We are here to help—and to assure you that you're not alone. As you read this book, you'll learn the stories of many women we've helped through WIFE and the Money Clubs. To ensure privacy, we have changed names and some details but the stories are all real. It is our hope that you will take the elements of these stories and apply the principles to your own lives.

Our Stories

There is tremendous power in helping each other. Over the years, we've been fortunate enough to find people who have believed in us and who share our vision. It is that combined energy that creates success. It worked for us, and it can work for you.

Our backgrounds aren't so different from most women.

Candace Bahr

I grew up in the Midwest, the middle daughter of three girls. My father was a cabinet-maker and my mother was a housewife. I didn't realize at the time how fortunate I was that my family openly discussed money (and often even shouted about it!). I now recognize that I had a tremendous advantage. While many women have been sheltered from money matters and are uncomfortable around money, I gained the confidence early on that I could be financially capable.

For more than 20 years, I have managed money for individuals of high net worth. Most of my clients are women who have gone through a transition, such as the heartrending death of a husband or an unfortunate divorce.

But it isn't just the wealthy who need advice. In reality, the less money you have, the more careful you must be. Through WIFE and the Money Clubs, I can share my knowledge and hands-on experience with lots of people who ordinarily wouldn't have access to my services.

I have been happily married to my husband, John, for almost 25 years, and we've worked together for more than 20 of those years! Obviously, we don't tiptoe around financial issues, and we strive to teach our teenage daughter, Carrie, that she can accomplish whatever she sets her mind to do.

Ginita Wall

My professional life as a financial planner has been devoted to helping people in transition, such as divorce or widowhood. When I moved to San Diego in 1987, after selling my large CPA firm in New Mexico, Candace was one of the first people I met. We immediately recognized that we had the same passion to help women, and together we started WIFE.

From an early age, I recognized my career path. I grew up on a dairy farm in New Mexico, the only child of two strong, independent parents. My father was a

Ph.D. and former college professor who decided to follow his dream of becoming a farmer around the time I was born. My mother was a novelist and an early feminist in the fifties and sixties who fought hard for women's rights.

My dad taught me about money. I fondly recall sitting at the kitchen table as he showed me how to read the business pages. When I became a teenager, I even started a business of my own raising chickens and selling the eggs through local grocery stores. Now, in my professional life, I've gone from selling eggs to creating nest eggs for people!

***

As you see, the two of us came together from different backgrounds. Our meeting was serendipitous. We all attract people into our lives who have the ability to help us grow and learn. From that concept of synergy comes the idea for the Money Clubs. Women in groups create a powerful and vibrant framework of support. In fact, most women like cooperation even more than chocolate!

"Our own success, to be real, must contribute to the success of others."

ELEANOR ROOSEVELT

A recent study at Emory University used an MRI brain scan during an experiment that involved alternating cooperation and conflict. The (male) scientists thought that conflict would bring more pleasure. To their surprise, they found just the opposite: Women's brains visibly light up when they cooperate rather than compete. The longer the women in the experiment engaged in a cooperative strategy, the more strongly the blood flowed to pathways of pleasure.

Scientists have long puzzled over the biological basis for women's simple niceness and cooperation. This new study may explain women's well-known attraction to group endeavors. Women have been helping women succeed in every land and every age—with everything from child rearing to weight loss. And now we know why. We're wired for it!

That's the concept behind the Money Club. The Money Club offers an exciting way to help yourself and your friends learn about money. It's completely free and nonfattening, and it will give you a chance to spend time with your friends. You can share ideas, good times, and even some chocolate.

You Are Not Alone—Join the Club

We go to health clubs to work out, we join book clubs and gather to play bunco. We join groups when we diet. It's been proven that this is a far more powerful way to succeed than going it alone. Yet isn't it odd that when it comes to money, we often struggle with it all by ourselves?

The Money Club is a way for women to have fun, take control, and change their lives. Amazing things happen in Money Clubs! The support of other Money Club members gives you a sense of community and belonging. With friends to assist you and keep you on track, you can help each other in a powerful, productive way. You are accountable to each other, and that keeps you motivated. Just as having a diet buddy helps you lose weight, your friends in the Money Club can provide the encouragement you need to succeed in securing your financial future.

"Alone we can do so little; together we can do so much."

HELEN KELLER

The Money Club is not your grandmother's investment club. In the 1990s, almost 700,000 people, mostly women, belonged to investment clubs. Jennifer was one of those women. She had been coaxed to join by a friend at work, and she enjoyed the camaraderie she found there. But because most of the discussions focused on buying and selling stocks, she felt it didn't address her needs.

Jennifer wanted more. She wanted to learn how to save money, pay off credit cards, shop for a mortgage, and achieve other goals that affected her daily financial life. Most importantly, she wanted to understand how money could help her accomplish her many dreams. When she heard about the Money Club, she was jazzed. It was exactly what she was looking for. She instinctively understood that as she and her friends explored what each of them wanted, they would help each other enrich their lives. That's a win-win attitude: If I help you win, I win too.

Through the Money Club, we have devised a way you can harness the power of the group to help you succeed financially. The Money Club is based on the ancient premise that the combined energy of several people focusing on the same problem is many times greater than the sum of individual energies involved. This concept has been used at high-level business meetings and in boardrooms around the country for years.

You don't have to know much about money to join a club. You just need a desire to improve your relationship with money. The Money Club is a grassroots phenomenon. Women (and men, too) create Money Clubs themselves using the framework and materials in this book and at the web site www.MoneyClubs.com. Amazing things happen in Money Clubs!

Money Truths and Dreams Questionnaire

This book is the beginning of your money journey, whether you join a Money Club or choose to travel the path alone. The Money Truths and Dreams questionnaire will provide insight into your feelings about money. It will show you where you stand, get you thinking and talking about your financial life, and help you determine about what areas you want to learn. At each question, we point you to the appropriate chapters in this book where you can learn more.

Each of these questions relates to a *Money Zone,* an area or interest in your financial life. Use Questionnaire 1.1 to figure out where you are right now. Don't be afraid to explore the truth about money. Remember, this is a snapshot. It's not a measure of your net worth or self-worth!

Though this questionnaire may take a few minutes to complete, it is worth it. Many women have told us that the Money Truths and Dreams questionnaire was pivotal in laying the groundwork for their financial journey. There are no right or wrong answers, so answer these questions honestly. The answers may not describe your situation exactly, but circle the one that comes closest to where you are right now. This is a guide to get you thinking. If the question doesn't apply to you, just ignore it.

We've left room at the bottom of every other page of the questionnaire for you to jot notes to yourself. What would you like to change or improve? If there's a disconnection between what you think you want and where you find yourself right now, write yourself a note. Don't edit or judge what you are writing—you can go back and clarify it later. You might currently feel stuck, but as you become clear about what you *really* want, you'll unleash an energy that will propel you forward along the path that leads from where you are to where you want to be.

After you have completed the Money Truths and Dreams questionnaire, go back over it again. Put a checkmark next to the topic headings for each question for which you circled *A* (Money Star-ter) or *B* (Getting There), or about which you made notes. By doing this, you are identifying the topics that resonate with you and that will help you improve your life.

Let this questionnaire be your guide to reading this book. At first, you may want to zero right in on the chapters that you've checked to find the answers that are key to you. Then read the book carefully from beginning to end for a complete 360-degree view of your financial life. You can also use your Money Truths and Dreams questionnaire to identify the Money Zones (areas of interest in your financial life) you would like to see covered in your Money Club, if you are in one.

In the future, as you learn more and progress through the chapters in this book, revisit the corresponding questions in the quiz. If your answer has improved, congratulations! Perhaps you moved up from your initial *A* answer (Money Star-ter) to *B* (Getting There). You might even skip from *A* to *C* sometimes. Amazing things really do happen in the Money Club!

"Life is what we make it; always has been, always will be."

GRANDMA MOSES

Questionnaire 1.1

Money Truths & Dreams

Couples and Money
(learn more in Chapters 2 and 13)

    1. Do you and your mate communicate well about money matters?

       a. When the subject of money comes up, it ends up sparking a disagreement.

       b. We don't talk much about money, but we don't fight much about it either.

       c. We communicate openly about our finances and together plan for the future.

Your Money Style
(learn more in Chapter 3)

    2. Do you know your money style?

       a. I think I'm a Libra.

       b. I know it affects my finances, but I don't think about it much.

       c. I know my strengths and weaknesses and try to improve upon them.

Fighting Your Money Fears
(learn more in Chapter 3)

    3. What are your emotional responses to money?

       a. I am paralyzed with fears and unmotivated to achieve my goals.

       b. I have some worries, but I generally feel okay.

       c. I feel in control almost all of the time, and I am moving forward toward my financial dreams.

Money Attitudes from Your Childhood
(learn more in Chapter 3)

    4. Are you aware of how your childhood money attitudes affect your current financial experience?

        a. No, I don't remember many money issues from my childhood. Anyway, there's nothing I can do about it now.

        b. I catch myself occasionally responding to money in negative ways from my childhood, but mostly I am doing okay.

        c. I understand how my attitudes were shaped, and I've done my best to maximize the positives and defuse unhealthy attitudes.

Careers
(learn more in Chapter 4)

    5. Are you happy with the direction your career is taking?

        a. As far as I'm concerned, work is a four-letter word.

        b. I have a steady job that pays the bills, but it's not particularly fulfilling.

        c. I challenge myself daily with a career I enjoy that provides sufficient income for my needs.

Notes

Questionnaire 1.1 *(continued)*

Earning Money Without a Job
(learn more in Chapter 4)

6. Do you have creative ideas to add to your income?

   a. Nothing legal.

   b. No, I wish I knew some interesting ways to make extra income.

   c. I have a home-based or part-time business that adds significantly to my income.

Net Worth
(learn more in Chapter 5)

7. Do you know your approximate net worth (the total of your assets minus the total of your liabilities)?

   a. Huh?

   b. I'm doing okay, but I haven't really figured it out.

   c. Yes, of course, down to the penny.

Budgeting
(learn more in Chapter 5)

8. Do you know your monthly household income and living expenses?

   a. If I get some of the bills paid by the end of the month, I'm doing pretty well.

   b. I have a rough idea, but I'm not always mindful of my spending.

   c. I have a written budget, and I stick to it.

Saving
(learn more in Chapter 5)

    9. Do you save at least 10 percent of your monthly income?

       a. I'm so swamped with debt I can't even think of saving.

       b. I don't save 10 percent, but I try to save something most months.

       c. Actually, I save more than 10 percent of my monthly income.

Getting Organized
(learn more in Chapter 5)

    10. Do you know where all of your important financial papers are located?

       a. In my house, I think.

       b. Yeah, in a big pile. (I really am going to get organized someday.)

       c. I have a filing cabinet with all of my paid and pending bills and permanent records, as well as a safe deposit box.

Notes

Questionnaire 1.1 *(continued)*

Buying or Leasing a Car
(learn more in Chapter 5)

11. Are you confident in your skills to buy or lease a car?

   a. I just pay whatever the salesperson tells me.

   b. I try, but I always end up feeling ripped off.

   c. I go into the negotiation fully informed, and I usually get what I want.

Cutting Expenses
(learn more in Chapter 5)

12. Do you live within your means?

   a. I live within my credit limit—isn't that the same thing?

   b. I try to stay out of debt when possible.

   c. I spend wisely in line with my priorities and beliefs, and I have money set aside for emergencies and charitable giving.

Banking
(learn more in Chapter 5)

13. Do you know how to choose the best bank and bank accounts for your needs?

   a. I use the International Bank of Mattress.

   b. I just choose from whatever my local bank offers.

   c. I choose the banks that have the best programs that fit my lifestyle and goals.

Buying a House
(learn more in Chapter 6)

14. Do you own your own home?

    a. I don't own a home, but I'd like to someday.

    b. I own a home, but I'm not entirely satisfied.

    c. I have a home, and it suits my family perfectly.

Mortgages
(learn more in Chapter 6)

15. Do you know how to choose the mortgage that is right for you?

    a. I just let the friendly local loan officer tell me what to do.

    b. I checked out some radio ads and Internet listings and found a mortgage that seems pretty good.

    c. I have chosen a mortgage that suits my needs—and I shop mortgages every year or so to see if I am still getting the best deal.

Notes

Questionnaire 1.1 *(continued)*

Insurance
(learn more in Chapter 7)

16. Do all members of your family have adequate insurance?

    a. No, I haven't gotten around to it.

    b. I have some insurance, but I'm not sure what it covers or if it's enough.

    c. Of course. We have adequate insurance for all of our needs, and review our insurance coverage each year.

Investing
(learn more in Chapter 8)

17. Do you know what your savings and investing objectives are?

    a. I don't have savings and I don't invest, so it doesn't matter.

    b. My objectives: save as much as I can and don't lose money on my investments.

    c. I regularly do a risk tolerance and asset allocation analysis to be sure my investments grow to meet my needs.

Reading the Financial News
(learn more in Chapter 8)

18. Are you confident in your knowledge of finances and the economy?

    a. There's so much information, I really don't know where to begin.

    b. I try to keep up but everything else in my life seems to take precedence.

    c. I read and understand at least one financial publication each month and keep up on current events.

Finding an Advisor
(learn more in Chapter 8)

19. Do you have relationships with good financial, legal, and tax professionals?

    a. Mostly, I just wing it. I don't have enough money for that.

    b. I know I need professional help, but I'm not completely comfortable with the advisors I'm using.

    c. I meet with my professional team as often as I need to do so. Their advice has been invaluable over the years.

Education Planning
(learn more in Chapter 9)

20. Do you have a plan to pay for your children's education?

    a. Plans? *What* plans?

    b. I could use some education myself in that area.

    c. Yes, I am saving, and I know all about the new educational plans that are available.

Notes

Questionnaire 1.1 *(continued)*

Retirement Planning
(learn more in Chapter 9)

21. Are you contributing the maximum to a retirement account in your own name?

    a. No, I never could understand those things.

    b. I'm contributing some, but it's probably not enough.

    c. Yes, I contribute as much as I need to so that I can retire comfortably.

Credit Card Debt
(learn more in Chapter 10)

22. Do you have credit card debt?

    a. How could I forget? I'm juggling as fast as I can, but I'm making very little progress.

    b. I am paying on each card every month, but the balances aren't going down fast enough to suit me.

    c. I am debt-free. Yay!

Establishing/Repairing Credit
(learn more in Chapter 10)

23. Do you have a good credit rating?

    a. I don't know; I'm afraid to look.

    b. I got my credit report, but I'm not sure how to improve my rating.

    c. I check my credit report each year to see if there are any errors, and I've taken steps to improve my FICO score.

Divorce
(learn more in Chapter 11)

24. If you are divorced, are you confident in your new financial situation?

   a. What do you mean, confident? I'm living on half of what I had before!

   b. I am learning to cope with my new situation.

   c. I have used the crisis of divorce to make changes that will improve my life.

Widowhood
(learn more in Chapter 12)

25. If you are widowed, are you confident in your new financial situation?

   a. Every time I start to deal with it, I just freeze.

   b. I go through the papers a little bit at a time.

   c. I am now more in control of my finances than ever.

Notes

Questionnaire 1.1 *(continued)*

Social Security
(learn more in Chapter 12)

26. Do you know your projected retirement benefits from Social Security?

    a. Nope.

    b. Don't they send those statements to me every once in a while? Where is that piece of paper?

    c. Yes, I read it and checked to make sure there were no errors in my earnings record.

Estate Planning
(learn more in Chapter 12)

27. Do you have a plan to take care of your loved ones after you are gone?

    a. I don't need one. I have a bumper sticker that says it all: I'm spending my kids' inheritance!

    b. I have a will somewhere, but I don't know where it is, and it was written so long ago that it may not even apply anymore.

    c. I have a will, living trust, power of attorney, health care directive, and other estate planning documents.

Providing for Parents
(learn more in Chapter 14)

28. Do you have a plan to care for your parents if they need help?

    a. Sure, it's called the government.

    b. My family hasn't come up with any workable solutions.

    c. Our family has discussed it and decided on a solution that meets our needs.

Financial Generosity
(learn more in Chapter 15)

29. Do you feel a sense of financial generosity?

    a. I've barely got enough for myself, never mind helping someone else.

    b. Charity begins at home. If relatives or friends need help, I try.

    c. I give money to charity, and I know how it's being used by the charity.

Kids and Money
(learn more in Chapter 15)

30. Do your children know how to handle money?

    a. No, they always come to me when they run short.

    b. Better than I did at their age.

    c. I am teaching them how to be Money Stars!

Notes

Questionnaire 1.1 *(continued)*

Using the Internet for Financial Education
(Appendix B)
  31. Do you know how to use the Internet and other resources
     for financial information?

     a. No, but I can find movie show times in my area in under
        five minutes flat. Impressive, isn't it?

     b. Well, I know how to find some things, but I don't really
        know what I need to know, so how can I find it?

     c. I know how to find whatever I need.

Scoring:
Add up your *A*s (Money Star-ter), *B*s (Getting There), and *C*s
(Money Star). Give yourself five points for every *B* answer and 10
points for every *C*.

*A*s _____ × _____ 0 = _____

*B*s _____ × _____ 5 = _____

*C*s _____ × _____ 10 = _____

Total   _____

Rating:

200 and above: You are well on the road to financial success. Use
this quiz to identify possible areas in which you can improve or
push yourself to even greater levels of financial acumen. Take the
lead in starting a Money Club so you can assist others who might
need a little help.

150 to 200: You are above average in your financial prowess. Identify
the areas that need improvement, and review those chapters of this
book to improve your financial skills. Start or join a Money Club to
hone your own skills and help others improve theirs.

100 to 150: You will need some help with your financial management skills. Start by reading this book in its entirety. Don't expect to be perfect. As you read and learn, take the quiz again to gauge your progress.

Below 100: You are heading into a danger zone and need to gather some facts about your present situation right away. Read this book carefully, fill in the worksheets, and take the quiz again. As you improve, you'll gain knowledge and confidence.

Small Steps to Becoming a Money Star

1. Get a notebook to use for the exercises in this book, in which you can jot notes to yourself. As you progress through this book, your Financial Security Notebook will chronicle how far you've come and will serve as a blueprint for your financial future.

2. Go back to the Money Truths and Dreams questionnaire. Look at the questions you answered with an *A* (Money Star-ter). Pick two or three areas you would like to improve on, and pick one or two small steps you can do in 15 minutes or less. (You can do anything for 15 minutes!) Focus on these areas, and later you can work on the others. You can't do everything all at once.

3. Write down your worst money fears. Once you have made your list, decide which fears are real, and which fears are beyond your control. Cross out the ones beyond your control. As you read this book, you can develop a plan to deal with your fears. Move past the fear and watch your whole world change.

4. Make a list of some of your best attributes and skills. Each day, choose one attribute on which to concentrate. Write it into the blank on this affirmation: "I am _____, and with each day, I am wiser, stronger, and more self-confident." Tape this affirmation to your mirror. Say it to yourself throughout the day.

5. As you read this book, think about friends with whom you'd like to share this information and who can act as a support system for you or join with you in a Money Club. Write their names here _____ _____ _____ _____ _____ _____

CHAPTER 2

The Truth About Women and Money

> Dear WIFE,
>
> Last year I married a wonderful man with two young children. I think I'm hap-pily married, but life is so much more complicated now. My husband says that marrying me was the best thing he ever did, and I agree—he's got me to help take care of the kids, to shop and cook, and to comfort him when he's had a bad day. Now my husband thinks I need to get more involved in handling the family fi-nances. Help!
>
> Frazzled in St. Louis
>
> Dear Frazzled,
>
> WIFE understands your dilemma. When a man takes a wife, he marries some-one to help him climb the ladder toward success. When a woman marries, she's taking on much more responsibility. You've discovered the dirty little secret of women's lives: behind every successful woman is a basket of dirty laundry wait-ing to be done and a family waiting to be fed. But your husband has a point. For your own sake, understanding the family finances is one of the most important things you can do. And it isn't that tough.

Women and Money

Whether you are single or married, life is much more complicated than it was in grandma's day. Women's relationships with men and money are more complex than ever before. The World War II generation revered stay-at-home moms and breadwinner dads who had company pensions to support them in their "golden years."

The rest of us are caught in the middle. Costly corporate pensions have been axed, expensive homes require two incomes to support, and easy access to credit cards is far too tempting. Here are some of today's truths about women and money.

Truth #1 A Man Is Not a Financial Plan

Whether you are married, single, or somewhere in between, you can't depend on Prince Charming. All marriages end in either death or divorce, and many women never marry at all. As a result, you are likely to be handling money on your own during a large part of your adult life. So what's a damsel to do? Taking responsibility is the key. If you are married, each of you needs the skills to be able eventually to stand on your own. That's doubly true for women, who tend to live longer, earn less, and save less for retirement.

Each month, after the bills are paid, figure out where you stand financially and discuss your plans for the following month. Failing to discuss financial issues can jeopardize your security individually and as a couple. Disagreements are inevitable, but using the tips in the rest of this chapter, you should be able to discuss your differences openly and settle them fairly.

"Men who have a pierced ear are better prepared for marriage—they've experienced pain and bought jewelry."

RITA RUDNER, COMEDIAN

Truth #2 You Can't Succeed Unless You Start

Procrastination is a common obstacle, especially for women. Men may put off taking important actions out of laziness or complacency. For women, procrastination usually comes from fear, not laziness. Many women avoid taking control of their finances because they're afraid they'll fail, and that means everyone will be disappointed. Other women are afraid of succeeding because of the responsibility money entails. Overcoming these fears is critical to ensuring your financial security.

If you are afraid to face your financial future, you'll spend your way from day to day. Get started now, and you can create financial security for yourself and your family.

Truth #3 Wealth Is Not a Four-letter Word

This Truth is a tough concept for many women. Women are great at feeling guilty! They blame themselves if they have too little, and whaddaya know, they also feel guilty if they have too much. This misplaced guilt stems from feeling inadequate, thinking they don't deserve luxuries, or fearing they will be judged for their excesses.

As a result, women generally shy away from wealth. Somewhere along the way, women got it into their heads that wanting money makes them greedy and cold-hearted and that the demure way to behave is to deny oneself any extravagance. As a matter of fact, in a study by the American Association of Retired Persons (AARP), 42 percent of women said they don't want to be wealthy.

But increased wealth brings with it the possibility of more than just additional clothes and vacations. Building personal wealth is how we can ensure a better future. Instead of fighting the power of money, we need to better manage it, channel it, and use it to change the world for good. It's more than money, it's your life!

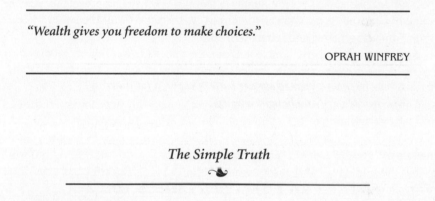

"Wealth gives you freedom to make choices."

OPRAH WINFREY

The Simple Truth

In a 2000 AARP study . . .

42 percent of women said they don't want to be wealthy.

41 percent of women said the main thing they would do with a million dollars would be to help friends or family or donate it to charity.

45 percent of women in the baby boom generation said they went to work because their families needed the money.

80 percent of married women save for the future; only 59 percent of divorced women do.

Truth #4 The Fear of Risk Can Be Costly

In a book called *Run Toward the Roar*, an African missionary told of seeing gazelles grazing in a field. As she watched, a pride of lions silently surrounded the field. When all of the lions were in place, as if by signal, two old, toothless lions roared loudly. The frightened gazelles swiftly stampeded away from the roar—and straight into the mouths of the younger waiting lions.

It is natural to fear risk. Fear is part of our instinct for survival, but take a lesson from the gazelles and focus on the *real* risks that affect you. Many women are so afraid of making investment mistakes that when the toothless lion of the stock market roars, they run in the opposite direction to low-interest savings accounts or even to the mall. They ignore the real risk of inflation gobbling up their savings. That guarantees they won't have enough money in the future.

Truth #5 Think Small for Big Success

The journey of a thousand miles begins with one small step, the Chinese proverb reminds us. The same is true of finances: The best way to begin is, well, to take one step forward, and then another. Small steps are the key to the Money Club way of improving your financial picture.

Sometimes we think we have to make major changes in our lives to get ourselves on track. But in reality, major changes are the result of a series of small steps. Don't feel overwhelmed by your finances. If you take at least one small step each day, you will begin to see real progress. We've suggested some Small Steps for you at the end of each chapter, and you'll find more small steps at The Money Club web site.

As you learn to think small, your confidence in your ability to handle your finances will grow. You'll see that you can learn new skills without fretting and worrying. You'll be able to take on new opportunities and to take better care of yourself while doing so.

Truth #6 Saving a Little Can Mean a Lot

The less you have, the more savvy you need to be when handling money. Many women feel they don't even have enough to get by, so there's no point in creating a plan for their future. A small salary shouldn't keep you from achieving financial security. Optimism and ingenuity are two key elements of making the most of your money.

Saving a little can mean a lot, over time. If you save just $1 a day, that's $365 a year. Not much, but more than you had before. If you saved $5 a day for your entire working life, you could retire a millionaire!

Truth #7 Money Talks

Money can't buy happiness, but it can definitely affect relationships. The last thing most women want to talk about when they fall in love is money, but it's one of the most important conversations you can have. The two of you must be in sync about money issues, or else you'll find yourself fumbling forward into the future with few clear-cut goals and no plan for how to achieve them.

To be a successful team, four factors are key: trust, shared goals, communication, and planning. You'll find out more about how to handle money as a couple later in this chapter.

The Simple Truth

A recent survey showed that 42 percent of married men and 36 percent of married women keep secrets from their spouse. The most common secret is how much the spouse paid for a particular item.

—*Readers Digest Survey, August 2001*

What Makes a Successful Marriage?

A study by Jerry M. Lewis (no, not that one), M.D., a research psychiatrist in Dallas, Texas, found that successful marriages share certain characteristics:
- *Power is shared equally by the partners.*
- *Partners listen to each other's side attentively.*
- *Partners respect their differences and their differing points of view.*
- *Couples don't keep secrets from each other and talk about their deepest feelings.*
- *Partners are empathetic and can step into each other's shoes.*

Disarming the Past *by Jerry M. Lewis (Zeig, Tucker, Theisen, 1999)*

Couples and Money

Love may be blind, but marriage is a real eye-opener. For a marriage to succeed, both partners must work together financially and emotionally rather than competing against each other. What's the answer? Repeat after us: communicate, communicate, communicate. Talk openly and frequently about your finances.

Quiz 2.1 will help you determine the areas in which you and your partner may be facing specific challenges. Have your partner answer the questions separately from you, and then compare the answers. The results may be surprising, and the discussion that follows the quiz will help you talk about financial issues and your financial future as a couple.

The answers don't have to fit you perfectly—just choose the one that is closest to what you feel. It's designed to get you thinking and talking. We wrote these questions in a humorous vein, so have fun with them.

Quiz 2.1

Couples Quiz: Test Your Money Relationship

1. My partner handles money
   a. like a bull in a china shop.
   b. according to our mutually agreed plan.
   c. in a way I have never completely understood.

2. My partner and I have discussed
   a. our long- and short-term financial goals.
   b. why we never seem to be going anywhere—and whose fault that is.
   c. the balances in our separate accounts.

3. I understand how to
   a. call my honey and ask for a larger allowance.
   b. tell a bill collector: "No! No cash for you!"
   c. pay bills, manage accounts, and talk to financial advisors.

4. My partner and I divide the money management tasks in our household
   a. by custom.
   b. by natural ability.
   c. by sheer neglect.

5. We have established a budget based on
   a. our current spending habits and our future financial goals.
   b. a document prepared fifteen years ago by a credit counselor.
   c. never mentioning the "B" word in our household.

6. I know my spouse's
   a. investment personality and risk tolerance.
   b. greatest financial foibles.
   c. name.

7. I am confident that
   a. I know everything about my partner's financial picture.
   b. I know where my partner stashes cash.
   c. I don't feel too confident about the whole thing, anyway.

8. My spouse and I have made a commitment to
   a. each other?
   b. never go to bed angry.
   c. discuss our finances regularly.

Scoring:
The answers that lead to better communication about money between partners are listed in the following table. If you and your partner have a different answer to the question, this is an excellent opportunity to discuss your feelings with your partner.

1. B
2. A
3. C
4. B
5. A
6. A
7. A
8. C

Now let's take a closer look at each question, and what the statements mean for your relationship.

1. *The way your partner handles money.* The way a person handles money is influenced by a number of factors, including his or her parents' attitudes about money and whether he or she grew up rich, poor, or middle class. For some people, money is a measure of their self-worth whereas others see it as a means of security. Some people splurge as a way to reward themselves whereas others are most proud of their ability to save. If you and your partner are on different financial wavelengths, pay close attention to the section in Chapter 3 that discusses your money style. Understanding your natural tendencies can help each of you learn to appreciate the other's traits and perhaps modify your own behavior. Discuss how you each feel about money and from where your beliefs stem and you will be better able to compromise on how money is handled in your household.

2. *Your discussion of future goals.* Whether or not you share a checkbook, sharing goals is one of the most exciting parts of being a couple. Together, you define and develop the type of lifestyle you will lead. Be honest with each other about your specific desires and priorities. For example, if you are young and you both want to have children, perhaps your spouse would like to go back to graduate school before you start a family. As a couple, you should reach an agreement about the goals you share, create a time line, and then determine the best saving and investment strategy to realize each objective.

3. *Your financial skills.* If either of you lacks financial knowledge, make the effort to master the basics and boost your confidence about money issues. Review all your personal finances together. Then learn about the basics of handling money using this book and the Money Clubs. Don't be afraid to ask questions and seek guidance along the way. The more you understand financial matters, the more confident and empowered you will feel in other aspects of your life. Knowing how to manage money wisely gives you a sense of control and security that is imperative to building a solid future as a couple.

4. *Dividing the money management tasks.* Who is in charge of paying the monthly bills, who balances the checkbook, and who files the paperwork? Is one of you in charge of your investment accounts, or do you make decisions as a couple? However you divvy up the financial duties, make sure you each understand what the other is doing. That way, you'll have the skills to manage your finances in case your spouse becomes ill or dies, or the marriage breaks up.

5. *Establishing a budget.* Without a budget, you may discover that one or both of you is spending beyond your means, which can make it nearly impossible to achieve your financial goals. Creating a household budget is relatively easy, and sticking to it will help you use your income wisely, safeguard your future, and avoid misunderstandings about how money should be spent. You'll get help with budgeting in Chapter 5.

6. *Your partner's money style.* As you will learn in Chapter 3, everyone has a different money style. Some people are natural born risk takers, whereas others are so afraid of loss, they'd rather sock their savings away inside their mattress. Talk openly with your partner about your attitudes regarding wealth, and how comfortable you are assuming risk with your investments. With patience and honest communication, you should fully understand each other's feelings and be able to reach an accord on the best way to manage your money together.

7. *Knowing your partner's finances.* Sit down together and review your financial picture. Order a copy of your credit report, and talk about how to improve your credit rating. If you have outstanding debt, pay it off as quickly as possible, even if it means cutting back on certain luxuries or postponing some of your other goals, such as buying a house or leasing a new car. But don't scrimp on your retirement savings!

8. *Your financial commitments to each other.* Disagreements are inevitable, and couples argue about financial issues more than anything else. By using the tools outlined in this chapter, you should be able to discuss your differences openly

and settle them fairly. Money is intertwined with trust in a relationship, so the more you can talk about money, the better relationship you will have.

Small Steps to Becoming a Money Star

1. Organize a regular family "money meeting" to discuss your financial situation, dreams, and goals. Use this time to brainstorm creative solutions to problems and generate ideas to improve your future. Make it fun and educational by holding back criticism and approaching problems with a can-do attitude.

2. Get your family's records in order. Set up a home office for bill paying and record keeping. A corner in the kitchen or a desk in the guest room is fine, as long as you have everything you need to pay bills, track tax-deductible expenses, and manage investments.

3. When discussing sensitive issues, try the timed-discussion technique. Set a timer for five minutes, and let your partner speak his mind on financial issues. Hear him out, without interruptions or criticism. After the five minutes are up, ask clarifying questions until you feel you really understand your partner's point of view. Then, take some time to think through what he has said. At another time, ask him to do the same for you.

4. Imagine your life as you would like to see it 10 years from now. Where will you live? What work will you do? What will you own? Visualize how you would like your life to change over the next ten years. Then, use this visualization as the starting point to develop specific financial goals. Would you like to go back to school? Start a business? Buy a house? Use your dreams to motivate yourself to get your financial house in order.

5. List five things you thought were important in life but you have found that you can live without. They can be physical things, emotional things, or qualities, such as status or prestige. What is more important to you now?

CHAPTER 3

Your Money Style

Dear WIFE,

My friend Emily is a such a saver she actually dislikes spending I'm just the opposite. I can't seem to stop spending until the money's all gone and the credit card has reached its limit. Now that we've discussed money styles in our Money Club, I understand why I've struggled with money all my life. It's my parents' fault! (Just kidding.) My mother was a spender and my father was a saver, and they had heated money discussions when I was a child. I guess I decided that the faster you got rid of money, the less you had to fight about. Thanks for the insight. It's nice to understand that we are all different.

Splurger in Boise

Dear Splurger,

We are glad you understand your money style a little better. Opposites attract, as your parents prove, and the same is true of friends in the Money Club. We have so much we can learn from each other once we understand our money styles and the money attitudes we learned as children. Now that you understand where your compulsion to spend comes from, you can work on developing some healthy attitudes toward money. You'll learn more about your money style and how to cultivate good money habits as you read through this chapter.

What's Your Money Style?

What money issues did you experience growing up? For most of us, money has hidden meanings beyond its purchasing power. Its meanings are bound up with our family backgrounds and our feelings of security, status, and self-worth.

Consequently, our emotional attitudes toward money sometimes cause us to behave inconsistently and to use money in ways that are nonproductive and self-destructive. Knowing we should save, for example, we instead go on a shopping spree. Knowing we should invest, we instead accumulate money in a low-interest-bearing savings account. When carried to extremes, this type of behavior can seriously endanger your financial life.

There is no "right" or "wrong" money style. Once you understand the hidden influences that shape your attitudes toward money, you may want to concentrate on altering some of your behaviors. On the other hand, you may prefer not to adjust your own money style, but to understand it as a means of accepting that what is right for other people may not be right for you. Either way, whether you modify your reactions or modify the advice to fit your individual money attitudes, you will have a clearer understanding of the role that money plays in your life.

"The only problems money can solve are money problems."

JAY W. FORRESTER

Take Quiz 3.1 to see if you are a Hoarder, Avoider, or Splurger. Circle the answer that best describes how you feel. The profiles are rendered in the extreme for quick recognition. Nevertheless, you will undoubtedly see aspects of yourself in one or more of them. Keep in mind that the categories are also useful for negotiating the more complex business of handling money with another person, whether a mate or business partner. Recognizing your personal money style can avert otherwise inevitable conflicts and confusion.

The Simple Truth

Oseola McCarty amassed more than $250,000 by saving the money she earned from washing and ironing clothes for $1.50 to $10 a bundle. McCarty, who died at age 91 in September 1999, willed a sizable chunk of her life savings—$150,000—to the University of Southern Mississippi, to which she had also made contributions during her lifetime.

—*Simple Wisdom for Rich Living,*
Long Street Press, 1996

Quiz 3.1

Your Money Style Quiz

1. You lucky devil! Upon arriving in Las Vegas for a weeklong vacation, you win $1,000 on your first bet. What do you do?
   a. Wire the money to your tax-free bond fund immediately and stick to your prearranged spending plan for the rest of the trip.
   b. Put it all on the next turn of the wheel or luck of the draw.
   c. Spend it all on shows, restaurants, and spa treatments before you leave town.

2. When shopping at your favorite store, you spot the perfect pair of pants. They suit you to a T! Only one problem: they are way out of your budget. What do you do?
   a. Buy them before your conscience says no. Plastic is power!
   b. Mutter under your breath about the store's outrageous prices and wait for the pants to go on sale.
   c. Buy them, agonize over your purchase all night long, and then take them back the next day.

3. Good news arrived in today's mail! You have inherited $10,000 from crazy old Aunt Minnie, who you have never even met. You
   a. start booking your vacation to Tahiti.
   b. increase your pretax contributions to your retirement plan.
   c. put it in your checking account to pay bills.

4. When it comes to saving money, you
   a. can't do it to save your soul.
   b. have set up a system that works for you.
   c. make (and break) a new savings plan every other month.

5. Honestly, how do you drive your car?
   a. Cautiously and safely—you are a defensive driver.
   b. Quickly and aggressively—you don't let anyone get in your way.
   c. Anxiously and hurriedly—there are a lot of crazy drivers out there.

6. If you could choose any one of the following occupations, regardless of income, it would be
   a. best-selling poet and novelist
   b. stuntwoman
   c. Supreme Court Justice

7. Regarding money, your best wish for your children is that
   a. they learn to control their spending. Someone's got to.
   b. they have good luck. That's what it really takes to make it in this world.
   c. they have a good education. They'll need to work hard to find a good profession.

8. Money-wise, what do you look for in a mate?
   a. A stable income and a conservative investment style
   b. A hot car in his driveway and a lot of shiny plastic in his wallet
   c. A lack of concern for material things

9. When you think of your retirement, you
   a. cross your fingers, close your eyes, and begin to pray.
   b. hope your investment plans work out.
   c. can't wait for the party to begin. I hear the weather is lovely in Florida this time of year!

10. Your worst money problem is your
    a. lack of financial education.
    b. shopaholic tendencies.
    c. procrastination.

11. Your worst fear about money is
    a. being awakened by the sound of creditors underneath your bedroom window, baying for blood.
    b. a tremendous stock and real estate market crash reducing your net worth by 90 percent.
    c. realizing that you are 55 and have no assets other than your car.

12. If asked how much is in your bank account right now, you'd say:
    a. "Do you want me to include the outstanding checks not yet posted to the account?"
    b. "I'm not sure of the exact balance."
    c. "I hope I didn't bounce any checks this week."

13. When you get a retirement account statement, you
    a. check it over very carefully.
    b. give up trying to figure it out after a few minutes.
    c. toss it in a drawer and assume the company must be right.

14. A quality that you admire in yourself is
    a. punctuality—you're always on time.
    b. spirituality—you're not a money-grubber.
    c. vivacity—you're the life of the party.

15. Why don't you have as much money as you want?
    a. You're too cautious. You miss out on great investments because you don't want to take a risk.
    b. You throw it away. You keep buying things you don't really need.
    c. You're not really sure why you don't have as much money as you want.

16. Guests are arriving for Thanksgiving dinner in one hour. In the kitchen, you're
    a. frantic, messy, and creative. You're trying to perfect a new recipe you created just for this occasion.

   b. disorganized, frustrated, and slow. You know the turkey is
      around here somewhere!
   c. organized, fast, and clean. Everything's in the oven already, and
      you're just setting up a few last-minute details.

17. When entertaining, you like
    a. spontaneous bashes with a few hundred of your closest friends.
    b. well-planned parties for your monthly dinner group.
    c. informal get-togethers with friends in the great outdoors.

18. Your attitude toward life is best summed up with which phrase?
    a. A stitch in time saves nine.
    b. He who laughs last laughs best.
    c. Ignorance is bliss.

19. When tipping in a restaurant, you
    a. tip in accordance with the quality of the service. You reward
       good servers and punish bad ones.
    b. tip lavishly. You expect to get the best service in the house next
       time.
    c. tip well even if the service is mediocre. You don't want to
       embarrass the server.

20. What you don't know about money
    a. can't hurt you.
    b. can be learned.
    c. will catch up with you one way or another.

Scoring
In the following chart circle the letter (H, A, or S) to which each of your
answers corresponds. Then count the number of circles for each type and
fill in the blanks next to each type. The type with the highest number is
your money style.

	a	b	c
1.	H	S	A
2.	S	H	A
3.	S	H	A
4.	S	H	A
5.	H	S	A
6.	A	S	H
7.	S	A	H

	a	b	c
8.	H	S	A
9.	A	H	S
10.	H	S	A
11.	S	H	A
12.	H	A	S
13.	H	S	A
14.	H	A	S
15.	H	S	A
16.	S	A	H
17.	S	H	A
18.	H	S	A
19.	H	S	A
20.	S	H	A

_____ Hoarder
_____ Avoider
_____ Splurger

Rating: From these scores, you can see which of the money styles dominates your personality.

*Our thanks to Olivia Mellan, whose groundbreaking work in this area appeared in her book *Money Harmony: Resolving Money Conflicts in Your Life and Relationships* (Walker & Co., 1994).

The Hoarder

The Hoarder is deeply attached to her money. Her hobby is saving money, and she loves to see her bank account grow. She is also apt to clip coupons, set budgets, and prioritize financial goals, although she may not be inclined to take on much risk. The Hoarder keeps her money "safe" in the bank, never considering that inflation is eating away at her savings every day. She is less concerned with having money now than with her security in the future, and although she appears successful, she often worries that she may outlive her money and end up in poverty.

The Hoarder also has a hard time spending money on herself and her loved ones, especially on luxury items or things that offer only short-term gratification. Many Hoarders worry about money and feel they will never have enough to feel secure. Others channel their thrifty tendencies into bargain hunting, always looking for the big sale. Getting a bargain makes her feel great, but finding out there was a better deal elsewhere makes her feel awful. Whatever outlet she uses to channel her anxieties, the Hoarder attempts to assert financial control over her life by focusing on details, and she is usually apprehensive about making mistakes.

If You Are a Hoarder

With obvious exceptions, the Hoarder is on to a good thing. Financial security is essential for creating and building self-esteem. But too much hoarding can be destructive and can lead to inner turmoil and bitter conflicts with family and friends.

If you are a tried-and-true Hoarder, you can take three positive steps toward a secure future. First, systematically examine your financial situation and assess your goals; then decide how much money you will need to reach your goals.

Second, take more risks with your money to gain greater rewards; make your money work as hard as you do. For example, channel the energy you might use looking for bargains into researching appropriate investment options for your financial goals and risk tolerance.

Third, once you know what you need to reach your goals and you have your money working for you, enjoy life! After saving and investing for your future, spend the remainder without guilt or anxiety.

The Avoider

The Avoider has trouble dealing with her finances, whether balancing her checkbook, budgeting, paying bills, or investing. She may have a fear of money that stems from a lack of self-confidence in dealing with financial transactions. As a result, the Avoider prefers to ignore the issue of money rather than confront her anxieties and take control of her finances.

Alternately, the Avoider might believe that money is evil and has the power to corrupt. She feels that having too much wealth or making a profit on investments means she is being greedy or selling out on her values and beliefs. Avoiders are not inclined to keep tabs on their current spending or invest for the future, and they may alienate their loved ones with their self-righteous attitude toward wealth.

The Simple Truth

One-third of women would rather talk to their grandmothers about their love lives than to financial consultants about investing.

Oppenheimer Funds Survey, 2001

If You Are an Avoider

First, you need to take an honest look at why you're evading money issues. Do you feel you lack the knowledge to make informed financial decisions? Or do you think that money and material possessions are superfluous and want to follow a more spiritually virtuous path of poverty?

If a lack of self-confidence is standing in your way, make an effort to learn about financial planning. You can find both basic and detailed information in books such as this one, in magazines and newspapers, and through the Money Club web site. If you haven't already joined a Money Club, start your own with a few of your friends. In the Money Club, you can figure out which financial issues need to be addressed immediately (like learning to balance your checkbook and paying your bills on time) and which you can tackle in the near future (like researching different mutual funds for your retirement plan).

If you think money is the root of all evil, remember that you can do a lot of good with your wealth. There is no sin in success. Consider investing in socially responsible companies or creating a charitable fund in your own name. Recognize that having money affords you the opportunity to help the people and causes that are nearest to your heart. You don't have to live extravagantly, but you shouldn't jeopardize your future security either.

The Splurger

The Splurger's credit cards are her best friends, but like some friends, they frequently talk her into spending she can't really afford. The Splurger hates to limit herself. After all, she works hard for her money and deserves to have money make her feel good. At the same time, however, she might feel frustrated that all her hard work hasn't garnered her more spectacular financial rewards, and she often splurges to cheer herself up or make herself feel more successful. Splurgers have a hard time budgeting and difficulty delaying gratification in the present to save for the future.

The Splurger is also prone to fantasies of financial rescue and fears achieving success on her own. She is afraid she will give up a certain emotional dependency that has been keeping her from being self-supporting. While she waits for the miracle person or event that will solve her financial woes, the Splurger may spend most of what she has at her disposal or rack up a hefty amount of debt.

The Simple Truth
~&~

Fifty-four percent of women are more likely to accumulate 30 pairs of shoes before accumulating $30,000 in retirement savings.

Oppenheimer Funds Survey, 2001

If You Are a Splurger

Although money is tightly intertwined with their definition of success, Splurgers never feel they have *enough* money, and they seldom have a clear perception of what money is. For many Splurgers, money is also a measure of love and approval. The Splurger uses money to make herself feel good, but when splurging undermines her financial security, it's time to get a grip on it.

If you share some of these characteristics, reward yourself for good performance with occasional splurges rather than all-out spending binges. Or perhaps you can learn to enjoy making sound financial purchases: Splurge on some smart investments that will grow in value in the future rather than buying more clothes you don't need. Similarly, instead of lavishing money and gifts on others, concentrate on building personal relationships on foundations other than money. Invest your time and your attention in your relationships with others, and invest your money in yourself. You will achieve considerably more satisfaction on both fronts.

"If we could sell our experiences for what they cost us, we'd all be millionaires."

ABIGAIL VAN BUREN

Your Money Attitude

A Healthy Approach Toward Money

Your financial future is up to you. Regardless of your financial history, you can begin today to build a solid financial foundation. Setting financial goals is the key to controlling your worries and keeping your finances healthy. If you don't have goals, you don't know how much you need to invest or where to invest. Once you set positive financial goals for yourself (you'll find out the secrets of how to set meaningful goals in Chapter 9), your healthy approach toward money will cultivate sound financial management.

Here are the signs of a healthy approach to money:

- You feel in control of money rather than being controlled by it.
- You use money in positive ways to enhance your life, not only as a means for providing necessities.
- You consider money a reward for an accomplishment, not an end in itself.
- You can use money spontaneously on occasion without feeling guilty.

- You realize that money cannot solve all your problems.
- In dealing with money, you adhere to your own general moral standards.
- You are aware of what money means to you and how you use it.

Few things in life are as empowering as the sense of security that comes with taking control of your finances. Like losing 20 pounds or finishing your first marathon, achieving a financial goal can boost your self-image and affect all facets of your life. What's more, wealth equals possibility. More than just buying yourself a nice car or putting a roof over your head, having money can mean sending your children to an Ivy League school, starting your own business, giving generously to charity, or providing for loved ones who may be in need. Best of all, having wealth means never having to fear for your financial security now or in the future. Instead, you can focus on the things that really matter.

Take Quiz 3.2 to help you assess your own money attitude.

The more answers you circled in Column A of Quiz 3.2, the more positive you feel about your financial situation. The attributes in Column A are your strengths that you can use to conquer the negative feelings in Column B.

The more answers you circled in Column B, the more work you need to do to improve your feelings about your financial life. Here's how you can work on the feelings you circled in Column B by using the strengths you circled in Column A.

Turn to a blank page in your Financial Security notebook. For each emotion you listed from Column B, write at least five possible solutions to the problem, from the simple to the sublime, beginning with "I CAN . . ." Focus on the strengths you identified in Column A as you devise your solutions.

For example, if you circled "Dependent" in Column B, because you don't have a job, some of the solutions could be:

- I CAN . . . talk to my spouse about my feelings.
- I CAN . . . call a community college to inquire about getting training to improve my job skills.
- I CAN . . . talk to my friends about trading off services in carpooling the kids, babysitting, etc.
- I CAN . . . develop a plan to find a job.
- I CAN . . . take one small step each day to help myself achieve independence.

As you read through this book and learn new ideas about finances, add as many statements as you can to your "I CAN" list. When you are done, choose the best ideas as a personalized list of small steps to get you on the road to financial security. As you progress through the "I Cans" you've listed, you will be able to utilize these strengths to build a positive financial future.

Quiz 3.2

How Do You Feel About Money?

Circle the words that best describe your feelings about money and finances at the moment. Circle as many as apply to you. I feel . . .

Column A	Column B
Secure	Helpless
Self-confident	Powerless
In control	Poor
Loved	Guilty
Respected	Worthless
Empowered	Worried
Independent	Dependent
In harmony	Inhibited
Peaceful	Restricted
Satisfied	Defenseless
Flexible	Depressed
Successful	Limited
Wealthy	Out of control
Capable	Lonely
Fulfilled	Overworked

"Money usually represents so much more than dollars and cents. It is tied up with our deepest emotional needs: for love, power, security, independence, control, self-worth."

OLIVIA MELLAN

Small Steps to Becoming a Money Star

1. Have a discussion with your parents, grandparents, or siblings about money styles. Who was the splurger in the family? Who was the hoarder? Who took risks? Who guarded the family's financial security? How are things different now than they were during your childhood? Asking these questions in an open, nonconfrontational way can stimulate interesting insights on your current financial situation. If you are married, ask your partner to discuss these issues with his family of origin as well.

2. If your spending sometimes controls you rather than you controlling it, decide one thing you can do to master your money. For example, when you take cash from the ATM, keep track of your expenditures. Or limit yourself to taking money only once a week at a specific time. As you gain mastery through your initial small step, decide on an additional action you can take. Step by step, your financial life will improve.

3. Build your financial "advisory board." Which of your friends can you count on for unbiased career advice? Who is good with investments? Who comes up with the most creative ideas for getting out of a financial jam? Start a Money Club to build on your strengths and help each other achieve your financial goals.

4. In quiz 3.2, look at the attributes in Column A that you didn't circle. Are there any to which you would aspire? Make this a goal by visualizing and vocalizing it. Say, "I am feeling more _____ each day." Say these affirmations 10 times in the morning and 10 times at night. This is the secret behind Money Magic statements that help bring prosperity into your life. Money Magic statements help you to change negative, money-repelling energy into positive, money-gathering energy.

5. If you are worried about something, ask yourself, "What difference will this make six years from now?" If it will make a significant difference, begin working to solve it. If it won't make a difference, recognize where it fits into your priorities.

PART TWO

Mastering Your Money Zones

CHAPTER 4

My Brilliant Career

Dear WIFE,

I'm the mother of a toddler, who said her first word yesterday. I missed it, and worse than that, it was the day-care provider she called "Mama." I'm heartsick. I need my job, but I'm conflicted about working when I could be home with my little girl. How can I resolve this dilemma?

Conflicted in Chicago

Dear Conflicted,

Join the club! Sixty-seven percent of mothers work, and we are sure that many of them experience the same conflict. And yet, surveys show that women who balance family and career are happier than those who focus on one or the other, because they end up doubly fulfilled.

Maybe you can integrate your motherhood and your career in ways you haven't thought about. Read on, and we'll help you explore ways you can mesh your career and your lifestyle, so you can enjoy both.

Tailor Your Career to Your Lifestyle

How you define success may depend on your gender. Often, a man's sense of accomplishment is closely tied to his professional achievements. A prestigious title, large salary, and material possessions are integral to his sense of self-worth. Generally, women are more multidimensional and place as much value on time spent with loved ones and on self-development as they do on their career accomplishments. Many women, whether single or married, believe a successful career is just part of the equation; a diverse and fulfilling personal life is more important to them.

Whether or not you have children, you need to strike a balance between pursuing your professional goals and feeling fulfilled on an emotional level. Let's take a closer look at some of the ways that women are balancing their career pursuits with their personal lives.

"I have yet to hear a man ask for advice on how to combine marriage and a career."

GLORIA STEINEM

Flex Time

Because so many women are in the workplace, employers have had to change their formerly inflexible attitudes for both sexes. More and more companies are recognizing that they need to offer flexible work hours so employees can focus on their families as well as their careers.

One woman we know starts her workday at 7 A.M. so she can leave the office by 3 P.M. to pick up her children from school. Her husband shifts his hours a little later in the day, freeing up time in the morning so he can send the kids off with a healthy breakfast and get the house in order before he goes to work. These adjustments help them both avoid the rush hour commute, so they can spend more valuable time with their family.

The Simple Truth

Married women with children under the age of 15 carry the heaviest workload of any group—about 77 hours per week.

—U.N. Human Development Report, Women & Diversity
WOW Facts (Business Women's Network, 2002)

Multiple Jobs

Many women work multiple part-time jobs to earn the equivalent of a full-time income. This might work for you. For example, if you are a part-time student, you could work three days a week at an office job and weekend afternoons in a retail store. This would leave you two days a week for classes and all of your evenings free for schoolwork. Your own situation and skills will determine the best part-time job arrangement for you.

Some women also choose a part-time schedule because it allows them the time and flexibility to focus on other interests and responsibilities, from raising a family to spending time with friends to pursuing hobbies or participating in charity work.

Job Sharing

When Doreen's teenage son started acting out, she needed to spend more time at home. Her friend Kathy wanted to work part-time, and Doreen convinced her employer to let them share her job. Doreen works mornings while her son is at school, so she can make sure he's home doing his homework in the afternoon rather than out with his friends. Kathy works in the afternoon, so she has mornings free for her yoga and other personal pursuits.

Job sharing is generally easiest to arrange if you have already been with a company for a while and have proven that you are reliable in your work. Talk to your employer about your need to scale back your hours, and ask if there is someone more junior who could help you fulfill your job responsibilities part-time. Your colleague has the opportunity to gradually improve her job skills and position at the company, and your employer knows that two trusted workers will be sharing the responsibilities.

Working from Home

Using modern technology, working from home presents few obstacles. When you talk on the telephone or use the computer, your customers and clients may not even know where you are. In fact, the technical support staff for a number of computer companies is in India, Ireland, or other countries. Only the accents give them away. If you want to work from home at least part of the week, speak with your employer. Together establish quantifiable goals that will show your employer you are still performing your job duties even as you work outside the office. Many telecommuters report they are actually more productive, since they waste less time chatting with coworkers in the office or sitting through unnecessary meetings.

The Simple Truth

In the workplace, men and women are equally likely to delegate authority. Women's management style often is more effective because they lead by example, motivating subordinates to reach performance goals. Men are likely to assign a task and put it out of mind.

*—HRG Consulting Group, Women & Diversity
WOW Facts (Business Women's Network, 2002)*

Can You Afford to Stay Home?

Can you live on one income? If you are like many couples, you can't even get by on two! But that doesn't mean you can't stay home to raise your children. It may be less expensive to run the household with only one spouse working. That's because two careers mean additional expenses for child care, commuting, clothing, meals eaten out, and taxes. Use Worksheet 4.1 to compute the cost if one of you stays home to look after your family.

In the end, the decision to work or stay at home is driven as much by your family and personal needs as your checkbook, and only you can determine what feels best.

Don't Abandon Your Career If You Decide to Leave Work

Putting your career on hold can come back to haunt you. You'll pay the price when you reenter the market. An interruption in your work history is likely to reduce your earning potential and cost you seniority. If your marriage ends in divorce or the death of your husband, you may not be able to reenter the job market quickly if you haven't kept up your skills and maintained your network contacts.

Here are some strategies to ease your transition into and out of the workforce:

- **Give notice and gather references.** Be sure to give your employer at least two to three weeks' notice when you leave your job. Ask for letters of recommendation from your boss and colleagues or clients before your last day.
- **Retain your benefits.** Under the federal law regulating employer-sponsored group health plans, COBRA, you likely are entitled to continue to receive the same health care benefits for 18 months after leaving a job. However, you will have to pay the premiums your employer may have paid or subsidized.
- **Time your departure wisely.** If you're only a few months from vesting in your employer's stock options or 401(k) matching contributions, consider waiting a bit before calling it quits.
- **Keep up your job skills.** Job sharing, consulting, or working part-time are great ways to stay active in your field. Keep up your professional certifications so you don't have to requalify when you decide to go back to work.
- **Stay in touch.** Keeping contact with previous bosses and colleagues will pay off. When you are ready to reenter the job market, you'll have a network of contacts to help with your search.
- **Take classes.** Attend continuing education classes to stay in touch and keep current. If you are planning to go into a different line of work, take classes in a new field so you'll have the right skills when it's time to look for a position.

Worksheet 4.1

Can You Afford to Stay Home?

Monthly income from working that would be eliminated:

Your after-tax wages, bonuses, commissions, profit sharing, etc. $_____

Employer retirement contributions lost (such as 401(k) match) +_____

Monthly expenses that would be reduced if you didn't work:

Child care (day care and/or after-school care) _____

Commuting costs (fuel, parking, maintenance,
   or public transit) _____

Convenience foods for children (you do fix lunch,
   don't you?) _____

Meals and snacks that you used to buy
   (before, during, and after work) _____

Family meals you won't eat out (now that you
   have time to cook) _____

Clothing and accessories you'll no longer buy
   (including uniforms) _____

Dry cleaning and other work clothing care _____

Out-of-pocket office supplies you'll no
   longer purchase _____

Other expenses decreased by staying home _____

Total −_____

Subtotal =_____

Expenses increased by staying home:

Medical and dental insurance premiums
   (if your employer paid them) _____

Life insurance premiums (if your employer
   paid them) _____

Increase in travel and vacations (now that
   you've got the time) _____

Career expenses (formerly paid by your employer) _____

Other expenses increased by staying home _____

Total +_____

This is the change in your income. =_____
Can you live without it?

How many hours did you spend at work and
commuting each month? _____

This is how much you were really making, per hour _____

Earning Money Without a Job

If you decide to put your career on hold, you can still bring home the bacon without a full-time job. Making money from your hobbies or using your skills on a part-time basis can be rewarding financially as well as emotionally. (See Worksheet 4.2.) Here are some ways you can earn an income without having to update your resume:

- **Use your special talents.** If you have a degree in math, advertise yourself as a tutor at the local high school. If you speak French, people will pay for private lessons. And if you're good at throwing a party, others may clamor for your services. One woman we know, a hobby seamstress, set up sewing classes for children. Post fliers at your local supermarket, student center, or church hall to attract customers at minimal expense.
- **Put idle hands to work.** Many companies need people to work from home doing simple but time-consuming tasks, like assembling products or stuffing envelopes. Although the work can be tedious, you can set your own hours and generate a steady income stream with little effort. Be careful, though, of the ubiquitous offers online, and even posted on telephone poles, that really are scams disguised as job offers; Don't send them your money.
- **Turn your hobby into a cottage industry.** Thanks to the wonders of the Internet, you now can share your handiwork with the whole world. Where once you might have marketed your home-sewn quilts, scented candles, or custom pottery exclusively through local gift shops and craft fairs, now you can expand your market. Use an outlet like eBay.com or even set up your own web site to advertise your wares to a global audience.

"Crafts make us feel rooted, give us a sense of belonging and connect us with our history. Our ancestors used to create these crafts out of necessity, and now we do them for fun, to make money and to express ourselves."

PHYLLIS GEORGE

"Choose a job you love, and you will never have to work a day in your life."

CONFUCIUS

Worksheet 4.2

Finding Your Passion

To figure out what you like to do and get someone to pay you for doing it, complete this worksheet. Don't dwell on each question or overthink each answer. Simply jot down any idea that comes to you, no matter how ridiculous it may sound. Brainstorm as many ideas as you can. A few days later, review the worksheet to see if you can come up with any additional ideas.

Once you have assessed your strengths, interests, passions, and assets, you can search for careers that seem appropriate. Start with your local Yellow Pages, looking up words from your answers or about which you feel strongly. Find businesses that might interest you, and start researching! Don't get discouraged if your search doesn't pan out right away. Remember, a chicken doesn't stop scratching just because worms are scarce.

Strengths

Things that people frequently compliment or praise me about:

Things that people ask me to help with or do for them:

Things people have told me that I ought to get paid for doing:

Things I've always thought were my "hidden talents":

Interests

Things I enjoy most:

Things I would still do even if I won the lottery:

Things I have always wanted to do:

Things I do in my spare time:

Passions

Things I've overcome that others struggle with:

Things that bother me deeply:

Things I know I could do a better way:

Things I could do to make the world a better place:

Things I am inspired to do:

Assets

Things I have done as a job or volunteer or through general life experience:

Things I have education or training to do:

Things I could do based on whom I know:

Things I could do based on equipment, facilities, property, or other possessions I own:

Starting Your Own Business

More and more women are discovering the excitement of being their own boss. The number of women-owned businesses grew at twice the national average between 1997 and 2002, and their employment rate is one and a half times the national average. According to the Center for Women's Business Research, an estimated 6.2 million women-owned businesses in the United States employ nearly 9.2 million workers and generate $1.15 *trillion* in annual revenue.

Women have been using their ingenuity to create opportunities for years. Bette Graham became a multimillionaire because she couldn't type. The one-time secretary got so tired of erasing her mistakes, she decided to cover them up with a white, water-based paint. Other typists clamored for her product, and in 1979, she sold the Liquid Paper Co. for $47.5 million.

Women in Charge

The number of U.S. companies owned by women grew almost 5 percent per year between 1997 and 2002, twice as fast as all firms.

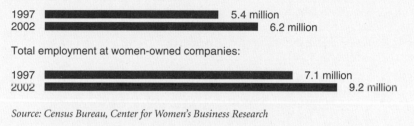

Number of women-owned companies:

1997 — 5.4 million
2002 — 6.2 million

Total employment at women-owned companies:

1997 — 7.1 million
2002 — 9.2 million

Source: Census Bureau, Center for Women's Business Research

Are You Cut Out to Be an Entrepreneur?

Before you decide to start your own business, figure out whether that's the right move, given your circumstances and personality. Remember, if you go into business for yourself, you will report to no one. While that may seem like a blessing, you must also be prepared to do many jobs yourself, at least in the beginning, because there will be no one else to do them. If you lack the discipline to work until the job is done or the flexibility to fulfill your work commitments before focusing on your personal life, you will be better off working for someone else.

Quiz 4.1 can help you assess your personality and determine whether you're ready to be an entrepreneur.

The Simple Truth

In 2002, more than one in eighteen women in the United States was a business owner. Seventy-three percent of all women-owned businesses are based in the home.

—U.S. Census Bureau and Center for Women's Business Research

Quiz 4.1

The Entrepreneurial Aptitude Test (EAT)
(Can you afford to quit your job and still EAT?)

1. Are you a risk taker?
   a. Never—I always avoid risk.
   b. If I have to—I'm uncomfortable taking risks and generally avoid them.
   c. Yes—Taking risks is sometimes a smart thing to do and I have no problem doing so when necessary.
   d. Yes—I enjoy putting it all on the line.

2. Are you likely to trust your instincts?
   a. No—I find my instincts are usually wrong.
   b. Sometimes—When I think I really understand the issue.
   c. Often—I have learned through experience that my gut is usually right.
   d. Always—I gather information, weigh the facts, and then trust my instincts.

3. Are you a good money manager?
   a. Extremely good—I watch every penny.
   b. Moderately good—I have a good idea of what I spend.
   c. Sometimes good—I try to live within my means.
   d. I really don't pay much attention to money.

4. Are you competitive at sports and work-related activities?
   a. Yes—I have to win at all times.
   b. Usually —I always give my best effort.
   c. Sometimes—If I care about the contest, I try hard to win.
   d. No—I don't usually care one way or the other.

5. When things don't work out, what do you usually do?
   a. Analyze the situation to figure out what I did wrong.
   b. Pick myself up and try again.
   c. Get depressed and angry at myself or others.
   d. Give up in defeat.

6. Do you look for creative answers to obstacles and problems?
   a. No—I usually just do what's easiest.
   b. Sometimes—I am only creative when there is no other solution.
   c. Usually—I'm pretty good at problem solving.
   d. Yes—I'm extremely resourceful at solving problems.

7. When I set goals, I usually
   a. write down small steps that progress toward meeting my long-term goals.

b. create a series of small steps in my mind.
c. develop the big picture without worrying about how I'll be able to achieve my goals.
d. don't set goals—I just go with the flow.

8. My time management skills are
   a. excellent. I am a dedicated goal setter and goal achiever.
   b. all right. Some days are better than others.
   c. poor. I don't manage time, it manages me.
   d. a source of anxiety. I never can seem to stick to a schedule.

9. Whether I succeed or fail is
   a. entirely out of my hands.
   b. mostly a matter of luck.
   c. dependent on a combination of luck and my decisions.
   d. entirely in my hands.

10. When faced with several options, I'm most likely to
    a. evaluate the pros and cons of each option before I decide.
    b. ask colleagues and friends for input, and do what they think.
    c. choose an option quickly and go for it.
    d. avoid making a decision until I'm forced to.

11. If I'm not making money after six months,
    a. I'll keep trying for at least a year.
    b. I'll figure out some alternatives to make extra income while I keep trying.
    c. I'll give up and find something else.
    d. I'll go into bankruptcy.

12. I know I have entrepreneurial aptitude because
    a. I have successfully done it before.
    b. I've done my research and think I've got a great plan.
    c. I've always been a good employee, and I'm good at managing others.
    d. everyone tells me I'd be good at it.

Scoring:

Add up your score using the numbers in the table below.

	a	b	c	d
1.	1	2	3	4
2.	1	2	3	4
3.	4	3	2	1
4.	4	3	2	1

	a	b	c	d
5.	4	3	2	1
6.	1	2	3	4
7.	4	3	2	1
8.	4	3	2	1
9.	1	2	3	4
10.	4	3	2	1
11.	4	3	2	1
12.	4	3	2	1

Rating:

37–48   Entrepreneurial Diva

You show a definite aptitude for entrepreneurship. Your money management skills, drive, and positive attitude will help pave the way for your success. Work hard to develop your strengths and to add members to your team who will complement any weak spots you may have.

25–36   Entrepreneurial Aspirant

You have some of the skills and attitudes necessary to become an entrepreneur. All you need is a bit of refinement. WIFE suggests that you review the answers with lower scores and set some small goals to improve them. This will improve your goal-setting skills and any other skill you need to become a more successful entrepreneur. For example, if you are not careful with money, you can review the savings chapter in this book and set a goal to cut your expenses and increase your savings this year.

12–24   Entrepreneurially Challenged

You need to learn and develop more to become a successful entrepreneur. Ask family members who are in business for help, or read biographies of great entrepreneurs. Attend a Small Business Administration or local community college course on small business development. After a bit of study, you can retake this quiz to see if you are ready for your new venture!

Every Business Needs a Plan

If you decide to start a business of your own, you will need an idea, a plan, and financial backing. Your business is unlikely to succeed without all three. While most people who go into business start with an idea, most businesses that fail do so because they didn't have enough financing to sustain them until they became established. A solid business plan can tie the idea and the financing together to create a successful company.

A critical element to entrepreneurial success is a well-thought-out business plan. The business plan explains your vision for your company and includes detailed information about your financial operations. A calling card for potential investors, it is your primary tool for raising cash and will also help you keep your business on track and focused on your original strategy.

Some plans are only ten pages, while others run 100 pages or more, depending on the nature and complexity of your business. Make the document concise but complete. Appendix B lists books and web sites to guide you through the process. Here is a general overview of what your business plan should entail:

- title page
- table of contents
- executive summary
- company's service or product
- marketing strategy/target audience
- competition
- financing requirements
- management
- advisory board
- future expansion
- financial forecasts

This list looks daunting, but it really is quite manageable. These sections are all important aspects of running your own business, and exploring them will help you develop your business ideas. Tackle your business plan one section at a time. Writing it merely requires discipline and patience, two important qualities you'll need to run your business.

Finding Seed Money

Once your business plan is complete, use it to drum up seed funding to get your company off the ground. Although it can be tempting to dip into your retirement fund because you're absolutely certain your business is a sure bet, keep your hands off your savings. Instead, follow these strategies for getting the money you need without jeopardizing your financial future.

Look Close to Home

Approach family members, friends, and colleagues about investing in your venture, either as a loan or in exchange for a percentage of profits. Have a lawyer draw up all the legal documentation to protect everyone involved if conflicts arise.

Take Out a Loan

If you can offer collateral such as your home or personal assets and provide a personal guarantee, you may be able to arrange a personal secured loan through your local bank. The bank will want to know exactly what you're going to do with the money and how you plan to pay it back, so be sure you have a written business plan before you start shopping.

Ask the Government

A loan guarantee by the Small Business Administration (SBA) will encourage banks to fund your business. Other state and local government agencies also offer economic development capital to build businesses and create jobs in certain areas. Contact your local Chamber of Commerce or the SBA (www.sba.gov) to find programs in your region.

Find an Angel

Angels may invest in your business if they believe it offers a serious growth opportunity. Expect to pay handsomely for this cash infusion. Angels generally expect to cash out after five to seven years with an annualized rate of return between 20 percent and 40 percent. You can locate business incubators and angel networks through your bankers, accountants, lawyers, or your local Chamber of Commerce, economic development authority, or business school. Make sure you have all your financial projections in place before you begin your search for investment funding, and create a clear exit strategy with the angel before you take a cent.

Three Critical Tips for Success

Once you have a clear vision for your business, it's time to start the financial planning process. After you've developed your business plan, here are some more things you need to know.

- **Keep personal and business finances separate.** Business and personal interests may collide. Don't sacrifice your other investments for the sake of your business. Don't dip into your retirement savings or your child's college fund to get your company off the ground. Set aside separate funds for business expenses that include separate checking and credit card accounts.

- **Stay two steps ahead.** When you are an entrepreneur, you do not have anyone you can depend on for a regular paycheck. Not only must you have faith in your undertaking, but you'll also need the character and financial resourcefulness to smooth out the bumps of an irregular income. A successful entrepreneur must have the discipline to save when the money comes in to create a cushion so that there will be funds available in lean times.
- **Keep an eye on your future.** When you start a new business, you'll probably use every spare cent you have. But don't forget about saving for your future. Now that you're the boss, part of your job is to set up your own retirement plan and perhaps one for your employees. Your financial advisor or accountant can help you determine which type of plan is right for you.

Small Steps to Becoming a Money Star

1. Describe in three sentences or less your own personal job description. If you are not earning money regularly right now, describe your most recent job or the next job you'd like to have. Are you providing a valuable service? How can you add more value? How can you learn more and improve your skills?
2. If you are changing careers, spend some time on the Internet or at your local library researching career choices. Don't forget to ask the reference librarian for research ideas.
3. Find someone who is successful in your chosen field, and ask for an interview. Find out what makes her successful, and what you can do to follow in her footsteps. What books does she recommend, and who else would she suggest you talk to?
4. It's sometimes hard to look at yourself objectively. Ask your friends in your Money Club to help you assess your talents and suggest what you can do in the future to make the most of them
5. List ten really great things you think you could do for people—either products or services—if you had the resources and the opportunity. Think of all of the things you have been trained to do and for which you have natural aptitude and/or a great idea. Everyone is creative—don't limit yourself to your current job.

CHAPTER 5

Saving for a Sunny Day

Dear WIFE,

My mother taught me a penny saved is a penny earned. The problem is, I earn so few pennies it's hard for me to save any! My salary is barely enough to get by, so how can I set aside money for bigger goals, like buying a house someday?

Feeling the Pinch in Birmingham

Dear Pinched,

WIFE knows what it's like to feel a crimp in your pocketbook, but you might be surprised at what's doing the squeezing. Keep a notebook for a week in which you write down where every penny goes. That includes groceries, magazines, gas, movies, and even sweet treats. Something as simple as cutting out junk food can really add up. Here's an example: Say you skip the soda ($1.00) and candy bar ($.65) you usually buy at work every day. In five days, that's $8.25, which is $33 a month. (And you spared yourself those empty calories!) Trimming back on the little luxuries can make a big difference in the long run. Save $33 a month, and in 10 years you'll have more than $5,000. Figure out some more places to save, and your money will grow even more. For example, take the change from your purse and put it into a jar each day. That could easily add another $50 a month, which is another $8,000 in 10 years. Read on, and you'll learn lots of tips for squeezing the most out of your budget.

Make the Most of Your Million Dollars

A lot of money passes through your hands each month. If you earn and spend $2,000 a month, that amounts to more than a million dollars during your lifetime!

Wouldn't you like to set some of that money aside for long-term goals rather than letting it sift through your fingers? By cutting back on some expenses, you may actually be able to live better and indulge in luxuries you didn't think you could afford.

The Simple Truth

❧

The average American handles about $600 of loose change annually. Combined, that's more than $140 billion. When was the last time you looked under the sofa cushions?

—US Mint

To cut back, you have to know what you have in the first place. Then tailor your expenses to fit within your income, including money to save. The best way to do that is with a budget. For many people, the term "budget" is synonymous with "deprivation." Budgeting is like a financial diet, and nobody likes to diet, financially or otherwise. But like a sound nutritional plan, budgeting is beneficial, and it doesn't have to be distasteful. With a budget, you can get more enjoyment from the money you spend, planning your finances rather than spending recklessly. You'll be happier, and your money will go farther.

Where Do You Stand Right Now?

Before you can plan for your future, focus first on your current finances. Use these seven simple steps to compute your present net worth, which is simply the total value of what you own minus what you owe.

Step 1: Cash.   Add the amounts in bank accounts, certificates of deposit, money funds, and cash in your wallet.

Step 2: Personal use assets.   Total the value of your home, personal furnishings, jewelry, automobiles, vacation cabins, time shares, and the like.

Step 3: Insurance values.   Look up the current value of all cash-value insurance policies.

Step 4: Retirement plans.   Add your IRAs, 401(k)s, SEPs, pension and profit sharing plans, and other employer-sponsored plans. Include only the portion you would receive if you left your employment, which is called your *vested share.*

Step 5: Other investments.   Stocks and bonds, mutual funds, investment real estate, limited partnerships, annuities, and the like, plus amounts owed to you by others and the value of your business go here.

Step 6: Debts.   List your debts, including mortgage, bank loans, and credit card debt.

Step 7: Net worth.   Add the assets, subtract your debts, and you have your net worth.

If your debts are greater than your assets, you will come up with a negative number. That means you have been living far beyond your means, and it is time for serious action to prevent further jeopardizing your financial future. A positive number doesn't mean you are off the hook, however. Is your net worth high enough? Even if your net worth is higher than you expected, you may still feel uncertain about your finances. For example, if your liquid assets in Step 1 are less than your debts in Step 6, excluding home and car loans, you may feel awash in debt and out of control financially. If your retirement assets in Step 4 are minimal and you are fast approaching retirement age, you may worry about your future retirement well-being. If the personal use assets in Step 2 constitute the bulk of your net worth, you may realize that funding your future needs could require selling some of these assets and scaling down your lifestyle.

Budgeting 101

Many years ago, Samuel Johnson advised, "Whatever you have, spend less." His words are just as true today. If you don't save, you will not have money to invest, and your financial goals will always be beyond reach.

A budget can help you get a handle on your finances. After all, if you don't know where your money goes, you'll live and spend from day to day with no clear idea of how much money is moving in and out of your accounts. You can use Quiz 5.1 (on page 69) to see if a budget will help you.

Devising a budget may seem a daunting task, but it really isn't that difficult. To help you figure it all out, follow these four simple steps.

1. Create a worksheet so you can analyze where your money goes. In your Financial Security notebook, list the budget categories that apply to you, one on each line, using the categories in Table 5.1 as a guide. Add budget categories that are uniquely yours: for example, if you are enrolled in school part time, you may have additional expenses for tuition payments, textbooks, and supplies.

2. Figure out where your money has gone. Go through your checkbook and credit card statements for the past year and list each check or itemized credit card charge in its proper category. Add the amounts in each category, and you will have a summary of your spending by category for the past year.

3. Create your budget for the coming year. Decide where you can cut back, and how much, and subtract the changes from the category totals. Divide the revised amounts by 12 to arrive at your preliminary monthly budget. Compare the total of all expenses with your monthly income, and adjust the expenses as necessary until your monthly budget equals your monthly income. Be sure you allocate as much as possible to the category "savings and investments"; 10 percent to 15 percent of your gross income is ideal. Getting the inflow and outgo to agree may take some doing, but persevere until your budget balances.

4. At the end of each month, see how close you came to your budgeted amounts. Use the Budget Worksheet in Table 5.1. Once you figure out whether your spending was over or under your budget, jot an explanation into the column next to major variances. If you consistently exceed your budget, you will have to adjust your spending habits or find a way to increase your income so you can accommodate your extra spending.

Using a computerized program such as Quicken or Microsoft Money will make tracking your expenses much easier, because it does the math for you as you go along.

A budget won't give you more money each month, but sticking to it will leave you with more at the *end* of each month. You and your partner should both be clear about the budget for your household. Setting guidelines together can go a long way toward helping you avoid conflict and achieve your financial goals.

"Beware of little expenses; a small leak will sink a great ship."

BEN FRANKLIN

The Simple Truth

❧

The most common spending cuts people made in the past year were reducing entertainment expenses (46 percent) and not eating dinner out (42 percent). More people 25 to 34 years old reduced eating out, possibly because they were spending more in that category than others.

—Retirement survey by G.E. Center for Financial Learning, 2003

Table 5.1   Budget Worksheet

Category	Budget	Actual	+ or −	Explanation
Paying Yourself First				
Cash savings				
Debt repayment				
Life insurance				
Disability insurance				
Retirement savings				
Education savings				
Auto payment or lease				
Residence				
Mortgage or rent				
Property tax				
Home insurance				
Utilities				
Repairs & cleaning				
Gardening				
Homeowner fees				
Other				
The Basics				
Food and clothing				
Groceries				
Household supplies				
Clothing				
Dry cleaning & laundry				
Health				
Health insurance				
Drugs & vitamins				
Doctors, dentists, etc.				
Other health costs				

Table 5.1   Budget Worksheet (continued)

Category	Budget	Actual	+ or −	Explanation
Personal care				
Grooming				
Other personal care				
Transportation				
Vehicle				
Insurance & registration				
Gasoline				
Repairs/maintenance				
Other transportation				
Tuition & education				
Legal & accounting				
Family and Social Life				
Child care				
Entertainment				
Meals out				
Club memberships				
Gifts				
Pet expenses				
Charity				
Miscellaneous				
The Extras				
Hobbies				
Vacations				
Sports				
Toys				
Pocket money				
Totals				

Quiz 5.1

The "Do I Really, Really Need to Budget?" Quiz

1. When you get a raise, you typically
   a. treat yourself to dinner out or something you've had your eye on and then allocate the rest to savings.
   b. go on a shopping spree.
   c. promise yourself again that you will draw up a budget.

2. You're at the mall. You find a beautiful, handmade sweater—at handmade sweater prices. You know you could live without it if you tried. What do you do?
   a. Keep your wallet in your purse—you know you don't really need it.
   b. Think about buying it, but decide against the purchase because there's something else you would prefer.
   c. Buy it immediately. Money exists to be enjoyed.

3. At the end of the month,
   a. there is always more month than money.
   b. you look forward to adding up your retirement plan contributions.
   c. you manage to pay all of your bills, save a bit, and not end up in the red.

4. When planning your annual vacation, you
   a. use the money set aside in your budget for travel.
   b. pay for your dream vacation with credit cards. You only live once, right?
   c. never take vacations. You just can't seem to spare the money

5. If your financial habits were a song, the title would be
   a. "The Low-Down, No-Dough Blues."
   b. "We Can Make It Through."
   c. "I'm Savin' It All Up For You, Babe."

6. The grapevine at work is full of news about layoffs. Sure enough, you're next. What do you do?
   a. Pat yourself on the back for accumulating an emergency fund.
   b. Try to arrange for higher credit limits and a home equity loan.
   c. Plan the vacation for which you haven't had time.

7. You know
   a. the approximate amount you have in the bank and how much you have charged this month.
   b. the balance of your accounts down to the penny.
   c. the exact starting date of the best sales in town.
8. When your favorite store announces a going-out-of-business sale, you
   a. get your plastic ready—you're going to shop until you drop.
   b. buy your dream stuff; you'll skip your vacation this year.
   c. go to the sale with your credit cards and come out with a bit more than you expected, but you'll pay it off within a month or two.

9. Credit cards are
   a. to be used for emergencies only.
   b. to be paid off every month.
   c. to be used to the max.
10. Which best describes your budgeting style?
    a. You've noticed a pattern of emotional spending—when you're happy, sad, or bored (or any other excuses you can think of).
    b. You spend according to your financial plan, keeping your long-term savings goals in mind.
    c. You spend in cycles—running up credit card debt and then paying it down.

Scoring:

Add up your score using the numbers in the table below.

	a	b	c
1.	1	3	2
2.	1	2	3
3.	3	1	2
4.	1	3	2
5.	3	2	1
6.	1	2	3
7.	2	1	3
8.	3	1	2
9.	1	2	3
10.	2	1	3

My total score _____

Rating:

10–16   You are a careful spender

You have good skills for restraining spending and getting wonderful deals. Since you are already in the savings habit, you may be motivated by seeing your savings grow. Add a special "budget bonus" category to your budget, and use it to save for something special, just for you or your family.

17–23   Careful spender-in-training

You have the basic skills, with just a few weak spots. Pick one or two categories in which you can improve, and keep track of your spending, cutting back where you can. When you have those categories under control, pick one or two more.

24–30   The careful spender is not in . . . yet

Let's face it: careful spending has just not been your forte. Set a detailed budget and keep track of all your spending for several months. Become more conscious of your spending. Before buying anything, ask yourself: Do I need this? Do I even want this? Do I want to dust this?

Choose Your Budget

Unlike stretchable gloves, when it comes to budgeting, one size does not fit all. A detailed budget will help you control every expense. But if you tend to overspend in just one or two categories, you may not need an elaborate budget. Here are five different types of budgets, one of which is right for you.

A Comprehensive Budget   If money is tight and you want to cut back on your spending, you will need a detailed budget that keeps track of everything you spend, and you'll want to monitor your spending against these budget categories frequently.

A Problem-Solving Budget   If you have trouble controlling money in just a few categories, such as clothing or entertainment, create a finely detailed budget for just these categories. For example, keeping track of clothing expenses for each member of the family by clothing type may help you pinpoint trouble areas.

A Planning Budget   If you want to save for particular goals, add budget categories to your spending plan that create pockets of savings to meet your objectives. Monitor your progress and adjust your savings as needed.

An Overall Budget   Perhaps you merely need a system for monitoring your overall spending from year to year. A budget with broad categories will help you monitor your spending habits so that your expenses stay under control as your income rises.

A Cost-Saving Budget   If saving more money year after year is your goal, analyze your past expenses, then create a budget that reduces your expenditures in each category gradually. For example, if your family vacations usually cost $5,000 per year, cut that figure to $4,000 for the coming year and $3,000 the year after that.

It's easier to save if you are saving for a pleasant goal. If your budget starts to feel constricting, think about your future plans in a positive light. For example, picture yourself moving into your dream home, envision your child's college graduation, or imagine yourself and your spouse walking along a tropical beach during retirement.

Use Your Computer

If you choose a more comprehensive budget plan, look into different kinds of software programs to help you keep track of your expenses. Programs like Quicken and Microsoft Money allow you to enter information about your spending in different categories, and then automatically calculate your total outlay. You can print checks using your home computer or make electronic payments online, entering them in the appropriate budget category. Some programs even automatically enter your credit card expenditures into your spending tally. You can also use these software applications to figure out potential returns on your investments, calculate the interest on a loan, and compute your tax write-offs.

Keep Track of Your Cash

If you're careful about expenditures you pay for by check but undisciplined when it comes to spending cash, keep close track of your cash expenses. Each time you take out your wallet at a cash register, before you put your wallet away, step to the side and jot down the expenditure in a small notebook you carry with you. The habit will soon become automatic, and by taking this extra step, you'll begin to think critically about each expenditure, rather than impulsively buying things you don't really need and may not even want.

Getting Organized

Got records? Most people do.

But can you find last month's bank statement? A copy of your will? The manual for your VCR?

If your answer was something unprintable, you need to get a bit more organized. Most people dread organizing their records because they keep far too much information. You don't have to keep everything. For tax purposes, keep papers that substantiate your income and expenses for at least three years in case of audit.

To keep on top of this year's tax receipts, start with a big mailing envelope. Label it "200_" and fill it with all of your deductible receipts, bills, cancelled checks, tax statements, and related information. At the end of the year you can categorize things, but just toss them in for now. When you are ready to refer to it at tax time, everything will be in one place.

You'll also want working files for these categories:
- *unpaid bills*
- *paid bill receipts*
- *current bank account, loan, and investment statements*
- *current cancelled checks*
- *credit card information*
- *employment records*
- *health benefit information*
- *insurance policies*
- *family health records*
- *manuals and warranties, and receipts for items under warranty*
- *inventory of safe deposit box (and key)*

When in doubt, keep it simple. Think: Why do I need this? When would I use it? Where will I look for it?

The Way to Save

Now that you know how to track and control your spending, it's time to start setting aside extra for the future. Of course, when we've told women this, many have said, "But I can barely live on what I make now!"

One of the easiest ways to save is to trim your paycheck. Have your employer automatically deposit a portion of your paycheck directly into a separate account without the funds ever passing through your hands. Money that is deducted from your paycheck and deposited into a credit union account, savings or stock purchase plan, or government savings bond is money you are saving for the future.

When you work overtime, don't spend the extra income frivolously. It represents your leisure time, so save it for something you enjoy, or add it to your retirement account.

The Simple Truth

Women are a dominant financial force. In 2002, they purchased more than 50 percent of all new vehicles, constituted 40 percent of all business travelers, influenced 80 percent of all travel, and owned 38 percent of all U.S. businesses, contributing $1.6 trillion to the national economy.

—*American Woman Road and Travel (www.roadandtravel.com)*

Clever Tips for Savvy Savers

Saving money takes some ingenuity and bargain-hunting acumen. *But don't confuse bargain hunting with saving money.* If you buy something on sale you didn't need or budget for, no matter how good the deal, you've just spent money you didn't have. The following strategies can help you trim costs across several categories, and keep your savings plan on track.

1. **Clipping coupons.** Coupons are great for saving money, especially for groceries and other items you buy regularly. Check your local paper and the weekly circular at your supermarket for the best deals, and if your store offers a discount club card, be sure to sign up. If you save even $5 a week, that's $260 a year—which is money that can be invested toward long-term goals.

2. **Stretching your clothing dollars.** It's easy to look like a million bucks without spending a fortune. Outlet malls and chain stores like Loehmann's, T. J. Maxx, and Filene's Basement offer designer clothing at a steep discount from retail rates. Update your outfits with accessories, rather than buying a whole new wardrobe each season.

3. **Finding furniture bargains.** If you need a houseful of furniture, buy your furniture by phone or Internet from North Carolina, where the major furniture manufacturers are located. Even including the cost of shipping, you can save money. Or look for used furniture at flea markets and thrift stores and have the items refinished or upholstered to make them as good as new.

4. **Conserving utility spending.** Installing proper insulation and modernizing equipment like your water heater can help lower utility costs. To reduce your phone bill, shop different long-distance carriers for the best rate. You might also want to cut out special services, like call waiting, three-way calling, and caller ID, which can save you as much as $30 a month.

5. **Curbing automotive costs.** Taking precautionary measures can help you keep your car running smoothly and save on big-ticket expenses down the line. Be sure to change the oil when necessary, keep fluids at their full-level marks, check your tire pressure often, and bring your car in for regularly scheduled maintenance. These simple steps can help you get better mileage and will extend the life of your car.

6. **Enjoying inexpensive entertainment.** These days, the cost of two movie tickets, popcorn, and soda can easily top $30, and if you go to dinner beforehand, you're looking at a $100 date. If you're looking for romance, try a home-cooked meal served by candlelight, followed by a long bubble bath or foot massage. You'll cut your cost in half, and double your pleasure!

7. **Locating travel deals.** Interested in staying in a French chateau for free? Trade your home for a few weeks at HomeExhange.com. You can book the

airline tickets at discount travel sites such as Orbitz.com, Expedia.com, Travelocity.com, CheapTickets.com, and Smarterliving.com. To save even more, schedule trips in the off-season, when rates are low.

8. **Saving on the small stuff.** Even small amounts saved regularly can grow into a sizable sum. For example, do you buy breakfast at the drive-through on your way to work everyday? The $2.50 you spend on a coffee and egg sandwich adds up to more than $625 a year. Invest that amount each year at a 6 percent rate of return, and in 25 years, you'll have nearly $35,000. It's true what they say: The little things mean a lot.

9. **Locking in the best rates.** Ideally, you should pay off your credit card balance in full each time you get your statement, but if you have to run a balance, make sure your interest rate is as low as it can be. If you transfer existing balances to a new card at a low introductory rate, read the fine print before you switch, so you don't fall into a hidden trap.

10. **Getting cash back.** Many credit cards now offer cash back on every purchase, or incentives toward new purchases. Shop for a card that offers cash or incentives like frequent flyer miles so you can save money as you spend.

11. **Extending your warranties.** Don't spend $50 for an additional 12-month warranty on the television set you bought for $250. But for major appliances like your refrigerator, washer, and dryer, extending your coverage can help you save big bucks on future repairs or replacement.

The Simple Truth

The web can help you scout out the best prices. Here are some of the best "shopbots" that also rate the stores on customer service: BizRate.com, Yahoo.com, DealTime.com, StreetPrices.com, and Froogle.com.

12. **Avoiding temptation.** Curb the urge to spend by avoiding temptation where you can. Make friends with the "mute" button on your TV remote control, and use it whenever there's a commercial break. Read a book or head for the gym when you're bored instead of going to the mall. Fill empty hours with volunteer work at a local charity or community center. You'll be helping others while you help yourself to save.

13. **Keeping away from credit.** Don't have too many cards at your disposal. Use credit cards sparingly, if at all, and avoid signing up for cards offered by different retailers, even if they come with a discount off your first purchase. The more cards you carry, the easier it is to let the money slip through your fingers.

14. **Doing it yourself.** You can save the money and improve your expertise in the process by tackling projects yourself. Enlist the aid of a handy friend, surf the Internet for information, or buy a book on the topic if you need a little help. If you're feeling adventuresome, you might also explore adult education classes and workshops to learn new skills and boost your self-confidence!

15. **Trading skills for services.** Consider bartering your time and talent for services you might need. For example, you could offer to tutor the 17-year-old next door in French once a week in exchange for him mowing your lawn. Many communities offer full-fledged bartering programs administered through local agencies, schools, and hospitals, so do some research in your area to find out how to sign up.

To Lease or Not to Lease

If you are in the market for a new car, you may have been tempted by the low monthly payments featured in the advertisements for leasing arrangements. With a lease, you can expect to make little or no down payment and make lower monthly payments. At the end of the lease period, you don't have to worry about the trade-in or sale of the used car. You can just turn back the keys to the leasing company, and walk away (literally, since you won't have a car). Or you can sign a lease on a new vehicle, and drive away.

That leads us to the major disadvantages of leasing a car. Granted, your monthly payment is less each month, but at the end of the lease period, you don't own the car. If you want to continue driving the same car, you must purchase it from the leasing company for its current market value.

Leasing a car has other disadvantages. A good credit rating is more important when you lease a car than when you purchase one. You must purchase special "gap" insurance that will cover the remaining lease payments on the car if it is wrecked or stolen. And at the end of the lease period, you may be charged for miles you drove in excess of the maximum specified in your lease, and you also may be charged for excess wear and tear on the car.

If you are planning to lease a car, don't be afraid to negotiate with the leasing company over lease terms, up-front costs, or monthly payments, just as you would when purchasing a new car. Here are some of the things to look for in an auto lease:

- *a lease term that corresponds to the length of time you'll want to keep the car*
- *no up-front "capital cost reduction" (read "down payment")*
- *closed-end lease so you won't be charged if the car is worth less than the estimated residual value*
- *mileage limit that corresponds to your driving habits*
- *no extra charge for moving with the vehicle out of state*
- *guaranteed-price purchase option*
- *security deposit not in excess of one monthly payment*

- *no up-front charge for sales tax*
- *payments that are less than you would pay on a car loan; comparison-shop for lowest costs*
- *no early termination fee*
- *ability to incorporate the cost of extra miles into the monthly payment at a reduced cost*
- *refund provision for cost of extra miles you buy but don't drive*

"Drive-thru banks were established so most of the cars today could see their real owners."

E. JOSEPH CROSSMAN

It's a Family Affair

The spending plan you create will be a unique reflection of you and your habits, needs, and desires. If you're creating a budget that affects other members of your household, you'll need to win their allegiance before you set down the guidelines. Try not to impose too many stringent spending controls on family members at one time, or you may have a mass mutiny on your hands! To keep the peace, each member of your family should have some money that he or she can spend without being accountable to the budget. To allow for this, add an expense category to your spending plan called "individual allowances."

How to Save on Checking Accounts

- *Choose a bank that offers a simple checking account that charges the least amount for your level of checking account activity.*
- *Compare the rates for bounced checks, in case you make a mistake, and for checks you deposit that are returned "not sufficient funds," in case you fall victim to someone else's error.*
- *Your bank should offer a regular savings account that allows a reasonable number of withdrawals.*
- *Inquire about auto loans, signature loans, and other small loans, so you can build your credit record.*

When Hubby Holds the Purse Strings

Budgeting can be tricky if you are married. In any marriage, it's best for both partners to be informed about where the money comes from and where it's being spent. Even if your spouse is the one managing the money, make a date once a month to review your respective checkbooks and bank statements. That way, you will both have a clear idea of how much you're spending separately and as a family. If your expenses outweigh your income, talk about the goals you have for the future and ways you can cut back on spending now to help you achieve them. And remember, everybody has his or her own money style. Review the information and tools in Chapters 2 and 3 so you can bring up financial issues while avoiding a battle.

Small Steps to Becoming a Money Star

1. Review budget categories in which you spend the most money. Trimming 5 to 10 percent from these categories will make a big difference in your savings. Prime categories to trim are groceries, entertainment, and clothing.
2. Break a habit. Pick a habit that you can do without: smoking, last-minute purchases, candy bars in the afternoon—something that doesn't give you much benefit and may even cause harm. Every time you resist the habit, put the money you would have spent into a cash jar or a savings account. After a few months, you'll be amazed at how much you've saved.
3. Create a "top three" spending priority list. Choose three areas you'd like to reduce. Write a list in big letters and post it in a prominent place, such as on the refrigerator or on the wall in your office. Spend as usual on other items, but keep a close eye on your top three.
4. Enlist your family's help. Have a family meeting and brainstorm ideas for saving money. Are dinners out really worth the expense? Or could you have a rotating "cooking night" and experiment with new foods at home? Does anyone in the family have a fun money-making idea that could help make ends meet?
5. Ask your friends about savings ideas. Does anyone have a great credit card deal? Know of an outlet store that's a little far away but has great bargains? Use the Internet to get great deals? Ask around and see if you and your friends can save money together.

CHAPTER 6

Taking Shelter: Housing and Real Estate Investing

Dear WIFE,

I'm in my mid-20s and unmarried, but I'm thinking about buying a small house. I make $36,000 a year, and I'm paying $750 a month in rent. What a waste! I've been in the same apartment for three years and have nothing to show for the $27,000 I've spent on rent. I'd like to buy a house, but can I afford it?

Seeking Shelter in Albuquerque

Dear Seeking Shelter,

WIFE commends you on your industrious attitude! Home ownership has many benefits, but figuring out how much you can afford can be tricky. WIFE thinks your mortgage payment shouldn't exceed 28 percent of your monthly income. You earn $3,000 a month, so your mortgage payment shouldn't exceed $840. At 7 percent, that's the payment on a 30-year mortgage of $126,000. Add your down payment to that (you can buy a first home for as little as 5 percent down), and that's how much home you can afford. Read on, and learn what you need to know about investing in real estate.

The Simple Truth

❦

The number of single women buying homes has skyrocketed in recent years. Twenty percent of all first-time home buyers are now single women, and today single women buy homes at twice the rate of single men.

—National Association of Realtors

Home Sweet Home

A tremendous sense of pride comes with owning your own place, and owning a home has financial advantages as well. You can deduct the mortgage interest and property taxes on your income tax return, your house may appreciate in value, and when you sell your home you'll likely realize that gain tax-free. Those are pretty great perks for investing in property.

But buying a house in an area where real estate values are deteriorating or spending more than you can afford are mistakes that can seriously derail your financial plan. Fail to pay your mortgage and you could lose the roof over your head. During a housing slump, renting is often your best bet, since property owners who are waiting for prices to rise will rent out their property, flooding the market with rentals and causing rents to drop.

Your decision to rent or own should be based on your own personal situation and finances. Worksheet 6.1 will help you get a better sense of the financial and tax consequences of owning versus renting.

Deciding to Buy

Decisions, decisions, decisions. Finding the right home at the right price can be tricky. To start, get clear on your vision. Do you want a quiet bungalow in the countryside, or a duplex in the heart of downtown? Are two bedrooms enough for your needs, or is your family growing? Visualize the perfect property, and then figure out how much you can afford for a down payment and monthly housing costs. Use Quiz 6.1 to help you get a clearer image of your new home and what life will be like after you move in. Grab a pencil and start planning!

If you are married, you and your spouse should discuss the questions in Quiz 6.1 together, to make sure you are in sync. If you disagree, figure out why. Are you concerned that you will lose touch with friends and family if you move too far away? Is your husband or partner afraid of the financial responsibilities or long-term commitment that come with owning a home? Hidden emotional factors may

Worksheet 6.1

Is It Better to Rent or Buy?

Step 1: Compare the costs

Monthly mortgage payment	_____	
Monthly property taxes	+ _____	
Monthly homeowner's insurance	+ _____	
Homeowner association fees	+ _____	
Routine maintenance	+ _____	
Monthly ownership cost	= _____	
Monthly rent	_____	
Subtract rent from monthly ownership cost		
Multiply by 12		$\times$ 12 _____
Annual savings of renting instead of buying		══════

Step 2: Compute lost earnings on down payment

Down payment	_____
Times rate you could earn if invested elsewhere	$\times$ ____ %
Annual lost earnings on down payment	══════

Step 3: Compute income tax savings

Annual mortgage interest (multiply the balance of your mortgage by the interest rate)	_____
Annual property taxes	_____
Total Interest and property taxes	_____
Times your highest tax bracket	$\times$ ____ %
Income taxes you will save by buying	══════

Step 4: Compute annual appreciation

Value of the home	_____
Annual appreciation percentage (can be negative)	$\times$ ____ %
Expected annual increase in value	══════

Option #1: Add bottom lines of Steps 1 and 2.	_____
Option #2: Add bottom lines of Steps 3 and 4.	_____

Which number is greater, option #1 or option #2?
If it's option #1, renting is better for you right now.
If it's option #2, buying is better for you right now.

Quiz 6.1

Dream Home Questionnaire

1. What's your price range for buying a house?
2. How many bedrooms and bathrooms should your house have?
3. What is the minimum size in square feet that you need to live comfortably?
4. Do you want a freestanding house, or do you prefer an attached unit, such as a townhouse or condominium?
5. Is having a yard important to you?
6. Do you want to live in a city, a suburb, or a rural area?
7. Do you want to stay within a certain distance of family and friends?
8. Are you concerned with the quality of schools near your home?
9. Will you need to commute to work, and if so, what's the farthest you are willing to travel?
10. Do you want easy access to public transportation?

---

lurk behind your disagreements, so put all your cards on the table and be honest with each other about your motives when making plans.

"The future belongs to those who believe in the beauty of their dreams."

ELEANOR ROOSEVELT

The Price Is Right

One of the most common questions we are asked is, how much house can I afford? A good rule of thumb is that your mortgage should not exceed 28 percent of your gross monthly income, and your monthly debt payments, including credit card and car payments, shouldn't be more than 36 percent of your income. Lending institutions will often let you make a down payment as low as 5 percent, but plan on putting at least 20 percent down on the purchase price of your new home to avoid the cost of private mortgage insurance (PMI). PMI protects the lender in the event that you can't make your mortgage payments and generally costs you about a quarter percent of the loan amount each year—money you'd surely rather spend decorating!

The Simple Truth

✧

Americans are devoting a larger share of income to keeping a roof over their heads. In 2000, an estimated 19 million American households spent 35 percent or more of monthly income on housing costs, compared to 16 million in 1990.

—2000 U.S. Census

Web sites sponsored by real estate firms and mortgage lenders often offer calculators to help you figure out how much house you can afford. Just enter your income, other debt payments, and today's mortgage interest rates, and these calculators will do the math. For example, go to www.homestore.com/Home Finance/Calculators/mortgagequalifier.asp? and play with the numbers to see what works for you.

"Before you try to keep up with the Joneses, be sure they're not trying to keep up with you."

ERMA BOMBECK

Shopping for a House

Now it's time to go house hunting! Before you begin, we have eight tips to help you get the best deal.

1. Start with the basics. Read the classifieds, visit open houses, and let brokers know what kind of housing you're seeking. Shopping for a home can be exciting; it's also time consuming and occasionally frustrating. Don't expect to find the perfect place overnight, and don't jump at the first house you see. Your decision will affect your lifestyle for the next several years, so shop judiciously.

2. Look online. The proliferation of web sites devoted to home listings makes it easier than ever to find the right residence. The resources in Appendix B list several sites that can help you narrow the search for a house, provide you with credit reports, put you in touch with real estate agents, and even let you apply for a mortgage online!

3. Shop strategically. You may be able to save thousands of dollars on the cost of your house by looking for sellers eager to offload their property. Perhaps the house has been on the market for a long time or is already vacant. A seller who is divorcing or has recently experienced a death in the family might be eager to make a deal.

4. Beware of hidden expenses. An extensive yard may be beautiful, but will you need an expensive gardener to keep up with the weeds? A pool is fun, but will the utility cost drown you? Country living is grand, but will it cost you an extra grand a year to pay for the gas you use in your daily commute?

5. Inspect before you buy. Hire a reputable home inspector to scrutinize the structure; the electrical, heating, and plumbing systems; and the property's general interior. Include a contingency clause in your contract so you can back out if your inspection reveals serious defects.

6. Think before you ink. When you sign a contract, include a contingency clause that the sale will be canceled if you are unable to obtain financing. Agree on which closing costs you will pay and which will be paid by the seller. Identify the items included in the sales price, such as draperies, chandeliers, and appliances, so there are no misunderstandings at closing.

7. Put as much down as possible. With 20 percent down, you'll save the private mortgage insurance, and you may get a better interest rate as well. Where can you get the money to beef up your down payment? Consider asking Mom and Dad to help foot the bill, as either a loan or a gift. Or if you haven't owned a home within the last two years, you can withdraw up to $10,000 from an IRA penalty-free to buy a principal residence. You can borrow from your 401(k) plan, but if you leave your job, you will have to repay the loan immediately.

8. Consider how to take title. Your home is likely to be one of your largest investments, so carefully consider how to take title, and consult with a lawyer if necessary. Here are some common ways people take title. If you are single, you'll probably take title in your name alone. In many states, married couples hold their property as *tenants by the entirety,* meaning they share joint ownership and the property cannot be sold to satisfy the debts of only one owner. In other states, *joint tenancy* is most common, and upon death the surviving owner inherits the entire property without it going through probate. Unmarried co-owners generally take title as *tenants in common,* with each owning a specified percentage of the property. The owners can sell their interests or will their interests to someone else without consent of the other co-owner.

Buying a house can be an exhilarating experience, but buyer's remorse is common, especially among first-time home owners. You may find yourself suddenly short-tempered, anxious, depressed, or thinking of backing out for silly reasons. If you suffer any of these symptoms, grit your teeth and ride it out. Adjusting to the idea of owning a house takes time, but if you did your homework in advance, you can rest assured you made the right decision.

How Would You Like to Pay for This?

It's smart to shop for financing before you shop for the house itself. Prequalification can be a valuable negotiating tool, since the seller will know you'll be able to close on the home quickly. Also, by prequalifying, you can make sure you're shopping in the right price range, so you don't fall in love with a house that costs far more than you can afford.

Qualifying for a Loan

A key factor in getting a loan is your credit history. Most lenders use a computerized system that assigns you a *credit score,* sometimes called your *FICO score.* A high score means you're more likely to repay your mortgage. If you're not overextended and you pay your bills on time, you should rank pretty high on the scale.

FICO is an acronym for Fair Isaac Corporation, which developed the concept of the credit score, a single number that represents your likelihood to repay a loan. To decide whether to loan you money, lenders run your credit report through a computer program with a built-in scorecard. Points are awarded or deducted based on many factors, such as how long you have had your credit cards, whether you make your payments on time, how much credit you have available, and whether your balances are near the maximum.

FICO scores range from the high 300s to the mid 800s. Studies have shown that borrowers with scores above 680 almost always made their payments on time, while borrowers with scores below 600 are fairly likely to develop problems. Banks use these numbers to determine whether or not to lend money and at what interest rate.

Some of the factors that affect your credit score are:

- delinquencies
- number of accounts opened within the last 12 months
- short credit history
- balances on revolving credit that are near the maximum limits
- public records, such as tax liens, judgments, or bankruptcies
- no recent balances
- too many recent credit inquiries
- too few revolving accounts
- too many revolving accounts

To get an idea of how your record looks so far, order a copy of your credit report from one of the three major credit bureaus—Equifax, Experian, or Trans Union—and make sure it is accurate. Chapter 10 provides more information about how to order and review your credit report and ways to improve your credit history.

Fixed vs. Adjustable Rate Mortgages

A big dilemma is whether to choose a fixed-rate mortgage or an adjustable-rate mortgage (ARM). With a fixed-rate mortgage, your monthly payment is set at the beginning and will never change. If you opt for an adjustable-rate loan, your initial interest rate may be lower, but the interest rate and monthly payment can climb quickly as interest rates rise.

If current rates are low, or if you expect to stay in your new home for at least five years, a fixed-rate mortgage is probably your best bet. But if rates are high, an ARM may tide you over until rates decline and you can lock in a fixed rate.

If you're planning to sell the house in less than five years, you may choose an adjustable mortgage with a lower initial interest rate. Do this only if that rate is 2 to 3 percent lower than current fixed rates, and there is no prepayment penalty, which is a charge for repaying the loan early.

If you decide on an ARM, you need to know not only the initial rate, but on what basis it will be adjusted and how often. Each lender may impose a different cap, or ceiling above which rates cannot rise. Generally, your interest rate shouldn't increase more than 2 percent at any one time, or 6 percent for the life of the loan. Also, make sure you'll be able to meet the higher monthly payments as they occur. Don't be caught off guard by higher housing costs in the future and blow your budget or, even worse, lose your house.

Consider a hybrid mortgage, with a fixed rate for a few years and adjustable after that. The mortgage payment is calculated over 30 years, but is fixed for the first five years or so at a lower rate than a fixed 30-year mortgage. If you plan to stay in your home less than five years before moving on, the hybrid mortgage with a five-year fixed rate will guarantee you a stable mortgage payment while you are there.

Another option is to pay your loan off faster than the traditional 30-year mortgage. If you choose a 15-year mortgage, the interest rate may be somewhat less than a thirty-year mortgage. In addition, the quicker you pay your loan, the less interest you will pay over the life of the loan. A $100,000 loan paid over 30 years at 7 percent will cost $139,400 in interest. That means your $100,000 loan actually costs you $239,400. Borrow $100,000 using a 15-year loan at 6.5 percent, and it costs $56,800 in interest. That's a savings of $82,600 in interest, which isn't chickenfeed!

Rules for ARMs (or, How Not to Lose an Arm and a Leg)

If you decide to use an ARM, here are some important rules to keep in mind:

- *Don't choose a loan with rates that change more than once per year. You don't want to get stuck in a cash flow crunch as your payment goes up month by month.*
- *Don't choose a loan with rates that can go up by more than 2 percent per year. Two percent may sound small, but it can create a big increase in your monthly payment. Be sure you will have time to adjust.*

- *Choose a loan with rates that have an increase limit of no more than 6 percent over the life of the loan and no decrease limit. You don't want to get stuck with a loan that will increase stratospherically. Conversely, you want to be able to take advantage of any interest rate decreases that might be in your future.*
- *Don't use negative amortization. Negative amortization means that you are not fully paying off the interest on your loan. In other words, you are getting deeper into debt each month. You want to pay down your mortgage, not increase it!*
- *Use a slow-moving index. To which index is your proposed ARM tied? Choose an index that is not as reactive to a rise in interest rates, such as the bank's cost of funds, instead of the Treasury index.*

Locking in a Good Rate

A lender will take some time to approve your mortgage loan application. You can protect yourself against a rise in interest rates by locking in a rate during the preapproval process. Be sure to get the lock-in deal in writing, and get a guarantee of at least 60 days. For a fee of about a quarter-point, you can also lock in a rate with a float-down option, which means you're protected from rate increases for a specified period, and your rate will drop if market rates go down before you close.

The "Dollar a Month" Plan

You can make painless prepayments on your mortgage and dramatically shorten the time it takes to pay it off if you pay just an extra dollar a month! Add one dollar to the first payment, add another dollar the next month, and then another dollar the month after that. At the end of the first year, your payment will have increased only $12 per month, $24 per month at the end of the second year, and so forth. Depending on the size of your mortgage, you can pay back your 30-year mortgage in 20 to 25 years and save thousands of dollars in interest.

Be Aware of Closing Costs

Closing costs on your loan can add up to thousands of dollars. When you apply for a mortgage, your lender should provide a good faith estimate of these costs, including *points,* which are the lender's one-time charge for transacting the loan. Each point represents 1 percent of the mortgage amount, and the more points you pay up front, the lower the interest rate should be for the life of the loan. If you plan

Worksheet 6.2

Your Effective Interest Rate

	Option #1	Option #2	Option #3
1. Mortgage points (e.g., 2%)	_____	_____	_____
2. Years you plan to own your home	÷_____	÷_____	÷_____
3. Annual cost of points	=_____	=_____	=_____
4. Interest rate (e.g., 7%)	+_____	+_____	+_____
5. Effective interest rate (line 3 + line 4)	=_____	=_____	=_____

to stay in your new home for several years, it's to your advantage to pay an extra point up front to get an interest rate that is a quarter to a half percentage point lower. But if you plan to move after only a couple of years, paying extra points for a lower rate may not be wise.

Use Worksheet 6.2 to compute your effective interest rate if you pay points. Use this worksheet to compare the various options that are offered to you by the lender, and you will be able to determine whether paying points to reduce the interest rate is worth the up-front cost.

Shopping for a Mortgage

You may want to hire a mortgage broker to help you find a suitable loan. The broker can help you determine how much you can borrow, the best interest rates, and closing costs and can answer any questions along the way. The mortgage broker is paid directly by the financial institution that provides the loan, and your only cost will be a small application fee. If you don't use a mortgage broker, consult several financial institutions to research the best loan for you.

You can shop for mortgages online, and compare quotes from several different lenders from the comfort of your desk chair. Women especially are turning to the Internet for mortgage information, because they can shop at their own pace without feeling pressured by slick salesmen or condescending loan officers. The Internet allows you to deal with lenders that have the best options for you rather than confining your mortgage search to a local mortgage company or bank.

But arranging a mortgage this way requires a certain amount of financial savvy, since you'll be shouldering much of the responsibility usually handled by a mortgage broker. Before you buy online, make sure you understand the following:

- how the loan process works
- how to compare costs and lenders
- which loan product and rate combination is best for you
- how lock-ins work and when to use one

Don't bother with lenders who won't quote rates unless you apply, and watch out for pricing gimmicks and hidden fees. Even if you don't go with an Internet lender, the competitive rates and fees quoted online can be a valuable negotiating tool when talking with conventional lenders and brokers.

When to Refinance Your Mortgage

Once you have a mortgage, you're set, right? Not really. Though your parents might have kept the same mortgage for 30 years, today's fluctuating mortgage rates keep you on your toes. When should you refinance? If you can get a no-cost loan at a rate that's lower than you are presently paying, why not refinance? Because it's a pain in the you-know-what, that's why. How much would you need to save to make it worthwhile to refinance? It's up to you, but most of us would be willing to settle for a clear 1 percent savings each year.

Assume the cost to refinance will average 1 percent of your loan amount (unless you choose a no-cost loan with higher interest rates) plus any points you pay. One important factor in deciding whether to refinance is how long you intend to keep your house. If you plan to keep your home just a year, it probably doesn't make sense to refinance at all, no matter how much your interest rate will decline. But if you plan to keep your home for ten years or more, even a 1 percent reduction in interest rates makes sense for you.

You can use Table 6.1 to decide whether it pays to refinance your mortgage.

Table 6.1   When Refinancing Makes Sense

Number of Years You Will Keep the House	Minimum Interest Rate Reduction
2	2.5%
4	1.75%
6	1.5%
8	1.25%
10	1%

Surfing Online Mortgage Services

Shopping online can demystify the mortgage process, but make sure you understand what kind of service providers you're dealing with before you submit an application:

- Direct lenders *underwrite the loans themselves.*
- Brokers *seek out the best deals for customers and process the applications.*
- Referral services *match borrowers to potential lenders and are not involved in the application process.*
- Mortgage auction sites *solicit bids from lenders based on a consumer's profile.*

The Resources section at the back of this book lists web sites where you can compare mortgage rates and other information. Bear in mind that most sites charge a fee or percentage of the loan when you apply.

"I am a marvelous housekeeper. Every time I leave a man I keep his house."

ZSA ZSA GABOR

Becoming a Real Estate Tycoon

Now that you own your own home, you may decide you want to invest in someone else's home. Investing in real estate is an attractive prospect for many, but it is not without its pitfalls.

Managing rental property can be a headache. It involves more time, money, and aggravation than many investors are willing to commit. You can take Quiz 6.2 to decide if you have what it takes to own and manage rental property.

If you like the idea of investing in real estate but don't want to play landlord, you can become a property owner from afar through a real estate investment trust (REIT), mutual fund, or limited partnership.

Real estate investment trusts pool the money of several investors to purchase many commercial or residential buildings and hire an independent company to manage the properties. Different kinds of REITs invest in different types of properties, from apartments to shopping centers, hotels, office buildings, and even mobile home parks. In addition, REITs are traded on major stock exchanges, so you can cash out easily at any time.

When shopping for a REIT, you'll need to do in-depth research. The best sources of information are the REIT's latest proxy statement and prospectus. The growth rate for *funds from operations,* or FFO, is more important than the earnings

Quiz 6.2

Are You Cut Out to Be a Landlord?

Being a landlord involves more than simply buying property, finding a tenant, and letting the cash flow in. Some people are comfortable with the kinds of activities that investors face almost daily. Others find them difficult. Answer these questions to see if you have what it takes to be a landlord:

	Yes	No
1. Do you deal well with people on a regular basis?	___	___
2. Do you deal well with risk?	___	___
3. Do you enjoy taking care of your own home?	___	___
4. Are real estate prices appreciating in your area (or do you expect them to in the future)?	___	___
5. Do you have spare cash (or home equity) to invest?	___	___
6. Are you good at keeping records and completing paperwork?	___	___
7. Do you have free time to spend on real estate investing?	___	___
8. Do you have any small business experience?	___	___
9. Can you juggle several tasks at the same time?	___	___
10. Are you willing to do repairs and maintenance yourself or are you willing to pay someone to have them done?	___	___
11. If the monthly expenses are greater than the rents, do you have the financial staying power to cover those expenses, year after year?	___	___
12. If the property becomes vacant for a month or more, do you have the resources to cover the mortgage payment?	___	___
13. Will you be able to manage the property on your own?	___	___
14. Have you talked with other local landlords about their experiences and challenges?	___	___
15. Will you treat this like a business, raising rents when market conditions allow?	___	___
16. Would you feel comfortable evicting a family with five hungry children if they didn't pay the rent?	___	___

If you answer "Yes!" to most of these questions, then you may have the personality and skills needed to be a successful landlord. Real estate investment, over the long haul, can be a rewarding activity, but it takes work and time.

per share, and the "same-space" revenue growth from year to year will give you an idea of the management's ability to cut costs and increase rents and occupancy. Also, check out the management's stake in the business; they should own a large portion of the outstanding stock. On the risk side, high yields can means less capital is going back into redevelopment and acquisitions, and too much debt can drag a REIT down quickly.

Real estate mutual funds are a way to diversify your investment in REITs. Real estate mutual funds generally hold shares of REITs and may also invest in companies related to real estate, such as builders and contractors.

Like other mutual funds, they are professionally managed, offer diversification, and typically require a small minimum investment. Before investing, be sure you know what the fees will be, and check the fund's earnings track record as you would for any other type of mutual fund.

Real estate limited partnerships are long-term investments. They pool the money from investors to buy properties, with the intention of selling within seven to ten years. Real estate limited partnerships usually charge hefty up-front sales fees and require a long-term commitment. If you sell your units before the partnership disbands, you may get back only a fraction of what you've invested, because they are not freely traded. Study the prospectus carefully before you invest, and check the results of the sponsor's past partnerships.

"Two rules (for investing):
  #1. Preserve the principal.
  #2. When in doubt, see Rule #1."

WARREN BUFFET

Small Steps to Becoming a Money Star

1. Use the worksheets in this chapter to figure out how much you can afford to spend on a house and the tax benefits of home ownership. There's no use limiting yourself to cramped quarters if you can realistically afford something more comfortable.
2. Take 15 minutes when you are alone at home to sit and be still. How do you feel in your home? Is it too cluttered for your taste or too sparse? Does it reflect your current personality, goals, and dreams? If not, what can you do to change your environment to suit you?
3. Take a short course in home improvement. Many local stores offer courses in tile setting, woodworking, spa maintenance, and other home improvement subjects. Even if you don't plan to do the work yourself, you can learn

a lot about the process and ensure that you don't get ripped off by contractors or maintenance people.

4. If you have a partner, make a copy of the Dream Home Questionnaire from this chapter for each of you, fill it out separately, and then compare your answers. Talk about the image each of you has in your head about your dream house and the area in which you want to live. By sharing your thoughts, you can merge your visions to find a home that meets the expectations of both of you.

5. If you already have an emergency fund, and you currently are contributing the max to your retirement funds, it may be time to start making extra principal payments on your mortgage. Paying just $40 a month extra on a $100,000 mortgage will slash five years off your loan!

CHAPTER 7

Insuring Your Future

Dear WIFE,

I'm just starting out as a freelance graphic designer, and I'm proud that I already have a couple regular clients. But my father isn't impressed. All he cares about is whether I have health insurance. It's like an obsession with him. I don't have insurance yet because I'm on a tight budget. How can I tell Dad to back off and let me focus on building my business first?

Creative in Salt Lake City

Dear Creative,

Sorry, kiddo, but Dad's right about this one. Forgoing health insurance is like walking a tightrope with no safety net below. So get a policy, pronto. If you can find group coverage through a professional association, that's your best bet. Otherwise, shop around for an individual policy. Read on, and we'll tell you what you need to know to get insured and get Dad off your back.

Conquering Life's Risks

A catastrophic loss can scuttle any financial plan. You might not be able to avoid unpleasant events in your life, but you can prepare to meet them head on by protecting yourself and your property.

The purpose of insurance is to protect you against major financial loss. Different people face different risks, so not everybody needs every kind of insurance. For example, if you are unmarried with no children, you may not need life insurance. But everyone who drives a car needs auto insurance.

The best protection is an informed decision before you sign on the dotted line. In this chapter, you'll find out how to identify the types of insurance you should have and the ones you can do without, and how to be smart about buying a policy.

Life Insurance

Some people buy life insurance for unusual reasons. Take the case of our client whose father left the proceeds of his $500,000 life insurance to a trust for the family dog, to be cared for by the housekeeper. Dad's will stated that the income from the funds was to be used for the dog's needs, and when the dog died, the $500,000 would go to the housekeeper. Obviously, he had not thought this through. Realizing that the dog's existence was the only thing standing between the housekeeper and her money, his son feared the dog might meet an early demise. Respecting his father's love for the dog, he petitioned the court to release the funds to the housekeeper right away, with the provision that she care for the dog for the rest of the dog's life. The court granted his wish, which was a doggone good thing: The dog and the housekeeper lived happy, long lives together.

Your insurance needs may be more conventional. With life insurance, you can provide funds to care for your dependents after you are gone. The proceeds can make up for the loss of the salary or other support you contributed to the household and also provide money to help your family meet future goals, such as education.

Deciding How Much Insurance You Need

How do you figure out how much life insurance you need? An old rule of thumb was that you needed five to seven times your annual salary. But that ballpark estimate doesn't take into account your family's specific needs, such as whether your spouse will continue to work, how your children will be cared for, and what college they will attend.

Worksheet 7.1 can give you a more accurate assessment of your family's financial situation and how much coverage may be appropriate. If your circumstances change—for example, if you marry, divorce, or have a child—revisit this worksheet and modify your coverage.

The Simple Truth
❦

The number of women more than 100 years old will double in the next 10 years.

—*U.S. Administration on Aging*

Worksheet 7.1

Your Life Insurance Needs

Immediate Expenses

Debts to be paid off immediately _____

Funeral and death costs _____

Estate taxes _____

Total immediate cash needed when you die _____

Education Fund for Children

Total cost of college (today's dollars) _____

Times number of children ✕_____

Total college costs to be provided _____

Less funds from other sources (existing college fund,
    grandparents, scholarships and loans, earnings) _____

Additional educational fund needed _____

Spouse's Living Expenses Until Retirement

Your annual earnings to be replaced
    (today's dollars) _____

Current age of surviving spouse _____

Times Multiple Factor (from *Table 1*) ✕_____

Spouse's total living expenses until retirement _____

Spouse's Retirement Needs

Total income needed in retirement (today's dollars) _____

Less social security benefits _____

Less pension benefits _____

Equals total retirement needs (today's dollars) _____

Times Multiple Factor (from *Table 2*) ✕_____

Total retirement needs of spouse _____

Less existing funds available for retirement _____

Retirement needs to be funded with insurance _____

Total Insurance Needed

Immediate Expenses, from above _____

Education Fund for Children, from above _____

Spouse's Living Expenses until Retirement,
    from above _____

Spouse's Retirement Needs, from above _____

Total Insurance Needed _____

Table 1			Table 2	
Spouse's Current Age	Multiple Factor		Spouse's Current Age	Multiple Factor
25	23		25	5
30	21		30	6
35	19		35	7
40	17		40	8
45	15		45	9
50	12		50	11
55	9		55	13
60	5		60	15
			65	17

How Jeanne Calment Lived to 122

Doctors tell us the keys to good health are regular exercise, proper diet, and getting rid of bad habits such as smoking. For Jeanne Calment, the secrets to long life were chocolate, olive oil, and port wine. She took up fencing at age 85 and still rode a bicycle at age 100. She finally gave up cigarettes in 1995, but her doctor said her abstinence was due to pride rather than health: She was too blind to light up herself and hated asking others to do it for her. Though blind, nearly deaf, and in a wheelchair, Mrs. Calment remained spirited and mentally sharp until her death in 1997 at age 122.

Selecting the Right Coverage

Now that you know how much life insurance you need to protect your family, you have to determine whether you want term insurance or permanent insurance, also called cash-value insurance.

Term life insurance is generally the least expensive life insurance you can buy. That's because it doesn't build any cash value. If you die during the period covered by the contract, your beneficiary will receive the death benefit. If you are still alive at the end of the term, the game's over.

Annual renewable term rates start low and increase as you age. Five-year and ten-year level term policies offer fixed premiums over the life of the policy. When shopping for term insurance, look for policies that are renewable for as long as you need coverage, or convertible to permanent coverage without a health exam.

If your family is young, term insurance is generally the best choice, because the premiums are lower than whole life and you can discontinue the coverage after your children are grown and your needs for insurance are less. However, the premiums can skyrocket if you continue to hold a term policy after age 50.

If you have a term policy that is several years old, look at current quotes for comparable insurance. Because of increased longevity, term insurance premiums have declined in recent years, so a new policy may cost less than your existing one. Never cancel your existing insurance policies until you have a new approved insurance policy in place.

The Simple Truth

The average life expectancy for a woman in the United States is 79.8 years, and the average life expectancy for a man is 74.4.

—*National Center for Health Statistics, 2003*

Permanent life insurance combines insurance coverage with savings. The two most common types of permanent coverage are whole life and universal life. The biggest benefit of permanent insurance is that you can borrow against the value of the cash account (the "cash value") or draw down the money as retirement income. But it can often take more than 10 years for the cash value to add up, and the premiums will be several times higher than comparable term contracts, because you're funding the cash account. What's more, although these policies accumulate cash value, to tap that value you must cancel the policy or borrow against it. And when you die, the insurance company pays only the face value of the policy, not the face value *plus* the cash value.

With a *whole life* policy, your premiums are fixed. When you take out the policy, the interest rate you earn on the cash value account is set. Some policies also pay a small dividend, which can be applied toward your premiums.

A *universal life* policy is like a whole life policy, except the interest rate set by the insurance company can vary from year to year, and the premiums and death benefit are flexible. Though the cash value buildup is not guaranteed, generally you'll have lower premiums than with whole life, while still retaining most of the same benefits.

A *variable life* policy lets you invest some or all of the cash value in stocks, bonds, and real estate through a variety of subaccounts that resemble mutual funds. Smart investment choices might yield a better return and a higher death benefit, but you're taking a risk because in declining markets, the cash value and death benefit of your policy can fall, or even disappear, with the market's performance.

A variation on this type of coverage, *variable universal life* (VUL), combines aspects of variable and universal policies by letting you control the investments and premiums while offering a guaranteed minimum death benefit. For all of these policies, investment earnings are tax-deferred until withdrawn, and income-tax free if paid as a death benefit.

How to Decide What's Right for You

Although term insurance is less expensive, permanent insurance is preferable in some instances:

- If you need insurance for more than 10 years, permanent cash-value insurance may actually be less expensive, since the cash value of a long-term policy will increase at a greater rate than the premium.
- If you expect to face health problems in the future that may make you uninsurable, permanent insurance might be best.
- If you are over 65, term insurance premiums will be so high that a permanent life insurance policy generally will cost you less than term.

Choosing the Right Insurance Company

Just like mortgage lenders and car dealers, insurance companies are turning to the Internet to lure potential customers and market their wares. Searching for a life insurance policy online may save you a bundle in annual premiums, and many sites offer added bells and whistles to help you calculate the right amount of coverage for your needs. Three useful sites include InstantQuote (www.instantquote.com), QuickQuote (www.quickquote.com), and Quotesmith (www.quotesmith.com). Each can provide price quotes from several different carriers, based on information you enter, such as your date of birth, the amount of coverage you need, and the duration of the policy. Although you can fill out an application online, you'll receive a hard copy of the contract by regular mail within a few weeks, and a medical technician will contact you about setting up an appointment in your home for a brief physical.

When choosing an insurance company, financial strength is important. You can look up your prospective insurance company in *Best's Insurance Reports* in your local library, or research online at www.ambest.com. The rating of your company is key, since you want to insure with a company that will survive to pay benefits should you ever need them. Choose a company rated A++, A+, or A—the higher the rating, the more financially sound the company.

Types of Insurance You Don't Need

- Accidental death insurance. *You are unlikely to use this type of insurance; less than 5 percent of all deaths are accidental.*
- One disease insurance. *Your health insurance should cover all types of diseases—not just one. What if you get the wrong disease?*
- Supplemental hospitalization policies. *Most of these policies do not pay enough to truly offset hospital expenses. A good major medical policy will pay for hospital expenses as well as other medical costs.*
- Mail order and TV insurance. *Most health and accident policies sold by direct mail or on TV have long waiting periods and high deductibles. Shop with a reputable agent to get the best price instead of relying on advertising.*
- Student health policies. *Before you buy, check to see if your student is covered under your existing health insurance. If so, you don't need another policy.*

Disability Insurance

Remember watching Christopher Reeve star in the Superman movies? He seemed charming and invincible in his screen persona, the Man of Steel, which made his horse-riding accident in 1995 and resulting paralysis all the more tragic. But accidents happen, as do debilitating illnesses, and they can pull you straight off the career track and park you on the sidelines for months or years at a time.

It's easy to tell yourself, "It won't happen to me." But at any point during your working life, you are more likely to become disabled than to die. For most people then, disability insurance is a must. It will provide a steady income stream in the event you're unable to work. In general, the policy benefits will replace about 60 percent of your annual earnings for as long as you are disabled.

The Simple Truth

❧

Fifty-four million Americans have some sort of long-term disability. Of this group:

- 73% are heads of household.
- 46% are married.
- 77% have no children.
- 58% own their own homes.

—*U.S. Census*

It's great if your employer offers group disability insurance coverage as a benefit. If not, investigate private coverage, which probably will cost between 1 and 3 percent of your annual income.

Before choosing a disability policy, here are several important considerations to keep in mind:

- Choose *own-occupation* coverage, which pays if you can't return to your former job, rather than *any occupation* coverage, which terminates when the insurance company feels you're able to rejoin the workforce in any capacity.
- Look for an *income replacement policy* that will pay the difference between your old salary and your new one for at least two years, if you go back to work at a lesser-paying job.
- To save money, choose a longer waiting period before benefits kick in. Most polices begin payments after 90 days, but if you have accumulated savings or accrued vacation days, you may be able to wait longer, perhaps 120 or 180 days. A longer waiting period may cut your premiums in half.
- Choose a noncancelable policy that is guaranteed renewable at least until age 65.
- A rider for a *cost-of-living adjustment* will ensure that your benefits increase each year to keep pace with inflation, but expect to pay an additional 20 to 25 percent for the premium.
- Choose a benefit period that covers your lifetime, or at least extends to age 65.
- Because disability insurance only covers part of your salary, review other resources as well. To qualify for *social security disability,* you must be unable to work at any job for at least twelve months. If you were injured on the job, you may be entitled to *worker's compensation* benefits, which typically replace two-thirds of your income and are tax-free. For those who qualify, other *government programs,* such as disability benefits paid by the Veterans Administration, armed forces, or civil service, can provide an additional source of income.

The Simple Truth

᪥

Seven out of ten social security disability claims are rejected because they do not meet the strict eligibility standards.

—Social Security Administration

Six Mistakes That Will Make Your Insurance Company Rich

Don't spend your money on unnecessary coverage. Avoid these common mistakes:

1. *Buying life insurance if you don't have children or other family members who are financially dependent on you. There are few reasons why you would need insurance if you are single and have no children.*
2. *Buying life insurance on your children. It would be a great emotional loss if one of your children died, but typically not a financial loss.*
3. *Buying mail-order life insurance unless you comparison-shop for the best rates.*
4. *Buying investment insurance, such as universal life or variable life, instead of contributing to your retirement plans. Retirement plan contributions are tax deductible, while investment insurance premiums are not.*
5. *Buying mortgage insurance, which pays off your mortgage if you die. Regular life insurance is cheaper, and your beneficiaries can pay off the mortgage or use the money as they see fit.*
6. *Buying expensive riders on your life insurance. Riders, such as waiver of premiums, accidental death benefits, and additional purchase options, are costly and are often not worth the extra money.*

Medical Insurance

"Be careful about reading health books. You may die of a misprint."

MARK TWAIN

A good medical insurance policy is a must, no matter what your age or income. But winding your way through the maze of insurance options can give you such a headache, you'll want to check yourself into the ER! We're here to help you find the right coverage to cure what ails you.

The Simple Truth

☙

The average adult, age 65 or older, spends nearly one-fifth of her annual income, or $2,400, on health care. Prescription drugs account for the single largest expense for older adults.

—AARP

Group Policies

Signing up for health care coverage through your employer is generally the cheapest and easiest route, and the premiums are deducted straight from your paycheck. Most employers offer one or more types of health care plans, such as *health maintenance organizations* (HMOs), *point of service plans* (POPs), *preferred provider organizations* (PPOs), or *fee-for-service plans.*

HMOs contract directly with a network of doctors, hospitals, and other health care providers. You must use one of the providers in the network, you pay only a small copayment fee each visit to the doctor, and there is no deductible.

POPs are like HMOs, but they also allow you to use health care providers outside the plan network, if you are willing to pay a deductible.

PPOs generally require you to pay an annual deductible. You also pay a coinsurance fee, typically 20 to 30 percent of the cost of service. However, the provider agrees not to charge more for services than the maximum allowed by the carrier.

Fee-for-service plans give you an unlimited choice of doctors and hospitals. After you reach your annual deductible, your coinsurance payment will typically be 20 to 30 percent of the cost. There's one catch: If your doctor charges more than the carrier's allowable rate, you may be responsible for the difference, in addition to your deductible and coinsurance.

If you and your spouse both work full-time, it is possible that you both have medical coverage through your employers. You may be able to cut costs and maximize your health care benefits by both enrolling in one employer's plan, rather than each of you maintaining a separate policy. Compare the different plans for price, flexibility, and covered services. Make sure your spouse can enroll, and understand the benefits for which he is eligible before canceling one of your policies.

If you are covered under your husband's policy and you decide to divorce, you may be able to continue coverage under his insurance plan for three years, as provided by COBRA (the Consolidated Omnibus Budget Reconciliation Act of

1986). You will be responsible for the entire premium, even if his employer subsidized the cost while you were married. But before you opt for the COBRA coverage, shop around. Private plans are usually less costly than COBRA coverage for healthy individuals.

Private Insurance Coverage

If you have to find a health insurer on your own, you'll find that comparing the benefits of various major medical insurance policies is complicated business. Here are a few features to look for:

A high upper limit—one that covers at least $1 million in medical coverage before it stops paying

An affordable deductible—the higher your deductible, the lower your premiums

Coinsurance clauses—the percentage of costs above the initial deductible amount you will be required to pay

Exclusions—what kinds of medical expenses are either limited or excluded from coverage, such as drugs, psychotherapy, and cosmetic surgery

To analyze a policy, begin by listing your medical expenses for a typical year by types of expense. (If you're choosing insurance for your household, do this for each family member.) Then, for each policy you are considering, estimate how many of these expenses for which you would be responsible. This will give you an idea of the expenses you would incur in a typical year. Next, assume that you or someone in your family were in an accident and required hospitalization, extensive surgery, and ongoing physical therapy. How many of these expenses would be covered by the insurance company, and how much would come out of your pocket? Add the cost of the insurance premiums to the medical expenses you would have to bear in each scenario, and you will be able to compare the policies.

Medicare Coverage

If you're nearing your golden years, you can look forward to receiving health care coverage under Medicare. Medicare becomes available when you turn 65, whether or not you're still working. The program has two parts: Part A is hospital insurance, and Part B is supplementary medical insurance, which covers expenses such as doctor fees and lab services. When you enroll in Part A of the program, you also enroll in Part B, unless you submit a written request to the Social Security Administration waiving the supplemental coverage.

Medicare does not cover all health care expenses, and certain expenses are covered only for a limited period, so you should have additional insurance to supplement your Medicare benefits. If you are not participating in an employer's plan, consider purchasing Medicare supplemental insurance, known as *Medigap*. There are ten standard Medigap policies, denoted by the letters A through J, each with a different mix of benefits. No matter which carrier you choose, the policy features will be the same, though the price and service will differ, so comparison-shop before buying Medigap coverage.

Insurance Coverage You May Not Know You Have

You may be covered and not realize it! Check to see if you are insured under the following policies:

- *Your home owner's policy may cover lost luggage as well as items stolen from your car and other locations, such as your purse. It also may cover items you have borrowed, property damage by vandalism, or property damaged in a move.*
- *Your credit card may provide accidental death insurance coverage for you if your airline tickets were purchased with the card.*
- *Some credit cards offer $1,000 in life insurance for cardholders, free for the asking.*
- *The American Automobile Association (AAA) insures its members for hospital and death benefits if they are in an auto accident.*
- *Your auto policy includes medical coverage, so if you are in an auto accident, your costs may be fully covered regardless of the co-pay and deductible provisions of your health insurance policy.*
- *Your health insurance may cover children who are away at college. Check before you buy separate insurance for your college-age kids.*
- *Clubs, fraternal organizations, credit unions, and other groups may offer free life insurance benefits with their memberships.*
- *Your auto policy or credit card may cover damage to rental cars, saving you money on expensive rental car insurance.*

Long-Term Care Insurance

We know you don't need anything else to worry about, what with working, caring for children, and being the only one who replaces the toilet paper roll when it's empty. But there is a crisis in long-term care coming to America that will affect you and your family profoundly.

The Simple Truth

~&~

By 2030, one in five Americans will be a senior citizen. Women over 65 make up three-fourths of the nursing home residents. That means that women are twice as likely to enter a nursing home than men are.

—U.S. Census and Older Women's League (OWL)

Long-term care is a woman's issue. Women often deplete their assets, financially and emotionally, caring for elderly parents and spouses. On top of that, they live longer than men, so they require more years of care themselves, with no spouse around to look after them.

When it comes to long-term care, don't expect the government to be there for you. With Medicare, you might get a few weeks of skilled care at your home or in a nursing home. After that, you're on your own. And Medicaid is a means-tested welfare program for the very poor, which requires that you spend or give away most of your assets before you qualify for benefits.

If you are building wealth, you may be able to pay for long-term care out of your own pocket when you are elderly. But many people who believe that they can self-insure forget to take into account the risk of becoming disabled while they are still young. An early disability can wipe out even a considerable fortune.

What's a woman to do? Long-term care insurance can help safeguard you and your family. Deciding when to start the coverage is a challenge: Premiums are much lower if you buy a policy before you're 50, but you'll be paying premiums for years for insurance you probably won't need until well after you retire. Consider waiting until you're closer to age 55 or 60 to buy a policy, even though the premiums will be more expensive and you run the risk of early disability.

When shopping for a policy, here are the features to look for:

- *Benefit triggers* based on mental and functional impairments, including Alzheimer's and dementia, or medical necessities, without the requirement of a prior hospital stay
- *Coverage period* of at least three to five years; lifetime is best, though more costly
- *Reimbursement for actual expenses,* not "prevailing expenses" or "usual and customary expenses"
- *Guaranteed renewability* for life
- *Waiver of premium* during the period of care
- *Cost of living increases* so the benefits will keep pace with inflation

- *Coverage for all kinds of care,* including home care, adult day care, and intermediate and custodial nursing home facilities
- *Protection against lapse* for failure to pay due to cognitive disorder, such as Alzheimer's or dementia

As with disability insurance, you can help keep premiums down by choosing a longer waiting period before benefits kick in, shortening the coverage period, and limiting the benefit amount. Customize your policy based on the coverage you want as well as how much you can afford to pay from your own pocket in the event you need continuing care.

Fun Insurance Facts

- *Many Japanese golfers carry "hole-in-one" insurance because of the Japanese tradition that golfers must send gifts to all their friends when they get an "ace." The cost of gifts can often reach $10,000.*
- *Benjamin Franklin invented crop insurance.*
- *Betty Grable's legs were insured for $1 million, and Fred Astaire's feet were insured for $650,000.*
- *A London insurance brokerage has begun offering insurance for alien abduction. A premium of $155 per year would pay about $166,000 to an abductee (provided the abductor was not from earth) and double if the insured was impregnated during the abduction.*
- *More money is spent each year on alcohol and cigarettes than on life insurance.*
- *The People's Insurance Company of China recently began offering a marriage insurance policy, in which a couple that divorces forfeits all premiums paid, but a couple that stays together 25, 40, or 50 years stands to gain substantial dividends.*
- *British employers can insure against two or more of their staff winning the UK national lottery and not returning to work. The policy provides 25,000 to 500,000 pounds to cover the costs of employing temporary staff or recruiting new employees.*

Protecting Your Property

Imagine coming home from a vacation and finding that a little connector under the master-bedroom toilet gave way, filling your house like a giant bathtub. Your furniture and carpeting are ruined, the floorboards and walls must be ripped out and replaced, and the total damage run tens of thousands of dollars. That's what happened to neighbors of each of us, and you probably have heard similar stories.

Home Owner's Insurance

If you own a home, you need *home owner's insurance* to reimburse you in case damage is sustained to your house or personal property, or someone is injured in your home. If you rent, your property and liability will be covered under a *tenant's policy* or *renter's insurance.*

These policies protect you against loss from most common risks, such as fire, windstorms, and theft. But standard policies don't cover special events, such as damage from sewage and drain backup, floods, or earthquakes. An "all risk" policy will cover damages caused by almost any situation, except those specifically excluded in the policy, but can add about 20 percent to your premiums.

The premium you pay will vary based on the risk rating of your property, the deductible you choose, and the amount and type of coverage you require. The best way to make sure your insurance is adequate is to buy a *guaranteed-replacement-cost policy.* The insurance company will adjust the amount of insurance each year and guarantees that you will receive full payment on any claims, even if the cost of replacing your residence exceeds the face value of the policy.

Normal home owner's policies cap the amount they will pay for personal property, which may not be sufficient to cover the loss of big ticket items, such as home office equipment, jewelry, furs, and artwork. If you have valuable possessions such as these in your home, you will need a *personal articles floater* to provide additional coverage. Be sure the coverage is based on the *replacement cost* of damaged items rather than on an *actual cash value* basis (what the items are worth today, based on how old they are, normal wear and tear, etc.).

Why You Need Renter's Insurance
Many people who rent don't have this key insurance. Here is what renter's insurance covers and why having this insurance makes sense.

- Personal property. *Your landlord's insurance policy likely covers the outside of the building and the grounds, but not your personal property. If you come home and find your stereo system gone, or four inches of water on the floor, unless you have renter's insurance, you'll be out the money needed to replace your stuff. Renter's insurance covers your possessions against losses from fire or smoke, lightning, vandalism, theft, explosion, windstorm, and water damage from plumbing.*
- Liability. *Renter's insurance also pays if other people are injured at your home or elsewhere by you, a family member, or your pet, and it pays legal defense costs if you are taken to court.*
- Other items. *Like home owner's insurance, renter's insurance sometimes has other clauses that cover the loss of property while traveling or property stolen from other locations, such as your car.*

Vehicle Insurance

"If all the cars in the United States were placed end to end, it would probably be Labor Day Weekend."

DOUG LARSON

If you own a car, you need vehicle insurance. There are four types of coverage: bodily injury liability, property damage liability, collision, and uninsured motorist coverage.

Bodily injury liability protects you against claims if your car injures or kills someone. Choose a policy with the highest limits available, since lawsuits are often for millions of dollars.

Property damage liability pays claims for property damaged by your car. This coverage is linked to the bodily liability coverage, with the coverage expressed on your auto policy with three numbers, such as 100/300/50, which means that you are protected for $100,000 of claims for injury to an individual in an accident, $300,000 of claims for all individuals in that accident, and $50,000 of property damage.

Collision insurance covers the damage done to your own car in a collision. The higher the policy's deductible amount (the amount you pay for each accident), the lower your premium for collision coverage will be. The same is true of *comprehensive insurance,* which covers damage to your car from causes other than collision, such as theft.

Uninsured motorist coverage pays for accidents in which you are not at fault if the other party is uninsured. Most policies cover only bodily injuries, while others pay for damage to your car.

Most auto policies also provide medical coverage, which will reimburse medical expenses resulting from an auto accident. Review your auto policy to make sure that the coverage you are paying for does not duplicate your health care policy, and eliminate overlapping medical coverage to lower your premiums.

The general premium you will pay for auto insurance is based on the location of your residence, your accident record, traffic violations, previous insurance claims, and the kind of car you drive. Here are a few quick tips to help keep your premiums down:

Shop Around   Premiums can vary widely from company to company, so take the time to comparison-shop. Call at least three insurance companies in your search.

Find Out About Discounts   Many carriers will knock a few dollars off your premiums if you take a driver training course, if you're a nonsmoker, or if you're a member of certain professions that statistically represent good risks. You may also get a discount if you have other insurance with the same company, or if you are a long-time customer.

Drive a Safe Car   If the type of car you drive has a good safety record, your carrier may offer a discount. By the same token, high-performance sports cars mean high-priced coverage.

Keep a Clean Record   Accidents and speeding tickets can send your premiums sky high; drive carefully to protect yourself and your finances.

Carpool to Work or Take Mass Transit   If you take public transportation to your job or ride in someone else's car, it can cut down on your average annual mileage, which will in turn help reduce your premiums.

Keep Teenagers on Your Policy   Insurance rates are sky-high for drivers in their teens and twenties; adding your children to your policy rather than buying them their own can help minimize this expense.

Carry an Umbrella

If you have significant assets, we suggest you carry an umbrella. An umbrella policy takes over if a claim exceeds your other policy limits, adding $1 million to $10 million extra coverage to your personal liability and automobile liability policies.

The umbrella covers you, your spouse, and any relatives living in your household and insured by your primary policies. This policy also includes coverage if you are sued for false imprisonment, wrongful eviction, libel, slander, defamation of character, or invasion of privacy.

The cost is only a few hundred dollars a year, and the peace of mind the umbrella policy provides is well worth the expense.

Small Steps to Becoming a Money Star

1. If you haven't already done so, complete the life insurance worksheet (Worksheet 7.1 at the beginning of this chapter) to determine how much coverage you should have. Then make a date with your insurance agent to discuss your needs and the options available.
2. If you and your spouse both have medical insurance, review your coverage to see if it would be less expensive for both of you to be on the same plan.

3. If you rent an apartment and do not currently have renter's insurance, research different carriers and coverage options and then purchase a policy so your property is protected.

4. If your employer doesn't offer health insurance, suggest the employer start a group plan in lieu of your next raise. Employer-paid health insurance is tax-deductible to your employer, but not taxed to you. It's a win-win situation.

5. Contact your insurance agent for a thorough review of your insurance coverage: life, health, home, auto, disability, long-term care, and liability. Get it done now so you can have peace of mind.

CHAPTER 8

Ready, Set . . . Invest

> *Dear WIFE,*
>
> *I know I need to start saving and investing, but I feel uncomfortable around numbers. Is there a quick and painless way that a numbers dummy like me can start?*
>
> *MathPhobe in Nashville*
>
> *Dear MathPhobe,*
>
> *Investing is easy as 1-2-3. (Oh sorry, didn't mean to scare you.) One, read this chapter to learn about how investments work. Two, read the next chapter to develop your own plan. Three, get your friends together in a Money Club. When you divide the tasks, subtract your fear, and multiply your knowledge, you'll find it adds up to a successful financial future. Money grows in groups.*

Making Your Money Grow

Remember your parents' stories from when you were young? "Why, when I was a kid, the movies cost a quarter and popcorn was a nickel!" Now you probably catch yourself telling others that when you were a kid, your allowance was a dollar a week, and it was plenty. Of course, these days, a dollar doesn't buy much, and ten years from now, it will buy even less.

Inflation is one of your major enemies when it comes to saving for the future. A mere 3 percent annual rise in prices will double the cost of everything within 24 years. So you'll need twice as much money then to live as well as you do now. But don't worry, the same dynamics have a positive effect on your investments. This positive dynamic is called the power of compounding, which makes your investments grow over the years, generally outpacing inflation. For example, if inflation were 3 percent overall but your investment grew at 8 percent, your account would grow much faster than a savings account that only matched inflation. Here's an example: If you invest $1,000 in a savings account earning 3 percent, in 24 years you'll have $2,000, just enough to counteract the effects of inflation. But if you invested $1,000 in an equity mutual fund that averaged an 8 percent return, in only nine years you would have matched the $2,000 your savings account earned over 24 years. In 24 years your equity mutual fund would be worth $6,300. Now you've got three times the buying power.

The Simple Truth

~❧

In a 2002 survey, 79 percent of women said they considered themselves more knowledgeable about investing than their parents, and 77 percent considered themselves more knowledgeable about investing than they were five years ago.

—Oppenheimer Funds

You can gauge the growth of your investments by using the Rule of 72. Divide 72 by the rate of interest you are earning on your money to determine how long it takes your money to double. For example, if your money earns 3 percent a year, it will take 24 years for your money to double. (Rule of 72: 72 divided by 3 percent equals 24 years.) But if you invest your money at 8 percent a year, your money will double in only nine years. And your money keeps doubling. A $10,000 investment earning 8 percent will grow to $20,000 in nine years, and nine years later you'll have $40,000, then $80,000, then $160,000. Money left to grow over years and years can be your ticket to a lifetime of financial security.

The Simple Truth

~❧

Many people know that the Rule of 72 can help them figure how long it takes for money to double. But not many have heard of the Rule of 115. Just divide 115 by your rate of return to see how long it takes your money to triple.

Risk vs. Reward

Losing money on risky investments is agonizing. Not only does it set you back, but it also takes a considerably greater rate of return to recoup those losses. For example, if your investment loses 10 percent the first year, it must earn 11 percent the next year just to break even. If your investment loses half of its value, it will need to double before you are back to even.

All investing involves some element of risk. The types of investments you should choose will be determined by your *risk tolerance*—that is, how much risk you're comfortable with—as well as other factors, such as your time horizon (how long you have until you need the money), current income, and future spending needs. It is better to invest wisely and accept smaller gains each year than to put all your money into a risky investment, hoping to make a killing. If you lose, it will be much harder to break even, never mind actually getting ahead.

At WIFE, we've found that investing stymies many women because they are searching for the perfect investment. Unfortunately, the perfect investment isn't out there (nor is the perfect man, but that's another story). One difference between romance and finance is that you don't have to search for the one best investment. Choosing a stable of investments with different features and benefits is the smartest way to go. That's the principle of diversification, or asset allocation, which we'll talk about later in the chapter.

"Don't be afraid to take a big step if one is indicated. You can't cross a chasm in two small steps."

DAVID LLOYD GEORGE

Three Types of Investment Risk

You face three basic types of risk when you invest your money:

Market risk is the risk that your investment will lose value due to market shifts. This type of risk is inherent in stocks and real estate.

Interest rate risk is the risk that a change in interest rates will cause your investment to lose value. This type of risk can be found in bonds.

Inflation risk is the risk that inflation will outpace the return on your investment, eroding its purchasing power. This risk affects savings accounts, certificates of deposit, and U.S. Series EE Savings bonds.

Risky Business

To help you figure out your relationship to risk, we've created Quiz 8.1. Take a few moments to complete it, choosing the answer that best describes you. The results should give you a good idea of how much comfortable you are (or aren't) with taking risks.

The Simple Truth

❧

Women see themselves less likely to be risk takers than men. Thirty-one percent of women label themselves conservative investors, compared with 21.7 percent of men.

—*Women's Financial Network*

Quiz 8.1

What's Your Risk Factor?

1. My primary goal is to
   a. protect my savings. I'm most concerned about preserving what I have.
   b. at least keep up with inflation.
   c. take some investment risk to get a good return.
2. If the stock market dropped 10 percent tomorrow, I would
   a. sell everything. I can't afford to lose it all.
   b. bide my time and see what happens.
   c. put more money in. Aren't you supposed to "buy low, sell high"?
3. If I had a choice between $1,000 cash and a one in ten chance for $10,000, I would
   a. take the money and run.
   b. consider my current financial situation. If I desperately needed the money, I'd take the cash.
   c. take a chance. Sometimes you win, sometimes you lose.
4. Would you invest in a start-up company?
   a. Only if the founder was Bill Gates.
   b. Yes, if I had extra cash to spare and the company had a good business plan.
   c. Of course. I'm always looking for new opportunities.
5. Short-term losses in my retirement account make me feel
   a. extremely worried. I just can't sleep at night when I know that I'm losing money.
   b. A bit concerned. But I know I have a long time ahead to make up the difference.
   c. committed to my investment plan. I know the market will go up over the long haul.

6. Do you like surprises?
   a. No, not even when I was a child.
   b. Only on my birthday.
   c. Half the fun in life is seeing what happens next.
7. When I make a bad investment,
   a. I brood about it for months, sometimes years afterwards.
   b. I try, sometimes successfully, to let it go.
   c. I focus on my next venture.
8. In my daily life
   a. I like predictability and routine.
   b. I try to do things differently every once in a while.
   c. I can't stand to do the same thing twice.
9. I am like the
   a. chicken—afraid to venture out.
   b. golden retriever—even-tempered and easygoing.
   c. cheetah—fast, solitary, and carnivorous.
10. My outlook on the future is
   a. pessimistic—things always seem to get worse and worse.
   b. half-empty and half-full—sometimes things work out,
      sometimes they don't.
   c. optimistic—things always end up for the best.

_____ *As*
_____ *Bs*
_____ *Cs*

If you listed more *As*:
You are very risk-averse. You tend to seek out conservative investments
with predictable returns. While it's important to work with your natural
style, it's also good to stretch yourself a bit. Try some learned optimism:
See the best in new situations, and take a risk once in a while!

If you listed more *Bs*:
You are a good balance between risk-averse and risk-seeking. You tend
toward prudent investments that take on an acceptable amount of risk.
Your challenge is to seek investments that suit your life stage and financial
goals.

If you listed more *Cs*:
You are a risk taker extraordinaire! You go for it—every time! Try to
temper your risk-seeking tendencies toward wildcat investments with a
sense of balance and realism. Be sure that you take care of the basics
before you go for the risky stuff.

The One, Two, Three of Investing

---

*"In the long run, it's not just how much money you make that will
determine your future prosperity. It's how much of that money you put
to work by saving and investing it."*

PETER LYNCH

From what we've seen over the past 20 years, women are more likely to be better investors than men. Here's why: They tend to research their investments more
thoroughly and invest to meet specific long-term goals. They are inclined to hold
onto their investments longer than their male counterparts and panic less easily,
even when the markets take a dip.

Although women can make better investors, they often lack investing confidence. If you're a novice in the world of investing, you may feel insecure about taking that first step and more than a little overwhelmed. Without guidance,
investment possibilities can seem both endless and confusing. But this is only an
illusion, because there are really only three major areas in which to invest: cash, real
assets, and financial assets.

- *Cash* includes the money in your wallet and your checking and savings accounts, money market accounts, short-term certificates of deposit, and Treasury bills.
- *Real assets* are tangible and include real estate, oil and gas, and antiques.
- *Financial assets* fall into two categories: stocks, through which you become a
  shareholder in a company, and bonds, through which you loan money to a
  company, government, or municipality.

Every investment fits into these general categories, and your investment portfolio eventually will include holdings in each of these groups.

---

*"A cow for her milk, a hen for her eggs, and a stock, by heck, for her
dividends."*

WALL STREET RHYME

Is Cash King?

Cash has a place in every portfolio. But is it possible to have too much cash? Many
financial advisors say you should keep three to six months of living expenses avail-

able, but that is just a rough rule of thumb. We say you should always have enough on hand to meet unexpected emergencies, and if your employment is in jeopardy or your income is irregular, you should also have enough to pay for several months of living expenses. Many people keep very little cash in savings accounts, and rely instead on credit cards for emergencies. That can be a costly way to feel secure, because that security is bought at the expense of high interest rates if they have to tap those credit lines.

Cash is a wise investment in a volatile economy, or when interest rates are sky high and going higher. Historically, those times are few. During normal economic conditions, cash loses buying power to inflation. To harness the positive power of inflation, you need to diversify your investments by putting some of your money into real and financial assets.

Let's Get Real

We find that for most people, their first real estate investment is their own home. For many people, it is also their biggest investment. As your wealth grows, you may invest in other real assets as well, such as rental real estate, artwork, antiques, and precious metals. But invest with caution. Real assets have their drawbacks. They can be hard to value, difficult to sell, and costly in terms of commissions. On the plus side, real assets tend to move in a different cycle than securities, so if the stock market is down, your real assets may be increasing in value.

Getting a Fix on Financial Assets

Financial assets include securities, such as stocks and equity mutual funds, and bonds, including corporate and government bonds. Each of these asset categories plays an important role in your investment strategy, because they tend to perform differently from one another. That means you can minimize the risk to your portfolio by *diversifying* your holdings, spreading out your money across several types of financial assets.

Stocks

When you buy shares of stock, you are buying a small piece of ownership in the company. As an owner, you have a say in the election of directors and other business conducted at shareholder meetings or by proxy. You are also entitled to *dividends,* if the company pays out its earnings to shareholders rather than retaining them to grow the company. Some stocks are riskier than others. Blue-chip and dividend-paying stocks are the least risky, whereas small company stocks and growth stocks are among the riskiest.

Bonds

When you buy a bond, you are lending money to a company, government, or municipality. In return, the issuer of the bond promises to pay you a specified amount of interest for a fixed period and to pay back the *principal* (the full amount of the loan) on the *maturity date*. Bonds provide continuing income, but they vary in safety. *U.S. Treasury bond*s are considered ultra-safe, because they are issued by government agencies. They also offer the advantage of being exempt from state and local taxes. On the other end of the spectrum are high-risk *junk bonds,* also called high-yield bonds, which are issued by newer companies or companies with questionable credit strength. Somewhere in the middle are *investment grade bonds,* which are those issued by companies that earn good ratings from one of the major rating agencies, such as Standard & Poor's or Moody's Investors Service.

The Simple Truth
❧

Your brokerage accounts are protected by the Securities Investor Protection Corporation (SIPC), which insures investor accounts in the event of the firm's failure. A broker's SIPC membership provides your account protection up to a maximum of $500,000, of which $100,000 may be in cash. Before you invest with a broker or financial advisor, make sure your investment will be covered by the SIPC. Many reputable firms purchase additional private insurance to insure your account up to $100 million of coverage.

Use What You Already Know
If you are choosing individual stocks, use the knowledge you have gained in your career or daily life to make your selection. For example, if you notice consistently effective ad campaigns for a particular product, do some research on that company. Is the company as sound as its products? If you are a physician, examine the pharmaceutical companies that are creating the hottest new drugs. If you are a plumber, flush out the companies that make the best tools. If your kids are clamoring for the latest new toy, find out the maker of that toy and last year's hottest toy too! If it's the same company, the stock might be a good investment play.

Table 8.1   Types of Investments

Defensive investments	Savings accounts
	Money market accounts
	Treasury bills
	Short-term CDs and bonds
Conservative investments	Intermediate-term CDs and bonds
	GNMA funds (Ginnie-Maes)
	Fixed annuities
Moderate investments	Long-term bonds
	Stocks
	Variable annuities
	Low-leverage real estate
High-risk investments	Junk bonds
	Options
	High-leverage real estate
	Precious metals
	Collectibles
	Penny stocks
	Venture capital
	Commodities futures

Each investment carries its own set of risks. Table 8.1 ranks investments in order of risk of loss from lowest to highest.

Investing in Mutual Funds

Most of the investments listed in Table 8.1 can be purchased through mutual funds. The concept of mutual funds is fairly simple. A mutual fund is a pool of money from investors with goals similar to yours; this money is invested by the mutual fund manager or investment committee. You buy shares in the mutual fund and then sit back and leave the rest to the experts, who invest your money in stocks or bonds of many different companies or government entities.

The Feeling Is Mutual

Mutual funds fall into a wide range of categories. Your choice will depend on your investment goals and your tolerance for risk.

Aggressive growth funds strive for large gains by investing in small companies or highly volatile stocks.

Growth funds seek long-term capital gains through investment in companies that are growing faster than inflation.

Growth and income funds emphasize growth, and they also concentrate on preserving capital by deriving income from current dividends.

Income funds invest in high-yield stocks, preferred stock, and bonds to produce current income.

Balanced funds invest in a combination of stocks and bonds to minimize risk.

Global and international funds invest in international stocks or bonds to obtain global diversification and higher returns when the dollar is falling.

Specialty and sector funds invest in stocks of companies in a particular field or sector of the economy, such as health, utilities, oil, and technology. Socially responsible funds fall into this category.

Corporate bond funds generally invest in the bonds of highly rated corporations.

Municipal bond funds invest in bonds that are issued by states and municipalities, most often to fund public projects, such as bridges and highways.

Government securities funds invest in U.S. Treasury and other bonds issued by government agencies.

Money market funds invest in short-term Treasury bills, commercial paper, certificates of deposit, and similar low-risk, short-term investment vehicles.

The Simple Truth

Women account for 60 percent of all socially conscious investments. More than $2 trillion is currently invested using some sort of social criteria. Socially responsible companies are ones with strong management and solid long-term prospects based on how these companies treat the environment, their employees, their communities, and the safety of their products.

—Social Investment Forum 2001 Report
in Socially Responsible Investment Trends in the U.S.

The ABCs of Fund Shares

All mutual funds charge operating expenses and management fees, which are deducted from the total return you receive each year. If you buy funds through a broker, you pay a sales commission, called a *load.* How the load is charged depends on the share class: A, B, or C.

- With front-end load funds, called *A shares,* a percentage of your initial investment (typically 2 percent to 5.75 percent) goes to your broker and the fund company as a commission, but you won't have to pay any fees when you sell your shares.
- With back-end load funds, or *B shares,* all of your money is immediately invested in the portfolio, but you pay a redemption fee (typically starting at 4 percent) if you sell the fund within six or seven years. The fee drops by 1 percent or so every year or two, and if you sell after seven years, you generally do not incur any additional charges. However, the internal expense charges can be up to 1 percent higher than on A shares for the first seven years.
- With level-load funds, or *C shares,* an extra 1 percent or so per year is added to the internal expense charges for as long as you own the fund, but generally there are no up-front or back-end fees.

Picking the Right Mutual Funds for You

Most money management magazines periodically publish performance surveys of major mutual funds, providing information about the fund type, performance, and minimum investment required. Following their "top picks" seems like an easy way to get a jump on mutual fund investing, but there is no guarantee the performance predictions will come true. In fact, many of those "must buys" have proven to be real busts.

The best way to get to know a fund is by requesting a copy of the fund's *prospectus* before you decide to invest. The Securities and Exchange Commission (SEC) requires all fund companies to furnish this document, which includes the fund's objectives and policies, the services it offers, the names of its officers and directors, its methods of purchasing and redeeming shares, the amount of sales charges and management fees, and its financial statements.

The Simple Truth

Women spend 40 percent more time than men researching a fund before they invest. Yet 70 percent of women investors feel they are too strapped for time to deal with finances. Only 56 percent of men feel this way.

—*Women's Financial Network and Women's Economic Status Report*

Here's what to look for when reviewing a prospectus:

Objective and Strategy   This section will tell you the objectives of the fund—whether it seeks income, growth, or undervalued stocks, for example—and the management's strategy for achieving these objectives, which will include information about what size companies the manager typically buys. For bond funds, the prospectus will indicate the average maturity of the underlying bonds.

Performance   This section includes a bar chart that shows the fund's return for the past ten years, and a table that shows average annual returns and total returns after expenses for one, five, and ten years. Although past performance is not indicative of future results, you can use this table to gauge the management's track record in the marketplace.

Fees and Expenses   Here you will find information about up-front or deferred sales charges and annually recurring fees, including management fees (what the managers collect for running the fund), which are listed as a percentage of each investor's assets. Pay close attention to any marketing expenses (12b-1 fees) and the "total annual fund operating expenses," which is the combination of all annual fees except any loads.

Management   This is an optional section, but it usually lists the names and qualifications of the portfolio managers.

Miscellaneous   The back pages of the prospectus include information about exchange privileges between funds in that family of funds, how to make withdrawals from the fund, and the potential tax consequences of buying, selling, or exchanging fund shares.

If all that sounds daunting, it is. We can't tell you everything you need to know about mutual fund investing in just a few pages. If you aren't willing to spend the time or don't have the inclination to research and choose funds on your own, consider hiring a financial professional to help you build and maintain a mutual fund portfolio. Even if you decide to go it alone, a periodic financial checkup with a financial professional is as smart a move as getting an annual physical.

Five Tips for Choosing a Mutual Fund

Investing offers no guarantees, but you'll sway the odds in your favor if you follow these five tips for choosing mutual funds.

- Check mutual fund ratings *to find several top-performing funds that meet your objectives.*
- Analyze the fund's performance *in both up and down years.*
- Look for consistency of performance *over a number of years. The less volatile the fund, the smoother the ride, and the better you will sleep at night.*
- Steer clear of new funds. *Once the fund has a track record and has shown its worth, you'll have plenty of time to invest.*
- Don't jump ship too soon. *When investments underperform for a short period, people tend to feel discouraged and uncertain, often deciding to take their losses or shift to a style that seems to be working better. But that's not wise: Give the fund manager a chance. If the fund fails to perform well in comparison to similar funds for a year or two, get out, but not before. Studies show that if you hop from fund to fund, you're likely to leapfrog past the manager's rebound and miss some of the fund's best performance.*

The Simple Truth

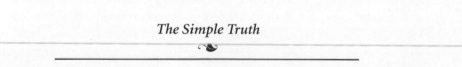

Frequently switching mutual funds can hurt your investment returns. Consider this: from 1984 to 2002, the average stock fund delivered an annual return of 9.3 percent, while the average stock fund *investor* earned only 2.7 percent annually.

—*Dalbar, Inc., and Lipper, Inc.*

Savvy Investment Strategies

Now that you understand the basic types of investments, it's time to look at how you can use them most effectively to achieve your goals. Building and managing a portfolio doesn't need to be complicated. It is similar to creating a sound nutritional plan for your family: The various food groups (investments) are combined to supply your nutritional needs (growth and income) and fit your individual tastes (risk tolerance and investment philosophies), while staying within your budget (portfolio size). The difference is that we are taught the major food groups and how they combine to create a balanced diet when we are in elementary school, but most people are never taught how investments can interlock to provide growth, income, and stability.

We often see that this is one of the places where people who invest by themselves fall short. They invest in several different mutual funds, thinking they are diversified, but when we review their portfolios, we find that many of those mutual funds have the same objectives and same types of stocks in them. That's like feeding your family a meal with six different types of bread, but no meat or vegetables.

Ingredients for Great Returns

In creating your investment portfolio, think carefully about your goals and time horizon (how long it will be until you need the money). Here are five essential strategies you should use as part of your investment plan.

Diversify Your Holdings   There's an old saying that you shouldn't put all your eggs in one basket, and that holds doubly true for your investments. The best way to minimize the amount of risk you incur is to diversify your portfolio—that is, to spread out your investments across several different asset classes. That way, if one area performs poorly, there's a good chance that some of your other investments will do well and balance out your losses.

Invest Systematically   If you invest systematically, you won't have to guess which way the market will shift or in what direction. Dollar cost averaging is a fancy term for investing money on a regular basis. With dollar cost averaging you invest a set amount each month, acquiring more shares when the price is low and fewer shares when the price is higher. The result is a lower cost per share than if you bought a set number of shares each month.

Don't Time the Market   One of the worst mistakes investors make is to try to second-guess the market by timing purchases and sales. One false move, and you can miss out on a great opportunity. For example, for the 10 years 1992 through 2001, the S&P 500 returned 175 percent. But if you were on the sidelines and missed the 5 best days out of that 10-year period, your returns would have been 117 percent—a difference of 58 percent! And if you missed the 10 best days during those 10 years, your returns would have dropped to 79 percent.

Rebalance Your Portfolio   Because the markets move up and down, you may find the asset allocation in your portfolio can get thrown out of whack. For example, if your portfolio consists of 60 percent stocks and 40 percent bonds, and the value of your stocks decreases substantially, your allocation might end up 40 percent stocks and 60 percent bonds. Rebalance your portfolio by buying stocks and selling bonds to bring your allocation back in line with your long-term goals and risk tolerance. You'll be selling assets that have increased in value (bonds) and buying assets that have decreased (stocks), which doesn't feel right. But in reality, you are selling high and buying low, and that's how money is made.

Reduce Your Tax Burden   You can minimize your annual tax bill by investing in tax-free or tax-deferred vehicles and also by timing the sale of your investments carefully. If you hold an investment for at least a year before selling, you'll pay long-term capital gains at a lower rate. For some investments, you won't pay tax at all. Tax-free investments such as municipal bonds and Roth IRAs can escape both state and federal tax. Traditional IRAs and 401(k)s let you avoid paying taxes on your earnings until they're withdrawn.

Asset Allocation Made Simple

Asset allocation—how to divide your money among the different types of investments—is the most important investment decision you'll make. But investors often approach the process in a haphazard manner, investing a little here and a little there, with no strategy, like the man who jumped on his horse and rode madly off in all directions. If you are saving for a goal that's just two years away, such as making the down payment on a house or sending Junior off to college, don't take risks in the volatile markets. Park your money safely in a certificate of deposit or money market account. But if your goal is further out, you can start taking some risks. Bonds are less risky than stocks in most markets, but stocks have a potential for greater returns. If you have long-term goals, don't be afraid to invest in stocks. Go out on a limb—that's where the fruit is.

You can use Table 8.2 as a starting point to determine how much you should invest in stocks and how much in bonds.

Here's how to use Table 8.2. Let's say you plan to send your nine-year-old to college in nine years. Look at the middle column of the chart and consider your risk pulse (you should have an idea based on Quiz 8.1). If you have a low risk tolerance, you would invest only 25 percent of your college funds in stocks. But if your tolerance is higher, you would invest 60 percent in stocks. If you can afford much more risk, then the high-risk allocation of 75 percent may suit you.

Once you have determined the ratio of stocks and bonds that is right for you, it's time to figure out more specifically what kinds of investments you should make in each category. You may wish to consult with a qualified financial advisor to help you make the right decisions.

Table 8.2   Nine Ways to Allocate Your Assets

Risk Tolerance	Investment Choices	Time Until You Need the Money		
		3–5 Years	6–10 Years	10+ Years
Low	Stocks	0%	25%	50%
	Bonds	100%	75%	50%
Medium	Stocks	30%	60%	80%
	Bonds	70%	40%	20%
High	Stocks	45%	75%	100%
	Bonds	55%	25%	0%

Finding Financial Guidance

The Simple Truth

Sixty-two percent of working-age women consult a financial professional when making investment decisions. Less than half of men do the same.

—Women's Retirement Confidence Survey, 1999

You may need professional help to get you moving and staying on track. Just as some people who diet are more successful in a diet program or with a diet coach than on their own, you might invest better when you have a professional with whom you can counsel. A financial advisor can help keep you on track and stay invested when your natural inclination is to cut and run.

Over the years, we've found that some investors simply don't have the time to devote to monitoring their investments, others lack the discipline to follow through, and still others tend to get carried away on a tide of emotions, buying when the market is rising without regard for proper allocation, and selling in a panic when prices drop. If any of this applies to you, you will probably benefit from the services of a qualified, ethical stockbroker, financial planner, or portfolio manager.

Every professional is compensated in one way or another, so hiring a professional will be somewhat more expensive than going it alone. But if a professional can help you create a personal asset allocation plan and help you rebalance periodically, the cost of the professional service will be negligible compared to the money you will earn by making the right decisions.

To choose a financial professional, ask friends, family, and other professionals for recommendations. Then interview several of the most highly recommended advisors. When interviewing prospective financial advisors, here are some questions to ask:

- *How long have you been in business?* You want someone with plenty of experience who has operated in bear markets as well as bull markets. That means someone who has been a financial advisor for at least six to ten years.
- *What services will you provide?* If you need help with goal-setting or retirement planning, you need an advisor who works in these areas, rather than a specialized portfolio manager.
- *What kinds of clients do you handle?* You are looking for an advisor who is familiar with your type of situation and who will give you the service you deserve. Some advisors specialize in advising women in transition, for example.
- *What types of investments do you generally recommend?* If you are looking for a full range of investment products, don't choose an advisor who recommends only annuities or insurance.
- *What financial planning process do you use?* Your advisor should be able to explain his or her techniques for guiding you to investments that suit your needs. Your investment plan should be customized to your particular situation, based on broad guidelines.
- *With whom will I work?* There should be one person you trust who will be primarily responsible for your account and with whom you will have personal contact.
- *How will you be compensated?* The advisor should be willing to disclose his or her fees and commissions. The advisor may be paid an hourly fee, percentage of capital being managed, flat fee, commission, or some combination of these. Don't balk because there are commissions, but beware of brokers that place you exclusively in funds and other investments that have high sales charges.
- *Will you furnish references?* Ask for the names and telephone numbers of the clients who have similar situations to yours and who have been clients for several years.

Money Grows in Groups

Whether you decide to hire a professional or go it alone, the more you know, the better off you will be. You may have joined an investment club in the past for exactly that reason.

Investing is often more fun and more fruitful when done with the aid of others who share similar goals and desires. An investment club is a good way to learn more about buying and selling stocks. But the concept of the investment club stops there. That's why we created the Money Club, to help women learn about all facets of their financial lives, not just investing.

The Money Club focuses on learning the dynamics of money, incorporating a 360-degree view of women's financial lives. Many investment clubs have added a Money Club component, spending some of their time on investment club activities and the rest on Money Club discussions and exercises. Consult Appendix A to learn more about Money Clubs, or visit the web site at www.moneyclubs.com.

Small Steps to Becoming a Money Star

1. Gather in one place information about all of your investments, whether in IRAs, brokerage accounts, savings accounts, or life insurance. Create a master list of all of your accounts, what they are invested in (stocks, bonds, cash) and the approximate amount in each. You can then create a picture of your present allocation and decide if you need to make any changes.

2. Start a program of systematic investing RIGHT NOW. Don't wait for the market to go up, or down, before you begin. Adding money each month to your investments is the way to build wealth. In fact, the rate at which you invest could be more significant than the rate of return you earn.

3. Consider using a DRIP (dividend reinvestment plan) to purchase stock. Use small windfalls, such as birthday gifts and tax refunds, to purchase shares, and reinvest your dividends in additional shares. Go to the Money Club web site (www.moneyclubs.com) and click on "Sharebuilder" to find an inexpensive way to get started investing in individual stocks.

4. Take a small risk with something you do each day—take a different route to work, try a new type of ethnic cuisine, experiment with a new hobby. Get used to taking small risks in life and seeing what happens. Increasing your tolerance for risk will help you expand your horizons and think more creatively about your investments.

5. Educate yourself by doing one thing every day to further your financial knowledge. For ideas, go to the Money Club web site, where you will find three Small Steps you can choose from each day. These steps take only five, ten, or fifteen minutes to do (and you can do anything for fifteen minutes). Small steps lead to big success.

CHAPTER 9

Reaching Your Goals: Investing for Education and Retirement

Dear WIFE,

My husband and I are in conflict: He wants to sock away the max into a retirement nest egg, and I think we should be saving for our children's college. Matthew is 14 and Caitlyn is 8. I'd like to save for both retirement and education, but I just don't think we can right now. Any suggestions?

Strapped for Cash in Peachtree

Dear Strapped,

You've got a nest egg dilemma. If you're saving for a retirement that's over easy, it could leave your kids' education scrambled. You can save for both. It's easy to say, "I'd like to, but . . ." Here's WIFE's advice: Get your "but" out of the way. Read on to find out some creative solutions that will help you figure out how to save for both goals.

Use the "Rocks" Method to Set Your Goals

On an outing to the beach, a grandmother decided to teach her granddaughter about the important things in life. She asked the girl to fill a pail with large rocks. Once the girl was finished, the grandmother asked her if the pail was full. "Oh, yes," said the girl, "I can't fit another rock in." Granny then told the girl to gather some small pebbles and put them into the pail. As she shook the pail lightly, her granddaughter saw how the pebbles rolled into the open areas between the rocks. She asked again if the pail was full. "Yes, of course, now it really is full," said her granddaughter. Finally the grandmother reached down for several handfuls of sand, which sifted through her fingers into the already-filled pail. "I guess the pail wasn't that full after all," said her granddaughter.

And so the grandmother taught her granddaughter a valuable lesson she carried with her the rest of her life. When setting goals, take care of the rocks first, the important things in your life. If you fill your pail with sand, the small stuff, there is no room for anything else.

What are the large rocks in your life? They are probably the things that are most important—your family, your health, your spiritual life, your security. The pebbles are the other things that matter such as your job, your house, or your car. The sand is everything else—the small stuff. If you spend all your energy and time on the small stuff, you will never have room for the things that matter most. Take care of the rocks. Set your priorities. The rest is just sand.

Make a list of your important goals. Open yourself to the possibilities, and create a vision of a future filled with abundance. As you write your list, don't hold back. There is no need to determine how you are going to get everything on the list just yet.

The Magic Wand Concept

If you have a tendency to limit your imagination, expand your horizons by using our special Magic Wand Concept. Pretend you have met a genie with a magic wand who will grant you anything you want. What *do* you want? That's a tough one, isn't it? Let your imagination run wild, and write down everything that comes to mind. Once you've listed all the possibilities, review them and discard the ones that don't seem that important.

Use the ROCKS method to turn your dreams into goals. Your goals need to be real and focused, so you can commit your energy to achieving them. The acronym ROCKS can help you remember the key elements you need to realize your dreams:

Realistic. Do you have the time and skills to achieve your goals? If they seem too lofty, don't abandon them. Just break them down into more manageable steps, and do the steps one at a time.

Obtainable. You must believe in your goal. Remember, if you believe it, you can achieve it.

Controllable. Your goal must be something that is within your power to do, not something that depends on outside forces.

Keep trying. If things don't go as you planned, revise your plans so that you can achieve what you set out to do.

Specific. Write down your goals. Use as many concrete and specific terms as you can to describe your goals and when you intend to reach them.

Consider the Roadblock Rule

Some goals may seem unrealistic and unattainable, but before you abandon them, consider the Roadblock Rule: You will never get anywhere if you let roadblocks define or limit your goals. If you really want something, the imperative of purpose will take over, and you can figure out how to get it.

Roadblocks make life interesting and give us feelings of accomplishment when we overcome them. Commit yourself to a certain path, and the dynamics of that commitment will propel you to accomplishment. It won't always be easy, and you might decide at some point to stop pursuing that goal. That won't be a failure to meet your goals, just a revision in what you want. As you travel the road to financial security, expect your goals to change and rearrange themselves along the way.

"There isn't a part of our lives that money doesn't touch—it affects our relationships, the way we go about our everyday activities, our ability to make dreams reality, everything."

SUZE ORMAN

Reaching Your Goals

It really is true that money is intertwined with everything in your life. To reach your goals, it is important to first identify them, then decide when you would like to achieve them, and figure out how much they will cost. Worksheet 9.1 can help you do just that.

Have Patience

Congratulations! By using Worksheet 9.1, you have now completed an important step that most people fail to do. Less than 1 percent of Americans write down specific goals each year. Writing down your goals is powerful. More than fifty years ago Harvard University polled a class of graduates. Fewer than 3 percent of them had written goals. When Harvard polled them again twenty years later, that small 3 percent had become wealthier than the rest of the class combined! Not only that, but they were also healthier and more content. That's the power of writing down your goals.

Worksheet 9.1

Reaching Your Goals

For each of your specific goals, write down the following information:

1. Goal _____ When? _____
2. How much do I need in today's dollars? _____
3. How many years do I have to save for my goal? _____
4. How much must I save each month to get there? (Divide today's cost by a number from Table 1) _____
5. How will I save for my goal? (From current earnings, raises, inheritances, etc.) _____
6. How will I invest those savings? (For example, children's education might be funded through a Section 529 plan, home purchases through mutual funds, retirement income through 401(k)s, etc.)
   _____

Table 1: Reaching Your Goals

Years to Goal	Low Risk 2%*	Medium Risk 4%*	Risk Seeker 6%*
1	12	12	12
2	25	25	25
3	37	38	39
4	50	52	54
5	63	66	70
6	77	81	86
7	90	97	104
8	104	113	123
9	118	130	143
10	133	147	164
15	210	245	291
20	296	365	462
25	391	511	693
30	496	689	1005
35	612	906	1425
40	741	1170	1992

*All returns are after subtracting the rate of inflation

You may have heard about this study and wondered how it could be true. We can't tell you the exact process, but we've seen the power of this in our own lives. Seventeen years ago, when Ginita wrote down that she wanted to be an author, she hadn't even written one book. This is now her eighth book. Candace and her husband create a collage each year to help them visualize what they would like to accomplish in seven areas of their lives. As they review the previous year's collage each January, it's amazing how closely their life accomplishments track their pictures.

The first step in achieving goals is to be able to visualize the goal and believe you can do it. But of course you have to follow up with action that will make those goals a reality. In the rest of this chapter, we will give you specific guidance to help you reach the two financial goals that many women believe are most important to them: their children's education and their own retirement.

Hi-Ho, Hi-Ho, It's Off to School We Go!

If you have children, chances are that providing a college education for them is high on your list of goals. With the cost of tuition, fees, and room and board for four years at a private university averaging $108,000 and state school costs averaging $42,000 for four years, it's no wonder parents are in a cold sweat. If today's costs make you nervous, Figure 9.1 will really get you shaking. It shows that when your preschooler is ready for college in 2021, the costs will have more than doubled.

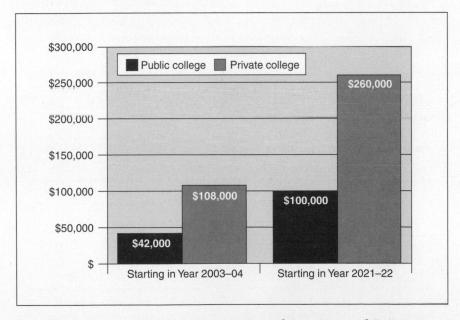

Figure 9.1   Present and Future Cost of Four Years of College

Stashing Cash for College

Fortunately, a smart savings strategy and a little help from Uncle Sam can make it possible for almost anyone to get the college education they deserve. The best thing you can do is to start saving while your child is still in diapers. The earlier you begin socking away cash, the more opportunity your money has to grow through compounding, which we discussed in Chapter 8. Even if you don't implement your investment strategy until your kids are in high school, you can make great strides toward meeting your savings goal. You'll just have to cut back in other areas and put every spare cent into your college fund.

Here's how much you will need to save each month to amass $100,000 for college. Table 9.1 shows that you have to save much less if you begin to save when your child is born versus waiting to save until your child is older.

Ouch! Those figures can really hurt your pocket book. At this point, you might be saying, "Why bother? I'll never be able to save enough." But ignoring the problem won't make it go away. There are lots of ways you can conquer the education cost woes. We know of someone who had their three-year-old at the driving range several times a week, practicing to be the next Tiger Woods and hoping to qualify for athletic scholarships.

If your child is not a star athlete, and you haven't saved enough, you'll need to supplement what you have saved. You can tap scholarship and aid programs, government-sponsored tax incentives, and plain old working your way through college. So start when you can to save as much as you can.

Here are some saving and investment vehicles that can help you make the grade.

Section 529 Plans   There are two types of 529 plans; college savings plans are the most common. These state-sponsored savings plans allow you to stash up to $55,000 during a five-year period for each of your children ($110,000 for a couple) without incurring any gift tax (and you can repeat this every five years). You can choose from a variety of investment portfolios, and if you live in certain states you may even be able to deduct your contributions on your state income tax return.

Table 9.1   Monthly Savings Needed to Amass $100,000 for College

Child's Age	Invest at 4%	Invest at 6%	Invest at 8%	Invest at 10%
Newborn	317	258	208	167
Age 8	679	610	547	488
Age 14	1,925	1,849	1,775	1,703

These figures represent the amount of money you have to save monthly at the stated rate of return in order to accumulate $100,000 by the time your child reaches age 18. The figures do not take into account any federal or state income taxes you may incur.

Distributions used for qualified higher education expenses are free from federal income tax. If you take the money out for any other purpose, the earnings will be taxed at your ordinary income tax rate plus a 10 percent federal penalty.

Section 529 prepaid tuition plans, offered by some states, let you lock in tomorrow's tuition at today's rate for designated schools. If your child decides to go to a different college, the money you invested in the prepaid plan may be refunded to you minus a fee, depending on the state's rules.

Education Savings Accounts　These accounts, also known as Coverdell ESAs, let you sock away $2,000 a year total for any child under age 18, if you don't exceed the income limitations. Withdrawals are tax free if the money is used for qualified education expenses (tuition, room and board, fees, books, supplies, and computer-related equipment) for elementary and secondary schools as well as college and graduate school. If the money isn't used for education by the time the child is 30, you'll have to transfer it to another family member or the earnings are subject to ordinary income tax and a federal 10 percent penalty.

UGMA/UTMA Accounts　The rules for these accounts are simple. Anyone can set aside $11,000 a year (in 2004) without incurring federal gift tax, and you can invest in almost anything. If your child is under age 14, the first $800 of the child's investment income is tax-exempt, the next $800 is taxed at the child's rate, and anything over that is taxed at the parents' rate. If your child is at least 14, all earnings are taxed at the child's rate. Here's the catch: If you're the account custodian, you only have control of the assets until your child reaches your state's age of majority (sometime between the age of 18 and 25, depending on the state and the account), at which point the money is theirs to do with as they please. In addition, these accounts are considered the child's property under the financial aid formulas. That can affect your child's eligibility for financial aid, since 35 percent of the child's assets count toward college costs, versus only 6 percent of your own assets.

Qualified U.S. Savings Bonds　A tried and true tool for setting aside money toward college, Savings Bonds provide a guaranteed payout at a future date, so you don't have to worry about the ups and downs of the market. You can set aside $30,000 per year in Series EE bonds and $30,000 per year in Series I bonds, and the earnings are exempt from state and federal income tax if used to pay qualified higher education expenses (although some income limits apply). Earnings are subject to federal income tax for nonqualified use.

Roth IRAs　Though Roth IRAs are generally considered retirement investments, some parents use them to pay for college. When you withdraw the funds for college expenses, those withdrawals are penalty free, and they will be tax-free as well if you are over age 59½ and the account has been established for at least five years.

This is a great way for older parents to save for their retirement and for education at the same time. But don't forget that if you withdraw from your Roth IRA for education, the money won't be there for your retirement. You can always go into debt to pay for college, but you can't borrow for your retirement. You will learn more about the income limits and contribution limits of IRAs in the retirement section of this chapter.

Taxable Accounts   You can always open any kind of account in your own name to save, and use those funds for your child's education, or whatever other purposes you wish. The income from the account will be taxed to you, as the account owner. This type of account gives you the most flexibility.

Table 9.2 helps you compare the features of these savings vehicles.

Two Tax Credits to Help You Fund College Costs

We've talked about the ways you can save taxes as you *save* for education. Here are ways you can save taxes as you *pay* for education.

The *Hope Credit* gives you a tax credit for 100 percent of the first $1,000 of tuition and fees you pay for the student's first year of college, and 50 percent of $1,000 of tuition and fees for the second year of college, if your income is under a certain level. The *Lifetime Learning Credit* provides a tax credit of 20 percent of up to $10,000 tuition you pay each year, for yourself or your child. Both credits are phased out for single taxpayers with income above $41,000 (in 2003) and for married couples filing jointly with an income above $83,000 (in 2003). These figures increase each year.

The Simple Truth

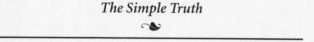

About $100 billion worth of financial aid is distributed to students in the form of loans, scholarships, and grants each year. The largest single source of aid is the federal government, which awards more than $40 billion to more than 7 million students annually. The next largest sources of financial aid are the colleges and universities themselves. They award about $8 billion to students each year. Other sources of financial aid are state governments, private agencies, foundations, corporations, clubs, and religious groups.

—*Peterson's College Money Handbook*

Table 9.2 Ways to Save for College Education

	529 Plans	Coverdell ESAs	UGMA/UTMA Accounts	Qualified US Savings Bonds	Roth IRAs	Taxable Accounts
Ownership for Financial Aid purposes	Account owner	Student	Student	Parent	Parent	Account owner
Taxes on earnings	No	No	Yes	No	No	Yes
Income limits	No	Yes	No	Yes	Yes	No
Contribution limits	Yes (varies by state)	Yes ($2,000/year)	No ($11,000 per year is gift-tax free)	Yes ($30,000 for I bonds, $30,000 for EE bonds)	Yes ($3,000 per year, $3,500 if 50 or older)	No
Control	Owner	Parent, until student reaches age of majority	Parent, until student reaches age of majority	Owner	Owner	Owner
Change of beneficiary	Allowed	Allowed	Not allowed	n/a	Allowed	n/a
Investment options	Varies by state	Mutual funds, securities, bank accounts	Mutual funds, securities, bank accounts	US bonds or EE bonds	Mutual funds, securities, bank accounts	Any investment

Table 9.2 Ways to Save for College Education (continued)

	529 Plans	Coverdell ESAs	UGMA/ UTMA Accounts	Qualified US Savings Bonds	Roth IRAs	Taxable Accounts
Uses	Higher education	Primary, secondary, higher education	Used only for minor's benefit	Tax free if used for education, but can have other uses	Retirement, but can also be used for education	Any
Penalties for early withdrawal/ nonqualified use	Yes	Yes	No	Earnings taxable if not used for education	Earnings taxable if owner under 59 1/2	n/a
Estate planning	Contributions removed from estate	Contributions removed from estate	Account remains in estate unless another person is named custodian	Account remains in estate of account owner	Account remains in estate of account owner	Account remains in estate of account owner

Finding Financial Aid

Even if you're a diligent saver, there's a good chance you'll still fall short of your funding goal, especially if you have several children. Fortunately, Uncle Sam and others are here to lend a hand. To qualify for aid, you will need to complete the *Free Application for Federal Student Aid,* which you can access online at www.fafsa. ed.gov.

To arrange your family's finances to maximize your chances for receiving financial aid, you'll want to make your move while your college-bound student is in the early years of high school. That's because the aid application forms ask about your finances for the calendar year starting in January of a student's junior year. Here are a few suggestions to increase your probability of receiving aid:

Pay Down Debt   Take out a home equity loan to pay off consumer loans, such as car loans, credit cards, and other obligations. Home equity loans reduce your assets, which is important in maximizing aid.

Get Your Kids to Cash Out   Students are expected to contribute up to 35 percent of their assets toward college costs, while you, as a parent, are expected to contribute only 5 to 6 percent of your assets. If your child has substantial savings, consider using some of the funds to buy things they can use in school later, such as a new computer or a car.

Structure Your Investments Carefully   Since retirement accounts and your personal residence don't count against you in determining the aid for which your student will qualify, maximize your retirement contributions or make extra payments on your mortgage. For every $1,000 you reduce your countable assets, you'll decrease your expected college contribution by about $56 a year.

Be Accurate, But Conservative, When Valuing Your Assets   Be sure you're not using inflated values when you fill out the financial aid forms. These rules apply to real estate you own and other property for which there is not a ready market.

Defer Income   If you're expecting a bonus or other lump sum payment, see if you can change the date you will receive it, so you will get the money before January of your child's junior year in high school, or after his or her junior year in college, to keep the money out of the financial aid picture. Even if you delay the receipt just until the next calendar year, at least you'll reduce your college contribution for one year.

Saving for Retirement

Retirement is another big goal for most people. Yet many women fail to plan strategically for their golden years. Here are the facts:

- Nearly one quarter of women erroneously think $100,000 or less will be enough to support them comfortably during a retirement lasting 20 years or more.
- Nearly half of all women investors have mostly conservative investments, which could result in smaller retirement account balances.
- Women over age 65 are twice as likely to live in poverty as men the same age.

These patterns are particularly disturbing because women live an average of seven years longer than men, and more than 90 percent of women will be solely responsible for managing their money at some point in their lives.

The Simple Truth

Nearly half of all women do not know how much money they will need for retirement, and 56 percent plan to rely on their husband, inheritance, or a stock market windfall to support them in old age.

—*A 2002 survey commissioned by Million Dollar Round Table, an association of insurance and financial services professionals*

Although most people say they'd like to retire early, in actuality, very few have the resources to do so. Sixty-two percent of women surveyed say they are behind schedule in their retirement planning and saving. Of women who expect to work post-retirement, 45 percent say it is because they need to, according to a survey by the American Savings Education Council.

How Much Do You Need for Your Retirement?

To estimate how much you'll need in retirement, look at several factors: the year you plan to retire, your longevity (and that of your spouse, if you're married), the income you will earn in retirement from part-time employment or consulting, your expenses in retirement, and the effects of inflation.

You can use Worksheet 9.2 to compute your retirement needs.

Worksheet 9.2

Retirement Planning

1. How much you will need each month, in today's dollars $_____
2. Add 20 percent for income taxes   _____
3. Total needed each month, in today's dollars (1 + 2)   _____

Monthly earnings and retirement benefits:

4. Earnings from employment during retirement   _____
5. Social Security from Table 1   _____
6. Pension plan monthly distribution
   (defined benefit)   _____
7. Total monthly earnings and retirement
   benefits (4 + 5 + 6)   _____
8. Other monthly income you will need,
   in today's dollars (3 − 7)   _____
9. Divide income needed (line 8) by 24
   (assumes inflation is 3%)   _____
10. Times years until retirement   ×_____
11. Additional income you will need due to
    inflation (9 × 10)   _____
12. Monthly income you will need, in future
    dollars (8 + 11)
    Multiply by 240*   × 240
13. How much you'll need at retirement to
    produce future income   _____

Amount saved so far:

14. 401(k) and other employer-sponsored plans   _____
15. IRAs   _____
16. Other investments earmarked for retirement   _____
17. Total saved so far, in today's dollars
    (14 + 15 + 16)   _____
18. Times investment growth factor from
    Table 2   ×_____
19. Amount saved so far, in future dollars
    (17 × 18)   _____
20. Investments still needed, in future dollars
    (13 − 19)   _____
21. Times monthly savings factor from Table 3   ×_____

22. MONTHLY SAVINGS NEEDED (20 × 21) $_____

*Assumes that investments will earn 4 percent more than inflation and will be exhausted in 40 years.

Retirement Planning Worksheet Table 1
Your Social Security Benefits (Monthly Social
Security Benefits You Will Receive in Today's Dollars)

Your Current Annual Income	Your Monthly Benefits at Age 65–67
$10,000	$615
$20,000	$887
$30,000	$1,151
$40,000	$1,423
$50,000	$1,598
$60,000	$1,722
$70,000	$1,849
$80,000	$1,969

Spouses generally will receive half of the above amounts at age 65 to 67, or benefits based on their own earnings records, whichever is greater.

Retirement Planning Worksheet Table 2
Investment Growth Factor (Amount One
Dollar Invested Now Will Grow to)

Years to Retire	Rate of Return			
	4%	6%	8%	10%
5	1.22	1.34	1.46	1.60
10	1.48	1.79	2.16	2.59
15	1.80	2.40	3.17	4.18
20	2.19	3.21	4.66	6.73
25	2.67	4.29	6.85	10.83
30	3.24	5.74	10.06	17.45
35	3.95	7.69	14.76	28.10

Retirement Planning Worksheet Table 3
Monthly Savings Factor (Monthly Amount Needed to Save One Dollar)

Years to Retire	Rate of Return			
	4%	6%	8%	10%
5	0.0150	0.0143	0.0136	0.0129
10	0.0068	0.0061	0.0055	0.0049
15	0.0041	0.0034	0.0029	0.0024
20	0.0027	0.0022	0.0017	0.0013
25	0.0019	0.0014	0.0011	0.0008
30	0.0014	0.0010	0.0007	0.0004
35	0.0011	0.0007	0.0004	0.0003

If Worksheet 9.2 showed you are saving enough each month for retirement, great. If not, step up your retirement savings, if you can. If it seems impossible to save enough each month, perhaps you can modify your assumptions. For example, you could plan to work longer, so you have longer to save and the period of time you are using your assets is shorter. Or you could plan to work part-time during retirement, reducing the amount of retirement income you'll need. Remember, the important thing is to start saving now, and keep saving as much as you can.

The Simple Truth
❦

The average monthly Social Security check for a woman over 65 is $697, which is $207 less than a man's. This is generally because women take time out of the workforce to care for families or ailing parents, and women often earn lower salaries while working.

—Social Security Administration

The Way to Save for Retirement

After you've calculated how much you should save for retirement each month, where should you invest it? Your choices include IRAs, employer plans, and other savings and investments. Here is a brief overview of the most popular retirement savings plans.

Employer Pension Plans   Some companies still have pension plans for their employees, though traditional pension plans are not as prevalent as they used to be. The benefit you will receive depends on your age at retirement, the number of years you have been employed, and how much you earned in the last years before you retire. Because women move in and out of the workforce more often than men do (for example, to stay home and raise their children or care for an elderly parent), they are less likely to work for an employer long enough to qualify for its pension plan. Statistics show it takes five extra years to make up retirement benefits lost for every year you spend out of the workforce.

The Simple Truth

Most retirement plans require five years of active employment to qualify to receive benefits. The median length of stay at a job for women is 3.8 years, vs. 5.1 years for men. As a result, less than one-third of women working in the private sector qualified for retirement benefits in 1998.

—*Women's Institute for a Secure Retirement*

401(k) Plans   You can contribute part of your salary to these plans and invest the money in mutual funds or company stock. When you contribute to a plan, you get a triple benefit. First, Uncle Sam subsidizes your retirement by deferring income taxes on the amounts you contribute. So for every dollar you contribute to your account, your net pay may decrease by only sixty or seventy cents. Secondly, the amount your 401(k) earns won't be taxed to you until you withdraw it in retirement. And finally, since the money is taken directly out of your paycheck, you won't be tempted to spend it now. If you work for a school or nonprofit organization, your plan might be called a 403(b) or a TSA. The letters and numbers are somewhat different, but the general rules are the same.

Some companies match part of your contribution, but may require you to stay with the company for a certain length of time before you are entitled to the matching funds if you leave. This is called *vesting*.

If you leave the company before retirement, you have four choices: You can leave your vested funds in the company plan (if the company allows), roll them into your new employer's 401(k) plan, roll them into an IRA, or cash out by taking a lump sum distribution. But cashing out is unwise: 20 percent of the funds will go straight to the IRS before you see a dime, and you may owe additional federal taxes, as well as state taxes, when you file your income tax return. If you are under age 55 and still working, you will pay an additional 10 percent early-withdrawal penalty.

The Simple Truth

The average women's balance in a 401(k) account is a little more than half of the average man's. And, neither fare very well as they approach retirement. On average, only 27% of their retirement needs will be covered by their savings in 401(k)s, IRAs, and similar plans.

—*Fidelity Investments report "Building Futures," March 2001*

Individual Retirement Accounts (IRAs)   An IRA lets you set aside up to $3,000 a year for retirement ($4,000 beginning in 2005). That amount will increase gradually to $5,000 in 2008 and then will be adjusted for inflation every year after that. If you are age 50 or older, you can also make additional "catch-up" contributions of $500 a year ($1,000 beginning in 2006).

There are two kinds of IRAs. A *traditional IRA* is tax-deductible if your income is under certain levels or you are not covered under another retirement plan. Your contributions and earnings are taxable to you whenever you withdraw them and you will pay a 10 percent federal tax penalty if you withdraw funds before you turn age 59½. You must begin taking distributions as of April 1 of the year after you turn 70½.

The other kind of IRA is a *Roth IRA*. Although contributions to a Roth IRA aren't tax deductible when you make them, you'll never have to pay tax on the earnings if you wait until 59½ to withdraw them. The Roth IRA has no mandatory distribution requirements, and you can withdraw your contributions tax-free and penalty-free at any time, once the IRA has been in place for five years. Just as with traditional IRAs, early withdrawal penalties apply to earnings on Roth IRAs. Under certain circumstances you can withdraw earnings penalty-free before age 59½: if you use up to $10,000 toward the cost of buying a home for the first time, if you pay college tuition costs, or if you pay extraordinary health costs. Because of its tax-free growth and more flexible withdrawal options, the Roth IRA is your best long-term savings plan other than an employer plan with matching contributions.

Don't Pay a Penalty If You Retire Early

Want to take out money from your IRA for early retirement? You can avoid the penalty for early distributions from your IRA if you follow the "72(t)" rule. Named after an IRS regulation, 72(t) allows you to take annual distributions from your IRA before age 59½, without the usual 10 percent penalty. If you want to retire in your forties or fifties, this could be an interesting option.

You must follow strict rules to qualify for penalty-free early distribution. The payments must continue annually for five years, or until you reach age 59½, whichever comes later. Once the payment schedule is set up, it cannot be changed except in case of total disability or death, so think carefully before you initiate this withdrawal option.

You can use a number of methods to calculate the amount of the payments: the life expectancy method (dividing the account balance by your life expectancy), the amortization method (using an amortization schedule, similar to a mortgage), or the annuity factor method (using the amortization method, but using insurance company life expectancy tables, not the IRS tables).

This method can become extremely complicated, so find a financial specialist who knows the ins and outs if you are considering using 72(t).

Savings Incentive Match Plans for Employees (SIMPLE)   If you own your own business, you can create a SIMPLE IRA plan that lets you and your employees contribute up to $9,000 per year ($10,000 for 2005) on your own behalf, and take a tax deduction for the contributions. If you are 50 or older, you can contribute an additional $1,500 ($2,000 for 2005). You can also contribute an "employer match" equal to 3 percent of your income, up to an additional $9,000 ($10,000 for 2005), but you'll have to match employee contributions as well. SIMPLE plans are flexible—you can contribute less in years when money is tight and more in years when cash is abundant. Contributions are tax-deferred and penalty-free if withdrawn after age 59½.

Simplified Employee Pension Plans (SEP)   If you are self-employed, you might want to consider an SEP plan, which lets you set aside 20 percent of your profits from self-employment (if you are incorporated, you may contribute up to 25 percent) up to a maximum of $40,000. As with a SIMPLE plan, contributions are tax-deferred and earnings are penalty-free if withdrawn after age 59½. You can also contribute less than the max or nothing at all, if you're strapped for cash in a particular year. Don't forget, if you have employees that have been with you for three years or more, you'll have to cover them too.

Keogh Plans   If you have an unincorporated business or partnership, it's likely a Keogh will let you put away more than any other plan. Your contributions are tax deductible and grow tax-deferred until withdrawn. All full-time employees who have been with you for three years or more must be included in the plan.

A defined benefit Keogh lets you choose the specific amount you'll receive at retirement, and then contribute to reach that goal, based on your age, expected retirement benefit, and years to retirement. These plans allow greater contributions on behalf of older employers and employees, since fewer years are left until they retire.

There are two kinds of defined contribution Keoghs. A *profit-sharing Keogh* lets you put away 25 percent of your compensation and that of your employees, up to a maximum amount of $40,000. As with the SIMPLE and SEP plans, you can choose to reduce your investment in any given year, which gives you an element of flexibility.

A *money-purchase Keogh* has the same contribution limits, but when you launch the plan, you have to pick a percentage of your net income you plan to contribute each year, and that percentage cannot be changed from year to year. Whichever kind of Keogh you use, you will need to file an annual tax form reporting the account's activity once the account balance hits $100,000.

Which plan is right for you? Now that you know the rules for all the plans, guess what? The amounts and limitations change each year. This also is a favorite place for Congress to fiddle as it tinkers with tax laws. So be sure to consult your business financial advisor before you decide which plan to use and how much to contribute.

Where Should I Invest My Retirement Contributions?

The investments you choose to fund your plans will depend a lot on your time horizon and your personal level of risk tolerance. If you're still young and have 20 or 30 years until retirement, you can afford to include more aggressive, growth-oriented investments, because you will have time to make up for any losses if the market dips along the way.

However, the closer you get to your golden years, the more risk averse your investments should become. As you get older, you should weight your portfolio more heavily toward fixed-income securities and cash equivalents to safeguard your wealth and make it easier to take distributions.

Figures 9.2A, B, and C offer three pie charts to show you possible allocations of your investment funds, depending on how close you are to retirement.

Protection and Growth Through Annuities

Annuities are most appropriate when you've maxed out the amount you can contribute to your retirement plans, yet you want to save more on a tax-deferred basis. Although you won't get a current tax deduction for the money you invest, you won't have to pay tax on the earnings until you withdraw the funds in retirement.

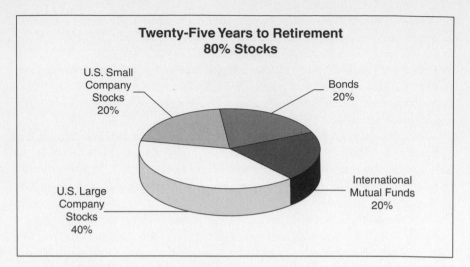

Figure 9.2A   Twenty-Five Years to Retirement 80% Stocks

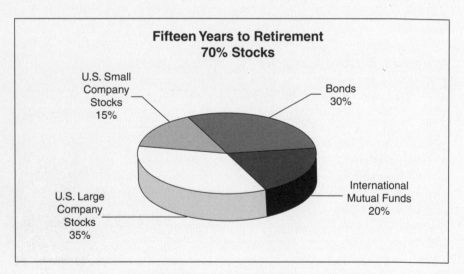

Figure 9.2B   Fifteen Years to Retirement 70% Stocks

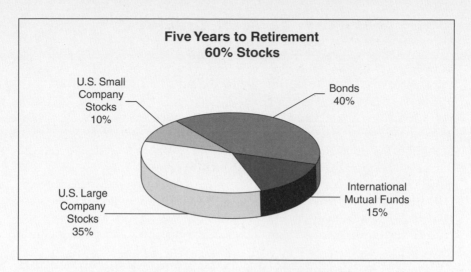

Figure 9.2C   Five Years to Retirement 60% Stocks

An annuity is a contract between you and an insurance company. Annuities can be flexible. For some annuities, you can make decisions about how often to make payments, how much to contribute (there are no limits), how those payments are invested, and how to receive retirement income from the annuity.

Types of Annuities

First, let's look at the types of available annuities.

An *immediate annuity* lets you deposit a lump sum with an insurance company or other financial institution, which in turn agrees to make payments to you for life, beginning immediately (hence the name). A portion of each payment you receive is considered to be a return of your investment and is not taxable. This type of annuity is most often purchased by people who plan to retire soon or are already retired, and want to know exactly what they will get each month for the rest of their lives.

A *deferred annuity* is used to accumulate funds to be paid to you in the future. When you purchase a deferred annuity, your payment is invested as you direct. Deferred annuities come in two basic forms, *fixed* and *variable*. A fixed annuity guarantees a specified rate of return each year. A variable annuity is invested in a variety of subaccounts that resemble mutual funds. The amount the variable annuity earns depends on how those accounts perform. With either kind of deferred annuity, the tax on earnings is deferred until you begin to receive the income.

Benefits and Drawbacks of Annuities

With a variable annuity, you assume the investment risk of the subaccounts: They may outpace inflation handsomely, or in a bad financial market, they could decline. But here's the good news: the annuity provides a safety net. If you die before you begin getting payments, your beneficiary will receive the greater of the current market value or the premiums you paid plus a specified interest rate, if you chose an interest-rate option when you purchased the annuity. If you are unlikely to need the money in your lifetime, it can accumulate for your heirs tax-deferred and with this safety-net guarantee of value. The internal expenses on a variable annuity are generally greater than the expenses of a comparable mutual fund. But for people who would like the peace of mind of having their principal protected in the event of their death, the annuity presents an excellent choice. Insurance companies now offer living benefit riders as an option, which will guarantee a specified income in retirement.

Annuities are attractive estate planning vehicles because they avoid probate. However, be aware that they don't have the beneficial step-up in tax basis as do mutual funds or stocks. You'll avoid the income taxes on the earnings while you are alive, but your heirs will eventually have to pay the income taxes once you die.

How to Get Retirement Income from Your Annuity

Once you reach age 59½, you can begin to receive distributions from your annuity without a 10 percent federal penalty for early withdrawal. You can choose to annuitize your deferred annuity, receiving fixed payments for life or for a specified number of years, but most people simply take withdrawals as they need them. If you annuitize your contract, then a portion of each payment you receive will be taxable, and part will be a nontaxable return of the premiums you have paid. If you take withdrawals as you need them, those withdrawals will be fully taxable until you have paid tax on all of the earnings of the annuity. After that, withdrawals will be considered nontaxable return of premiums.

Investigate Before You Buy

If you are interested in purchasing an annuity, be sure to investigate the following features carefully:

- the current financial strength and track record of the insurance company issuing the contract
- the current interest rate and guarantee period for a fixed annuity, and the insurance company's record of investment returns for a variable annuity
- the minimum guaranteed rate of interest and principal guarantees
- bail-out provisions that allow you to surrender the contract without penalty if the interest rate falls below a specified amount

- the amount you can withdraw from the contract each year without being subject to withdrawal charges imposed by the insurance company (though withdrawals before age 59½ are subject to IRS penalties of 10 percent)
- the internal charges, which are the cost the insurance company charges to manage the portfolios and provide the guarantees and insurance
- surrender charges, the period for which they apply, and the circumstances under which they are waived (death, disability, or annuity payout)

Small Steps to Becoming a Money Star

1. Review the list of financial goals you created at the beginning of this chapter. Use the ROCKS method to focus on the key elements of both short-term and long-term desires. Create milestones in your savings plan so you can track your progress and feel a growing sense of accomplishment as you move forward.
2. If your children are older, discuss their education planning with them. Does your daughter dream of going to Harvard, or does she plan to attend the local state college? Is your son hoping for an athletic scholarship? Discuss your dreams and plans together so you'll all be on the same page.
3. Start saving, or increase your current contributions now. Make a deal with yourself to contribute to a retirement or education savings plan today. Calculate how much money you'll need, and what your contribution should be.
4. Gather up all your retirement plan statements and review them. Coordinate your retirement plans with your spouse to make sure that you are both on track to meet your savings goals.
5. Planning your retirement is more than just dollars and cents. Take some time to visualize how you would like to live when you retire. Where do you want to go? What would a typical day be like? Mentally explore your options. Make a collage of images related to retirement. Include a photo of your favorite retirement destination or whatever images help you to focus on achieving your goals.

PART THREE

What to Do When Life Happens

CHAPTER 10

Hope Is Not a Strategy: Dealing with Money Troubles

Dear WIFE,

Eighteen months ago, my dream of owning my own restaurant became a reality. I thought my business was successful, because I had lots of customers every night. I was too busy to pay attention to the money. Now my accountant tells me I've been losing money, and I'm $20,000 in debt. How can that be?

In Hot Water in Minneapolis

Dear Hot Water,

Running your own restaurant is a brave undertaking, but you've learned that it isn't as much about managing menus as managing money. When you find yourself in a hole, the first thing to do is to stop digging. Take a good hard look at your finances, and cut expenses where you can. You're not alone: There are lots of folks who find themselves in debt, for many different reasons. Read on to find out how to pay off your debts while protecting your credit history.

Dealing with Debt

Getting into hot water financially is one of life's unpleasant surprises, but you can handle it, no matter how serious the situation seems. Most of us are in debt at one time or another.

Debt can be a useful financial tool. It allows you to make necessary purchases that you otherwise could never afford. Imagine if you couldn't buy a house until you had saved enough to pay in cash! Each year, you would save and save, and each year, the cost of your dream home would escalate as inflation continued to push it beyond your grasp. But by incurring debt, you can purchase that home now, and enjoy the appreciation as the house goes up in value. What's more, the tax-deductible interest you pay on the mortgage saves you income taxes.

Still, too much debt can be a nightmare. Debt becomes a problem when you get in over your head. If you end up with credit card debt that seems overwhelming, it's not your credit card's fault, any more than it's your car's fault when you get a ticket for speeding.

If you find yourself with too much debt, keep your cool. By rethinking your financial strategy, you can get back on track to a secure future. In this chapter, we'll examine ways you can slash debt and repair credit, so that any setbacks will be brief. Remember, you have the power to manage your money wisely in good times and bad. There is always a solution to the problems you face.

The Simple Truth

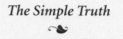

The average American household has 14.27 credit cards and carries an average outstanding credit card balance of $7,034.

—U.S. News & World Report, June 17, 2002

You Have Too Much Debt When. . .

How do you know if you have too much debt? Answer Quiz 10.1 to find out if you are in over your head.

How to Get Off the Credit Card Treadmill

In times of crisis, people often rely on credit cards to bail them out of a financial bind. Although having access to a line of credit can be beneficial for just this reason, relying too heavily on credit cards can get you into a heap of trouble. Financial advisor Andrew Tobias says, "Remember Aesop's tale of the ant, who saved food for the winter, and the grasshopper, who figured the future would take care of itself? Now imagine a grasshopper with credit cards!"

If you are caught in a whirlwind of credit card debt, here are some tips to put you back on the road to financial security.

Quiz 10.1

You Have Too Much Debt When...

True	False	
❏	❏	Your monthly payments (car, credit card, etc.) exceed 25 percent of your monthly take-home pay.
❏	❏	You borrow from one credit card to pay another.
❏	❏	Your credit cards are always maxed out.
❏	❏	You shop at stores that will take credit cards because you don't have the cash.
❏	❏	You feel overjoyed when you receive a solicitation in the mail for a new credit card.
❏	❏	You avoid opening your credit card bills because you're afraid of what you'll find inside.
❏	❏	You don't have any idea how much you owe on your credit cards.
❏	❏	Your debt is increasing each month instead of decreasing.
❏	❏	You keep having one emergency after another that drives credit card balances up.
❏	❏	You can't imagine living without your credit cards.
❏	❏	You have been refused additional credit by a credit card company or turned down for a mortgage.

If you answered True to any of these questions, you may have a problem with debt. Read on to learn how to pay down your debt and get your finances back on track.

- If you can, quit using your credit cards: Instead, use a debit card so the payment comes straight out of your bank account.
- If you must continue using your credit cards for now, charge only what you can pay in *full* within 30 days, when the bill comes.
- Put the money for each charge slip into a savings account as you make the purchase. That separate account will be used to pay the bill when it comes. As an alternative, deduct each charge slip from your checking account balance as you make the charge. Where you would normally write in the check number, put "CC" for "credit card." When your checking account balance reaches zero, quit charging.
- When the bill comes each month, if possible, pay all the current charges plus the monthly finance charge. In addition, pay 5 to 10 percent of the old balance due, or as much as you can afford.

By using these steps, you will get off the credit card treadmill and out of debt in a year or two. This regimen is difficult, and you may have to scrimp to do it. Do it anyway. The financial relief you feel as your credit card balances disappear will be well worth the sacrifice.

"To shorten winter, borrow some money due in spring."

W. J. VOGEL

Dealing with Creditors

When you have too much debt, you may have lots of creditors. That means lots of payments: the house payment, the car payment, the three credit card payments, the gas card payment, the department store payment, the student loan payment, and the payment to your parents for the money they loaned you last year.

The worst thing to do if you are having trouble making your payments is to ignore them. Sorry, but they won't go away! Prepare a detailed budget so you can show your creditors that you have a realistic plan for getting out of debt. You may be able to convince them to take smaller payments for a while, especially if you have experienced a recent financial emergency, such as illness or job loss, which has put you behind.

With so many bills, how can you determine which to pay first or how much to pay toward your debt each month? As a first step, create a debt reduction worksheet, on which you list your creditors, the amount owed to each, the interest rate, and the minimum monthly payments due. You can use Worksheet 10.1.

There, that wasn't so hard, was it?

Now, on Worksheet 10.1 list the extra monthly amount you plan to pay on each debt. Begin with the debt with the highest interest rate. Once that is paid off through extra monthly payments, begin paying the debt with the next-highest interest rate, and so on. Just be sure to make the minimum payments required on all your cards. As you dig out of debt, don't fall behind on your mortgage or car payments, which would result in foreclosure or repossession.

In addition to paying down your highest rate cards, make sure you are getting the lowest interest rates available. Call each of your creditors, and ask if they would be willing to reduce your interest rate. Or transfer your balance from higher-interest cards to lower-interest ones. It is amazing how much difference the interest rate makes, as Table 10.1 demonstrates. For example, if you pay $100 per month toward a $5,000 credit card balance, you'll see that at 5.9 percent interest, it will take you nearly five years to pay it off and you'll pay

Worksheet 10.1
_____

Tallying Your Debts

Creditor	Balance	Interest Rate	Minimum Payment	Account Number	Phone Number	Extra Monthly Payment

Table 10.1   Time and Interest to Pay Off a $5,000 Credit Card Balance (paying $100 per month)

At This Interest Rate	It Will Take You This Long	And You'll Pay This Much Interest
5.9%	4 years, 10 months	$753
7.9%	5 years, 1 month	$1,084
9.9%	5 years, 5 months	$1,474
12.9%	6 years, 1 month	$2,212
15.9%	6 years, 11 months	$3,252
18.9%	8 years, 4 months	$4,911
21.9%	11 years, 3 months	$8,470

$753 in interest. Raise that interest rate to 21.9 percent, and it will take you more than eleven years to pay it off. You'll pay an astounding $8,470 in interest on a $5,000 purchase!

Monitor your progress, and revise your debt worksheet often. Dealing with debt is like tackling a weight problem: It's as easy to rack up too much debt as it is to put on unwanted extra pounds. And just like losing weight, paying off the debt takes time and persistence. By monitoring your progress, you'll reach milestones along the way and eventually bring your debt back down to a manageable level.

Restructuring Your Debt

Another way to handle excessive debt is by consolidating the money owed to several different lenders into one lump sum and making regular payments toward this amount. Tax laws may tempt you to use the equity in your home by taking out a home equity loan to consolidate credit card balances, auto loans, and other personal debt into a more manageable whole. Your payment will be reduced, because most home equity loans allow you to pay just the monthly interest to stay current. Unfortunately, after consolidating what they owe, many people incur additional credit card debt, and they end up once again facing mounting bills *plus* the extra burden of a home equity loan.

Another option is to work with a credit counselor. Legitimate credit counseling agencies will charge only a nominal sum, and they won't make any promises about eliminating the blemishes on your record. Instead, they will help you set up a regular payment schedule with your creditors and provide you with additional tools that can help you stay on track with your spending and debt in the future.

These companies can negotiate with creditors on your behalf to reduce payments and interest rates. Generally, you pay a monthly lump sum to the counseling agency, which then distributes the money to your creditors. Credit counselors also can set you up with a debt management program to help you climb back out of the hole you're in. Some of the 1,300 Consumer Credit Counseling Service Centers charge a nominal start-up or monthly fee for their services, while others receive a portion of the debtor's payments to creditors as compensation for their services.

To find a suitable credit counselor, contact the National Foundation for Credit Counseling (www.nfcc.org) or the Association of Independent Consumer Credit Counseling Agencies (www.aiccca.org). Make sure you have a clear understanding of any fees involved up front, and as an added precaution, check with your local Better Business Bureau to determine whether the agency you choose has a solid customer service record.

Disadvantages of Debt Consolidation Loans

You may be tempted to borrow to pay off several existing debts and lower your monthly required payment. Here are the disadvantages of such loans.

- *The lower monthly payment and the zero balance on your credit cards may lure you into spending more.*
- *Although the interest rate on the consolidation loan may be lower than on your existing debts, the extended period of the consolidation may create more finance charges over the life of the loan.*
- *Most debt consolidation loans require you to pledge collateral, which limits your future borrowing power and may be disastrous if you declare bankruptcy.*

Bankruptcy

The Simple Truth

᠅

More than 1.6 million Americans filed for personal bankruptcy in the year ended March 31, 2003, according to the Adminstrative Office of the Courts. That's a 7.1 percent increase from the previous year, and a 500% increase since 1980. Two out of three of those filing had lost a job, and half had experienced a serious health problem.

—BankruptcyAction.com

If all else fails, personal bankruptcy may be your only answer. Chapter 13 of the federal bankruptcy law, called the *wage-earner plan,* allows you to repay part of your debt over several years, and the rest will be forgiven. Under Chapter 7, known as *straight bankruptcy,* your assets are sold and used to pay debts, and the rest of your debts are forgiven. Under settlements negotiated in bankruptcy cases, you may be able to keep a few assets: some equity in your home and car, the tools of your trade, retirement benefits, and a small amount of jewelry and household goods.

Certain debts are not dischargeable in bankruptcy, including federal and state taxes, child support, alimony, traffic tickets and criminal fines, student loans, debts for $500 or more of luxury goods or services purchased within forty days of filing for bankruptcy, loans of more than $1,000 made within twenty days of filing for bankruptcy, and loans obtained fraudulently.

Bankruptcy should be viewed as a last resort. Bankruptcy is a viable option if you are facing foreclosure on your house that you can't avert, or if your dischargeable debts are at least a third of your income, you won't have additional debts coming due in the future, and your income will be enough to support you after bankruptcy.

You can file for bankruptcy only once every six years, and the information will stay on your credit record for a whopping ten years. For this reason, bankruptcy really should be viewed as a last resort. Don't declare bankruptcy if your debts are small or if you have a large number of debts that are not dischargeable, such as income taxes. Bankruptcy also is not a good option if you expect to incur sizable debts in the future, such as for large medical bills. That's because you'll end up in the hole again with no options this time.

Misery Loves Company

Filing for bankruptcy is always a tough decision. Most of us feel embarrassed when our finances spin out beyond our control. But if your money troubles have you on the brink of bankruptcy, don't despair. You are in famous company. Many successful people have gone broke at some point in their careers: the painter Rembrandt, circus showman P. T. Barnum, author Mark Twain, singer Willie Nelson, ketchup mogul Henry Heinz, auto manufacturer Henry Ford, movie stars Burt Reynolds and Kim Basinger, talk show host Larry King, singer Wayne Newton, filmmaker Francis Ford Coppola, and many, many others.

Oops, I Blew It! How to Repair Bad Credit

Is Big Brother watching you? When it comes to your credit history, it seems that way. Most people go merrily on their way, living their lives, while computers in back rooms are keeping track of their every financial move. Only when they get turned down for credit do many people realize that someone's been keeping track, and it's not them.

Why Your Credit Report Is Important

The accuracy of your credit report is critical, because it can be used by lenders to decide the interest rate on a loan, by prospective employers to screen job applicants, and by insurance companies to price policies. In addition, your creditors regularly review your credit profile, even if you have a good payment history.

Your credit report reveals many things about your financial habits. It shows how many bank cards and charge accounts you currently have, how many you have had in the past, and whether they were paid when closed. For each card or account, your credit report tells the current amount you owe, when you made the last payment, whether your payments have been made on time, and what your credit limit is, or the largest amount you have owed on the card or account. Your credit report also lists any judgments against you, liens, bankruptcies, and foreclosures on real estate you owned.

What Hurts Your Credit History
These will ding your credit standing, so avoid them if you can:
- *too many credit cards, or cards with zero balances*
- *high debt other than your mortgage*
- *delinquent accounts or frequent late payments*
- *frequent job or address changes*
- *bills marked uncollectible*
- *bankruptcy*

How to Read and Correct Your Credit Report

What can you do to improve your credit standing? First, get a copy of your credit report and read it. Obtaining and reviewing your credit report also guards against identity theft. You can check to make sure no one has obtained a credit account in your name and is merrily spending away your creditworthiness.

You can get a copy of your credit report from credit bureaus listed in the Yellow Pages under "Credit Reporting Agencies," or online. The three major credit bureaus are:

Trans Union: (800) 888–4213, www.TransUnion.com

Equifax Information Services: (800) 525–6285, www.Equifax.com

Experian: (888) 397–3742, www.Experian.com

These agencies compile information about your credit history from public records on foreclosures, bankruptcies, tax liens, and other court judgments, as well as from merchants and lenders.

By federal law you are entitled to a free copy of your credit report if you have been denied credit based on information in the report and request a copy within 60 days. You may also receive a free copy if you are unemployed and intend to apply for a job within sixty days of your request, if you're on public assistance, or if your report contains errors due to fraud. Otherwise, the cost to order a credit report is generally around $15.

When you receive your report, go through it carefully and be sure you understand fully the various codes and abbreviations that are used. If you find incorrect information, contact the credit bureau immediately and ask that it be corrected. The report you receive should have a form you can fill out to dispute an entry, or you can do this online.

If the source of the incorrect information is a lender or credit card company, you will need to ask that company to furnish corrected information to the credit bureau. If the information cannot be corrected or doesn't tell the full story as reported (such as extenuating circumstances for delinquent payments), you may put a written statement of 100 words or less in your file at the credit bureau, to be transmitted along with your payment history whenever a potential creditor accesses your file.

When you take action to correct a mistake in your credit report, be sure to keep a copy of the correspondence in your files. Also, realize you may have to make the same request again in the future, since credit reporting agencies are notorious for taking their time to make corrections. If at any point you speak to a credit bureau representative on the phone, make a note of the date and time of your call and exactly what was discussed. With patience and persistence, you can resolve disputes and clean up your credit history, so you can move forward with your plans for the future.

"A bank is a place where they lend you an umbrella in fair weather and ask for it back when it begins to rain."

ROBERT FROST

How to Improve Your Credit History

Improving your credit history takes time. You must create a record of timely payments, reduce the balance outstanding on your accounts, reduce your required monthly payments, and give past credit problems a chance to fade away. Eliminating the tracks of identity theft from your credit history can also take months, even years. Because bankruptcies stay on your record for ten years and other credit problems may remain for seven years, bankruptcy, skipped payments, and foreclosures should be a last resort in dealing with financial woes.

Clean up any legitimate debts you still owe. Contact your creditors to see if they will settle for less than the full amount, or perhaps wipe the past-due status off your record in exchange for payment. Negotiate to get the best deal you can.

Once all of the negative items are cleared up, work on getting the right number of credit card accounts. You don't want too many and you don't want too few. Keep a few accounts open, use them regularly, and pay them off every month, with no late payments.

Don't do business with companies that promise to "fix" your bad credit or improve your credit rating for a fee. Only you can do what is needed.

Small Steps to Becoming a Money Star

1. Take stock of your situation. Don't be afraid to face your bills and make a list of what you actually owe. Being willing to analyze your situation objectively will make it possible to resolve the problem. Knowledge is power!

2. When you are in the middle of a financial crisis, it's easy to blame yourself, but try to resist the urge. Always remember, keep your head held high and your eye to the future. Tell yourself that "this too shall pass" and reward yourself in small ways for the progress you make. Your self-worth is not dependent on your net worth.

3. Pay attention to interest rates. Don't throw those credit card solicitations out without looking for cards that have a lower interest rate than your current debt. If you find a good offer, transferring your debt can save you a

bundle. You can also check out www.bankrate.com to find the lowest available offers and submit your applications.

4. Freeze your debt. If you're trying to tighten your belt, consider putting your credit cards out of service temporarily. Simply place your card in the middle of a container full of ice cubes and put a few cubes on top to keep the card from floating to the surface. Fill the container with water, and put it in the freezer. In order to use your credit card again, you'll have to wait for it to defrost, which will give you a "cooling-off" period to consider your expenditures.

5. Order a copy of your credit report and that of your spouse, and sit down together to review them. If there are any inaccuracies or inconsistencies, decide which of you will take steps to correct the problems. Don't put it off—it will only get worse, not better.

CHAPTER 11

When the Vows Break: Getting Through Divorce

Dear WIFE,

When my husband left me, I was a stay-at-home mom and thought the world had ended. Then a friend told me about your program Second Saturday: What Women Need to Know about Divorce. From that moment on I have been empowered! Now I've taken control of my life, and it feels great. I still have difficult days, but that's part of the process, I think. Thanks so much for your support. I now understand that a man is not a financial plan!

It's Never Too Late in Sedona

Dear Never Too Late,

For most people, divorce is the largest single legal and financial just transaction of their lives. This process has probably taught you that divorce isn't just about the law. It's also about three things: family, emotion, and money. In this chapter we'll share the powerful lessons from Second Saturday that have helped thousands of women through divorce.

Divorce Basics

The Simple Truth

∾

Two-thirds of all divorces are initiated by women.

—*American Law and Economics Review 2-1 (2000)*

You might be happily married, or divorced, or may find yourself somewhere in between. Or perhaps you have a friend or family member going through divorce. Divorce touches almost everyone's life at some point. As devastating as divorce can be, it is also a time for growth and new opportunity.

Divorce certainly can take a bite out of your lifestyle. In the first year after divorce, the wife's standard of living drops almost 27 percent while the husband's increases by as much as 10 percent. That's not our opinion; that's fact. That's why we started Second Saturday: What Women Need to Know about Divorce. It's been used as the model for programs across the country, educating thousands of women. The proceeds from the program go back into the community and are used to give scholarships to women who are returning to college after years of being out of the workforce.

Over our combined 40 years of working with women going through divorce, we've encountered many unusual stories and situations. The couple who fought about dividing furniture for so long that the husband finally sawed the dining room table in half. The couple who fought over custody of the refrigerator magnets. The couple who spent more than $200,000 in legal fees arguing about custody of the family dog. The woman who contemplated having her children "kidnapped" so her husband would feel sorry and come back home. The man who stole his wife's wallet full of credit cards "for her own good," because he thought she spent too much on groceries. The woman who wanted alimony on the basis that she couldn't work because her cats would be home alone all day.

You've probably heard stories like these or even lived through some of them. It all boils down to this: Divorce is not fair. It's an uphill battle, fought in a language that you don't understand, using money you can't spare, for a prize that's only half of what you had before, and it all takes longer than you ever imagined. Those are the realities of divorce, and if you can shortcut the process by figuring out what's really important to you and compromising on the rest, you'll come out miles (and dollars) ahead.

Every family situation is different. Before you can figure it all out, you need to understand the rules of the game. Understanding divorce laws is the starting point to navigating the intricacies of divorce.

Divorce laws vary from state to state. How you divide your property will probably depend on the laws of your state. In most states, equitable-distribution laws apply. That means each spouse gets a fair share of marital assets. It's not always 50/50, but you should get what's rightfully yours. The problem is that some assets are easier to divvy up than others. Things like pension plans and securities can be tricky to split, especially when you take timing and tax considerations into account.

It Isn't the Money, Honey

Each year, nearly 2.8 million people go through divorce, but contrary to popular opinion, financial issues are not a leading cause—at least not according to recent findings by Jan Andersen, an associate professor at California State University in Sacramento. After studying a wealth of research on the topic for his doctoral dissertation at Utah State University, Andersen found that money took a backseat to other marital woes, such as lack of emotional support, verbal or physical abuse, and sexual problems. When couples do fight over finances, it's generally symptomatic of deeper issues, such as feelings of insecurity or a need for control.

The 12 Financial Pitfalls of Divorce

A bit of advance planning goes a long way. Before you begin the divorce proceedings, take steps to prepare for what lies ahead. When you divide property and income, each of you will have only half of what you had before, or perhaps less. If you don't have your own regular income, you will need money to live on until you can get an award of alimony or until the divorce is finalized and you have access to your share of the marital assets. As a result, you will need to gather information and time your actions strategically.

By familiarizing yourself with the 12 financial pitfalls of divorce, you can save yourself a lot of hassle and heartbreak in the future.

Pitfall #1. Not Enough Cash

In divorce, everything always costs more and takes longer than you expect. Expenses begin to mushroom as soon as the divorce process starts. If you feel a split is imminent, start stashing the funds you'll need for attorney's fees and living expenses. The more money you can set aside before the divorce proceedings begin, the less anxiety you will face when the big day comes. One affluent woman, married for more than 40 years, had been planning her getaway for 25 of those. She regularly stashed money from her healthy household allowance.

When she was ready to leave, she came to us for advice. As we reviewed her financial situation in preparation for the divorce, we tallied up the total—her nest egg was almost a quarter of a million dollars. And her husband thought she was a bad money manager, because no matter how much he gave her, she always ran short!

If you are afraid your husband will seize your joint savings, transfer your share to a new account. This money will still be a marital asset, but at least it will be under your control. Be aware that this act of self-protection may be perceived by your spouse as hostile and get your divorce off to a bad start. Do what you have to do to feel safe: Divorce is not about good manners. It's about survival.

If you don't already have a credit card in your own name, apply for one at your local bank. If you have shared credit cards with your spouse, close out as many as possible. If one of you continues to use any of those accounts after the split, the other is still legally responsible for the debt.

Pitfall #2. Too Little Preparation

Divorce is a long, complicated process that requires careful preparation. Don't just pack your bags, load up the kids, and drive away in a car that needs four new tires. Instead, prepare by using joint funds to undertake any necessary car repairs, to pay for necessary dental work for the children, and to buy any career clothes you will need. Otherwise, you'll be paying for all of that from your share of the bank account once you leave. One woman at Second Saturday confessed she had used joint funds to pay for plastic surgery before leaving. She considered it an investment in her future.

In some states, income received after separation belongs to the spouse who earned it. If that's true in your state, think about the timing of the separation. Is your husband due any bonuses or other windfalls in the near future? Don't separate until after they arrive, so you can get your share. Of course, if you're the one scheduled to get the bonus, well, there's no time like the present.

Don't forget about Social Security. You can collect retirement benefits based on your ex-spouse's earnings history if your marriage lasted ten years or longer. So if you've been married nine years, you might want to stick out the last year, so you can collect when you reach retirement age.

Pitfall #3. No Records

The three most important words during divorce are: document, document, document. When you divorce, you must identify the assets you and your husband have accumulated and establish their value. Even if your husband was in charge of the finances while you were married, it's now up to you to find those records. You are entitled to your share of any marital property you find, and any additional income you discover may increase the amount of earnings that are used to calculate alimony and child support.

Gather as many financial records as you can before your divorce begins. Make a clear copy of tax returns for the past three years, loan applications, wills, trusts, financial statements, banking information, credit card statements, deeds to real property, car registrations, and insurance policies. Also copy records that you can use to trace your separate property, such as from an inheritance or gifts from your family. These assets will remain yours as long as you can document them.

As you are taking stock of what your family owns, carefully inventory any safe deposit boxes. Track down bank and brokerage accounts and loans to friends and family members. Also obtain copies of pay stubs, retirement and pension plan statements, and documentation regarding investments. Make a list of personal property, including artwork, furniture, jewelry, and computers.

If you suspect your husband is hiding cash, copies of your spouse's business records and business tax returns can be a treasure map showing you where the hidden assets are buried. It's time to play super sleuth! One woman snuck into her husband's office one Sunday when he was out of town, hoping to copy records and leave, with no one the wiser. Oops! The door locked behind her and the alarm went off. She had to explain to the police that though she was sneaking around, she was only copying the information to which she was entitled.

Pitfall #4. Overlooking Assets

Don't overlook any assets—half of everything is yours! Small assets, such as frequent flyer points and vacation pay, can add up. Even if you don't want an asset, it can be used to trade for something you can use. Don't overlook hobbies or side businesses that might use expensive equipment or generate income. If you have a PHT degree (Putting Honey Through), you might be entitled to compensation for the expenses you paid to get your spouse through school.

A business is generally valued based on a combination of its net income and assets, so you may want to engage a forensic accountant to look for telltale signs of additional income or overstated expenses. In looking through a dentist's expense records, Ginita found lots of unreported income and overstated expenses. In addition to a highly paid dental assistant (read "girlfriend"), Ginita found his new golf clubs classified as dental tools. We visualize the dentist shouting "Open wide" instead of "Fore!" on the golf course as he plays through.

Your spouse may try to hide assets. He may collude with an employer to delay bonuses or raises, arrange a false debt repayment to a friend, or pay a salary from his business to a nonexistent employee. Even if he does, don't try to hide assets yourself. You'll likely be found out and incur the wrath of both your ex and the judge. Your divorce will be more straightforward and less expensive if you tell the truth and reveal all your assets.

Pitfall #5. Ignoring Tax Consequences

Though divorce is not a taxable event you have to report on your tax return, it can still have tax consequences. If you've owned your house for a number of years, it's probably gone up in value. Up to $250,000 of gain on your principal residence escapes tax when you sell, but if your gain is more than that, you'll owe money to the government. If your gain is greater than $250,000, you are probably better off selling while you and your husband still own the house together, so you each can claim a $250,000 exclusion.

Rental real estate can have even more of a tax bite. Ginita once counseled with a client who was about to sign her final divorce papers. She had agreed to take the rental they had owned for years, letting her husband take their home. She intended to sell the rental and use the proceeds to buy herself a condo. The problem was that over the years the couple had refinanced, taking money out each time. Now, with the rental fully depreciated, when it sold, the taxes would eat up all the proceeds, and then some. By taking the rental, she had thought she was getting $50,000 in equity, but in reality she'd owe $60,000 in taxes when it sold. Armed with new information, she hurried back to her attorney to renegotiate the deal.

Another huge asset in most divorces is the money in the retirement plans. Dollar for dollar, money in retirement accounts is generally worth less than money in bank accounts, since retirement money will be taxable when withdrawn. One exception is the Roth IRA, which won't be taxable when withdrawn for retirement.

Other assets that might have hidden tax traps are securities that are worth much more than they cost, stock options, annuities, cash value of life insurance policies, and vacation homes. Your attorney is versed in marital law but may not know all the ins and outs of current tax law. Your situation may require the help of an accountant or financial planner knowledgeable about divorce to determine if you are really getting a good deal.

Pitfall #6. Not Taking an Active Role

During divorce, being uninformed can be very, very expensive. Learning as much as you can and negotiating directly with your husband, if possible, will help you recover more quickly from the divorce. That is because you will have a healthy sense of control over the process, be focused on practical things, and be working with your ex to get things done. Taking an active role in the negotiations will help you to reach a better settlement than letting the attorneys handle it. You will have less conflict and litigation after the divorce, better compliance from your ex, and better sharing of information about the children.

Don't do what one woman did. She took two tranquilizers before a settlement conference. As a result, she was in a semi-stupor while her soon-to-be-ex ran the show. It wasn't until the next day, after the settlement had been reached, that she realized she missed out and wanted to renegotiate. Don't be a passive observer of your own divorce. Your attorney may give you legal advice, but all the decisions are ultimately up to you.

Here are some recommendations for being active in your divorce:

- Read a book on divorce, such as *The ABCs of Divorce for Women* by Carol Ann Wilson and Ginita Wall, even if you plan to use an attorney.
- Take a divorce class, such as Second Saturday, at a local college or university.
- Share financial information related to divorce with your spouse.
- Set appointments with your spouse to discuss specific issues. Prepare an agenda ahead of time, meet in a neutral place, set the length of the meeting, and don't exceed it.
- Take a class in negotiation skills or in dealing with difficult people. Chances are you'll need both during this challenging time.
- If there is something you don't understand, ask. Don't make assumptions or jump to conclusions.

Pitfall #7. Mixing Money and Emotion

During this trying time, it's easy to confuse your feelings with the facts. Try to be as dispassionate and businesslike as possible. View your attorney as a paid professional rather than a friend or confidante. When your grief is overwhelming, go home or to a friend's house, not to your attorney, who is billing you at an hourly rate.

Make property division decisions based on your own long-term best interests, not out of revenge. It won't make you happy to declare war on your ex. Make an effort to bring the divorce to a successful conclusion with as little rancor as possible. A nasty divorce benefits only the attorneys.

Here's a sad story about a woman who was forty-nine when she left her husband. After a couple of years of negotiations, unable to settle, her case went to trial. She was unhappy with the judge's decision, so she appealed her case to the appellate court. Then her husband disagreed with the appellate court's finding and appealed to the state Supreme Court. The Supreme Court remanded the case back to the lower court to be retried, at which time Ginita was brought in as a forensic accountant. The case was finally over seventeen years after it began. The client was sixty-six years old, broke and bitter. Why did these proceedings last seventeen years? Neither she nor her physician husband could accept the courts' decisions and move on, and they had the financial wherewithal to keep fighting until the money was all gone.

Pitfall #8. Not Fighting for What's Yours

Women tend to be supportive and sensitive to the needs of others, to build bridges, and to "make nice." These tendencies often get in our way during divorce. Divorce is about survival, not making friends. You have to insist on getting what you need and deserve. Even if you hope that you will eventually be able to reconcile with your ex, don't bend over backwards to make it happen. Stand up for yourself and get your share. If you reconcile, that's fine. If you don't, you'll still be able to take care of yourself financially.

Don't forget the four "gets" that can trap you. Fighting just to *get* even, giving up to *get* it over, being conciliatory to *get* him back, and trying to *get* your old life back. All these "gets" trap you into old ways of being and rob you of your ability to move forward as a whole person in control.

Sometimes women don't feel entitled to a share of their husband's retirement. "He worked all those years and I didn't," one older woman told us. "Besides, he needs it because he's almost old enough for retirement, and he's been counting on that money." She was so busy focusing on his retirement that she didn't realize that her own retirement years would be bleak, not golden, without her fair share.

"I don't know the key to success, but the key to failure is trying to please everybody."

BILL COSBY

Pitfall #9. Not Taking Control

Unfortunately, you can't call your attorney and say, "I want a divorce. Please call me when it's over." The only way out is through, and you are in charge of getting there. Going through a divorce can sometimes make you feel like the captain of a leaky boat on stormy seas—there seems to be a new crisis at every turn. Use this time of upheaval to start taking control of your life. Vow never to worry in the dark. If you can't sleep, turn on the light, pick up a pencil and paper, and write down your worries. Then, you can go back to sleep and deal with them first thing in the morning. Listen to your attorney, but make your own decisions. This is your divorce, so take control of the process!

Write everything down. That's one of the key things we talk about in Second Saturday. One woman really took it to heart. She kept track of all her expenses, notes from her meetings with attorneys and accountants, and promises made by her husband. And when he made threats, she wrote those down as well. Annoyed by the ever-present notebook, he snuck into her house one night and stole the notebook out of her purse. She woke up to see him bolting out of the bedroom, and she dialed 911. In his anger he grabbed the phone from her hand and ripped the cord from the wall. When the police arrived, she didn't want to press charges, but they had to arrest him anyway, because ripping the phone out of the wall is considered a felony. He spent the rest of the night in jail.

Pitfall #10. Not Being Ready for the Worst

During divorce, prepare yourself mentally for the worst that can happen. How will you cope if you have to move in with your parents? If divorce proceedings last for years and you lose all of your money? If your ex remarries within two weeks, moves to Tahiti, and refuses to pay any support? Face the worst so what actually happens will seem easy by comparison. Don't panic and let your fears rule your life. Face them, and take control.

There's a story about an old mule that fell into a dry well. The farmer, thinking it wasn't worth the trouble to get the mule out, decided to fill the well with dirt. As he and his farmhands shoveled dirt into the well, the mule started to panic. But rather than giving up, the mule shook off the dirt as it rained down. With each shovelful that came down, the mule shook it off and then stepped up onto the accumulating pile. "Shake it off and step up, shake it off and step up, shake it off and step up," he repeated to encourage himself. Bit by bit, step by step, he fought panic and kept on going. Eventually the old mule, exhausted but triumphant, made it to the top and walked right out of that well. The moral of the story: If you have a plan and follow it through, no matter how tough it gets, small steps combined with persistence will eventually get you out of the hole.

Pitfall #11. Not Developing a Career

Many women put their careers aside to concentrate on their families. After divorce, you will probably need to figure out a way to support yourself and your children. Divorce is an excellent time to get some career counseling at the local job center, university, or community college. There's nothing like new knowledge and a fulfilling career to bolster your self-esteem.

Over the years, it has truly been a joy for us to see women come full circle as they navigate their lives. Just recently we heard from a woman who received a Second Saturday scholarship years ago. The scholarship allowed her to take courses at the community college to rebuild her confidence and skills after a long hiatus taking care of her children. Before long she finished her degree and started a new cosmetic packaging business. As the business grew, it supported her and her children well. Last year she sold her business to a large corporation for almost $2 million. Sometimes the paths we take are not necessarily what we had planned in the beginning, but often they move us toward where we really need to be.

Pitfall #12. Not Getting Good Professional Advice

Right now, you need all the help you can get! Divorce can be complicated, so don't try to do it all yourself. Get the best advice you can afford. Hire an attorney who can give you excellent guidance, even if you plan to negotiate part of the divorce yourself. Engage a forensic accountant if you think there might be hidden assets.

Find a good therapist to help you emotionally. Hire a financial advisor who specializes in divorce to help determine the best settlement options for you and to help you determine how best to invest the assets you receive in the divorce. Don't skimp now on matters that will affect the rest of your life.

One woman came to us, having negotiated her divorce herself. Her husband agreed to give her $400,000 as a property settlement, plus $3,000 a month for three years. That seemed like a lot to her, and it is a lot of money, but not in comparison to their joint net worth. He was giving her $400,000 as a settlement, but it turned out that he earned $400,000 *a year* from their distribution business, which was worth millions. He was keeping the business as well as the family home and their rental property. The settlement wasn't fair, and the $3,000 a month wasn't enough to support her while she went back to school and developed her career. We steered her to an attorney who, with our help, was able to renegotiate to get a much better property settlement plus the income she needed and deserved.

Dividing Retirement Funds

Some of the most difficult assets to divide are retirement plans. If both of you worked throughout the marriage, and you have similar amounts in retirement plans, you might each simply keep your own retirement stockpiles. However, if your husband accumulated a significantly larger retirement plan, perhaps because you left the workforce to raise your children or care for an elderly relative, you'll need a significant share of his retirement assets to help meet your future financial needs.

If you are to receive a portion of the retirement assets held by his employer, you may need to file a Qualified Domestic Relations Order (QDRO, pronounced "kwa-droh") with the plan administrator to segregate the portion of the account that belongs to you (the nonemployee spouse) and arrange the payment schedule. If the QDRO provides that you will take a lump sum payment, you can roll over the money into an IRA in your name without paying current income taxes or penalties.

How to Keep Attorney's Fees Low

Divorce is expensive emotionally, and it's also expensive monetarily. Next to the emotional fallout, one of the most difficult aspects of divorce is the steep legal expense. Most lawyers charge an hourly rate of $150 or more, and generally you have to give them a retainer of at least $1,000 before they'll even start work. If your divorce goes to court, it can take months, even years, of legal wrangling before you see a settlement.

Although attorney's fees can be astronomical—the average cost is about $20,000 per spouse—read on to learn ways you can keep the cost of your divorce low. The key is to research your options and play an active role in the process.

The Simple Truth

∾

The average duration of marriages ending in divorce in 1998 was 11 years for first marriages and 7.2 years for all marriages—remarriages that end in divorce are shorter than first marriages that do so. The average age at divorce was 42 years for men and 39.4 for women.

—Vanier Institute of the Family

Should You Do Your Own Divorce?

With all this expense, you may be tempted to negotiate your divorce yourself. But even if you feel comfortable going it alone, your personality and personal situation may be such that you need professional advice.

Should you use an attorney or file for divorce yourself? Quiz 11.1 can help you assess your situation. For each question, answer true or false.

Consider Mediation

If you and your spouse don't agree on important issues, such as the division of property or child custody or support, it doesn't mean you need an expensive lawyer. You can try to resolve your disputes through mediation. The mediation process pits the two of you against the problem of figuring out the divorce, rather than pitting you against each other. This is especially advantageous for couples who will have an ongoing relationship after the divorce, such as parents of minor children.

Mediators charge by the session, hour, or day, and may be marriage or family counselors or attorneys. Those who are attorneys generally charge their standard fee ($150 an hour and up). Those who are therapists, psychologists, ministers, or social workers usually have much lower fees, and some even have a sliding scale based on a person's ability to pay. To find a qualified mediator, ask a trusted financial professional or attorney for referrals, or contact your local family or domestic relations court. You can also contact the Association for Conflict Resolution (www.mediators.org) or the Academy of Family Mediators (781–674–2663) for a list of practitioners in your area. After you and your husband come to an agreement in mediation, you should have a lawyer review the agreement before you file the divorce papers.

Quiz 11.1

Should You Do Your Own Divorce?

True   False

❑   ❑   You or your spouse have complicated property issues, such as a family business or farm, pension plan valuation, stock options, future royalties, disputed titles, or separate property.

❑   ❑   You have children and are having difficulty coming to an agreement about custody, visitation, or living arrangements.

❑   ❑   You feel confused about your rights or overwhelmed by legal complexities.

❑   ❑   Your spouse files legal papers that contradict your previous agreements, takes unilateral action that threatens you personally or financially, or otherwise acts in an aggressive or dangerous manner.

❑   ❑   You and your spouse are so hostile that you are unable to have any rational discussions and come to any kind of agreement.

❑   ❑   One spouse is unwilling to accept the process of divorce and won't cooperate.

❑   ❑   Your marriage has been punctuated by affairs, abuse, and/or extreme conflict.

❑   ❑   One spouse is on active military duty or is a military retiree.

❑   ❑   One spouse has managed the family finances and the other has little or no information or financial sophistication.

If you answered True to any of these questions, a do-it-yourself divorce is probably not for you. If none of these statements apply to your situation, you may be able to do your own divorce.

Do Your Homework

If you decide to use an attorney to do your divorce, you can still keep the fees down by staying actively involved throughout the process. Here are some tips for saving time and money:

- Have a written fee agreement with your attorney about rates, retainers, and how and when the balance of the fees will be paid. (A retainer is a sum of money, often several thousand dollars, you give the lawyer and from which the lawyer pays court costs and satisfies your first few bills.)
- Gather as much information and as many financial documents as possible. Paperwork should include information showing what you own and what you owe (i.e., a net worth statement or balance sheet) and information about your income and expenses.
- Reduce paperwork costs. If your lawyer needs to make copies of original documents you provide, you may be charged up to $1 per page! Save the money and provide photocopies yourself. Similarly, ask that your attorney use regular mail rather than fax or overnight delivery for information you don't need immediately. Postage and other costs incurred by your lawyer are passed on to you.
- Separate emotions from economics. Remember, whenever you speak with your attorney, whether on the phone or in person, you're on the clock. It's very expensive to cry at $200 an hour. Your discussions with your lawyer should be succinct and focus on the essential information to manage your divorce efficiently.
- Bunch your phone calls. Lawyers generally bill time in increments, generally six-minute segments or quarter-hour segments. Either way, you'll find that rather than calling three times and talking four minutes each (which may be billed to you at three 15-minute increments), you'll save money by bunching your questions and calling just once. Keep a telephone log of conversations with your attorney, including the date, the time and duration of the call, and the matters you discussed, and compare your log with the bill you receive.

Consider Collaborative Divorce

Collaborative divorce is a team approach to divorce that includes divorce coaches, financial specialists, collaborative law attorneys, and when needed, child specialists and therapists. Although more professionals are involved in the collaborative divorce cases, the cost is lower overall because you receive comprehensive assistance that lessens misunderstandings and disputes after the divorce.

In collaborative divorce, both spouses have specially trained attorneys whose only job is to help them settle the dispute. All participants agree to work together respectfully, honestly, and in good faith to find "win-win" solutions. No one may go to court, or even threaten to do so, without terminating the collaborative divorce process.

Collaborative divorce differs from mediation in its comprehensive team approach. In mediation, a single mediator helps the disputing parties settle their case.

The mediator cannot give either party legal advice and cannot help either side advocate its position.

Currently about 3,000 lawyers in twenty-five states offer collaborative divorce services. To find one in your area, contact a local collaborative law institute or family law office.

Agreeing on Alimony and Child Support

Deciding on Alimony

Alimony, sometimes called *spousal support* or *maintenance,* is designed to help you get back on your feet again financially after a divorce. It is most often used when one spouse has a high earning ability or the other has stayed home to raise the children. If your marriage lasted only a few years, if you're both able to support yourselves, and if you're both in good health, it is unlikely you will receive alimony.

In most states, when alimony is awarded, it is based on such factors as the length of the marriage, each person's needs and earning capabilities, and their age, health, and standard of living. The tax advantages or disadvantages of paying alimony are also taken into consideration. You can maximize what you receive or minimize what you will pay by carefully documenting living expenses and identifying all sources of income for yourself and your husband. You can use the budget worksheet in Chapter 5 to do this. If you are negotiating your alimony, this information will help you justify to your spouse why you should receive more. Likewise, if you're paying alimony, a detailed summary of your expenses may help your spouse understand and accept lower payments. You and your spouse will each need to provide a clear picture of your taxable and nontaxable income from all sources to reach an equitable alimony agreement.

"Whenever I date a guy, I think, 'Is this the man I want my children to spend their weekends with?'"

RITA RUDNER

Calculating Child Support

When a marriage ends, you cease being husband and wife, but if you have children, your roles as parents continue. Issues regarding children often touch deep nerves, and child support can be a source of contention in many divorces. Understanding the guidelines and process for determining support may help you come to an agreement that will be in your children's best interests.

Most states rely on two factors to determine how much support is merited: the parents' ability to pay and the child's needs. The amount of time the child spends with each parent can also come into play, as well as extraordinary expenses relating to education or health care.

If you want to calculate the amount of child support required by your state, you will need a copy of your state's formula. You can obtain the formula through your attorney or at your county clerk's office. You will need to know each spouse's income and expenses, as well as any extraordinary or extracurricular needs of your children that your state factors into the child support formula. These can include expenses such as orthodontic work, tutors, sports lessons, therapy, or transportation to special schools. Make sure your settlement agreement specifies which additional expenses will be included in your child support formula to prevent future court battles and expensive attorney fees.

Your settlement should also spell out who will pay for common expenses that may not be included in the state's formula, such as:

- health insurance for the children
- medical expenses and deductibles
- therapy or substance abuse treatment
- special school expenses, such as sports uniforms and equipment and activity fees
- future college costs

You may also want to provide a contingency plan for how the children will be financially supported if one of you dies. Be sure you have adequate insurance to provide for this possibility.

Time to Rebuild . . . and Flourish!

---

*"Divorce is the psychological equivalent of a triple coronary by-pass.
After such a monumental assault on the heart, it takes years to amend all
the habits and attitudes that led up to it."*

MARY KAY BLAKELY

Divorce is not just an ending, it's also the beginning of an exciting new chapter in your life. In the months and years after divorce, a myriad of new options will unfold. And the best part is, you're in charge. Whatever your goals may be, remember that your life is uniquely your own, and you're in the driver's seat. Don't let the naysayers sway you from pursuing your dreams. Only you can decide what is right for you.

That is not to say you won't have low times. Everyone does. But the bad days will get fewer as the good ones become more frequent. We know that divorce is one of the most emotionally difficult events you will ever experience. But believe it or not, over the years we have seen thousands of women who went through the divorce process and not only survived, but thrived. That is what we wish for you.

Small Steps to Becoming a Money Star

1. If you think divorce is inevitable, start taking the appropriate actions to prepare for filing. Set aside cash reserves to cover the costs of legal bills and living expenses during the first few months of separation. Also, make sure you collect complete records and documentation on all marital assets, so you can determine your future needs and ensure you get your fair share in the divorce settlement.

2. Think of divorce as a business transaction. You were involved with your spouse in a business partnership that did not work out, so wrap up the loose ends cleanly. If you have children together, your lives will be intertwined forever, so work things out and separate on good terms.

3. We go through marriage together, but we go through divorce alone, and it can feel lonely. Join a group of women who are going through the same thing you are. Better yet, join a co-ed group, so that you can hear the male viewpoint. It will help you better understand your husband's position.

4. Cut as many ties as you can. The fewer assets you own together and financial involvements you and your spouse have, the better relationship you can maintain, and the better parents you can be to your children.

5. Set goals. Take a class, plan a trip, or find a new job. Creating goals for yourself, learning new skills, and keeping busy will help you feel a sense of purpose and empowerment! Spend time with your children, creating new relationships and new family traditions to replace those that no longer work.

CHAPTER 12

Suddenly Single: Getting Through Widowhood

Dear WIFE,

My husband and I were married 32 years before he passed away a few months ago. We lived comfortably, and he left me a large inheritance, for which I am grateful. One major problem: My husband was briefly married to another woman while he was in the Navy, and together they had a son. Although my husband left him a small amount of money, his son is now contesting my husband's will and claims that he has the right to half of his estate. I do not know this individual, and he had not spoken with my husband for more than 30 years. Is he entitled to an inheritance?

Grieving in Palm Beach

Dear Grieving,

You are already dealing with tremendous heartbreak, and the claim made by your late husband's son makes matters that much more painful. It is unlikely that he is entitled to half of the estate. Some of your property probably passed to you directly, because you were a joint owner or a beneficiary. The rest will pass in accordance with his will, if the probate court finds it is valid. Work closely with your attorney. And remember, the probate process takes time. WIFE suggests you surround yourself with family and friends who can offer emotional support and help you keep a clear head as you work to get your life in order.

Widowhood

Widowhood is a stressful experience. At a time you feel least able to cope with life, you must often make serious financial decisions that will have a lasting impact on your future well-being.

If you're fortunate, you will be surrounded by loving friends and family, and you will have well-established relationships with legal and financial professionals who will help you through this difficult period. Even their presence, however, may not prevent you from encountering those who may attempt to control your funds or otherwise mismanage your assets.

Nine out of ten women are on their own financially at some point in their adult lives, and often the quality of their lives depends on their financial skills. The traumatic early days of widowhood should not be spent scrambling to catch up on your financial education. The earlier you begin to take responsibility for your financial affairs, the better off you will be.

We started the Women's Institute for Financial Education in the 1980s after we had met several recent widows who were desperate to get their feet on the ground financially. They had nowhere to turn for unbiased financial information. There were support groups to help them with the emotional facets of what they were going through, but none to help them with the financial issues. We created a non-profit educational organization that would enable them to get the knowledge they needed in a safe, supportive environment. Our seminar, Suddenly Single: What Women Need to Know about Widowhood, is just one of the important cornerstones of our educational series. In this chapter, we will share with you what we teach in that fundamental program.

The Simple Truth

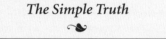

A woman born during the baby boom will likely be widowed by age 67 and remain a widow for 15 years or longer.

—*Dr. Nancy Dailey, www.DrNancyDailey.com*

Contingency Day Planning

What would happen if, heaven forbid, you were widowed tomorrow? Would there be enough money to continue your present standard of living? Who could you turn to for advice? Don't think it couldn't happen to you: 48-year-old Lisa came to us after her husband died suddenly as he was doing his daily laps in the swimming pool. Though he had handled all the finances, fortunately she knew where his will was, and where he had neatly filed their important papers. They had talked about finances in a general way, but never really talked about whether there was enough in life insurance to see her through if the unthinkable happened. We were able to help her through the initial settlement process, which gave her time to come to grips with what had happened and clear her head. When she was ready, we helped her create a long-term plan so that she could feel financially secure and continue her teenage sons' educations.

Because you never know what might happen in life, we encourage everyone to schedule a "contingency day," a day on which you and your partner discuss your finances frankly and openly. After going through the process once, you should update your discussion by having a contingency day meeting each year. The most caring activity in which you and your husband can engage is to share your financial condition and your knowledge with each other. (And your husband thought it was sex!)

"Live as if you were to die tomorrow. Learn as if you were to live forever."

M. GANDHI

If you have adult children, you may want to include them in these discussions. If you are not married and have no adult children, plan an annual contingency day anyway, and make the same kind of reckoning for yourself. That way, you can assure that the future will be as comfortable and uncomplicated as you can make it for those you leave behind. If you have relatives who will be responsible for your estate, make their task as simple as possible. Remember, they will be mourning your death at the same time they will be dealing with your financial assets and the responsibilities you leave behind.

Here are some important steps to take when planning your contingency day with your spouse:

- Decide what information you must gather to prepare for the discussion, and designate which of you will be responsible.
- Set a date to meet, and schedule several hours for your contingency day planning. You might want to decide in advance to follow the discussion with some form of entertainment, like dinner and a movie, to help you both unwind.
- If your husband resists setting a date for the meeting, ask him if he will help you gather the documents to proceed yourself. Discuss with him what information you have and what you need, and then begin the process on your own. Your progress and determination may spark his enthusiasm for the project.

- If discussions about money have caused conflicts between the two of you in the past, ask your accountant or financial planner to be present to facilitate your financial discussions. The money it costs to have a professional present will be well spent if it results in a productive discussion and lays the groundwork for future planning meetings between you and your husband.

Topics for Discussion on Contingency Day

What Are Our Financial Assets?   It is important to identify everything you own and what you owe before you can begin to plan for the future when one of you dies. Use the steps in Chapter 5 listed under the headline "Where Do You Stand Right Now?" to help you identify and list all your assets, cash, and the current income that will be available if either spouse passes away. Be sure to include insurance policies and retirement assets, such as deferred annuities and employer death benefits.

Are Our Assets Sufficient?   Now that you know how much you have, you can determine whether it's enough. How much would you need to live on? How much cash would you need immediately? Use the worksheet in Chapter 7, "Your Life Insurance Needs," to compute your urgent cash needs, the funds you will need to educate your children, your living expenses until retirement, and your retirement needs. Any shortfall should be covered by insurance.

Where Are Our Assets Invested?   Discuss each asset you own so that you and your partner understand the nature of the investment, how much income it produces, what the long-range growth potential is, how safe the investment is, and how marketable the investment is. This is a good look at your current circumstances, and you should do this on a regular basis anyway.

Should Any of Our Investments Be Sold?   Examine each investment critically. Does it fit your long-term goals? What are the growth and income potentials of the investment? Too often, a widow is left with investments that her husband made and controlled, and she is unsure about how he would have managed them if he were still alive. Give careful consideration to the criteria that will indicate the time to sell investments you may currently own, so that you can decide whether to hold them as you review your portfolio every year.

Will Either of Us Be Able to Manage This Investment Alone?   An active business or real estate investment requires time and skill to manage. If your husband has managed the business or property in question, you may need to identify and develop the necessary management skills to run it or to keep it going until it can be sold. Here are some of the questions you will need to answer:

1. What are the specific management requirements of the investment?
2. If the asset is to be sold once your spouse dies, what steps must be taken to sell it?
3. If the asset is to be kept after your spouse's death, what skills will be required to maintain and supervise it?
4. If you lack the requisite management skills, list those you will need to acquire and how you plan to attain them.
5. If either you or your spouse is involved in a lawsuit, review the progress of the lawsuit, the expected outcome, and the procedure the other spouse should follow if one of you died.

Whose Advice Should We Solicit? Which key advisors know the most about your financial and legal affairs? Both you and your husband should meet with your advisors, and each of you should feel comfortable with them. Make a list of all your advisors, including their contact information (addresses, phone numbers, and e-mail addresses). On the list, include your accountant, attorneys, stockbrokers, financial advisors, insurance agent, banker, mortgage broker, executor of your will, and any other advisors on whom you depend.

Estate Planning

If you don't have a will, you don't have a way . . . to control your own estate and ensure that your assets will be distributed as you wish. Yet millions of Americans don't have a will or trust in place. You shouldn't add to those numbers. Providing for what happens after you go is the responsible thing to do, and it's not that difficult. At the very least, you can create a simple will that states how your assets will be distributed and who will care for your children and their money. If you have significant wealth or your situation is more complicated, estate planning can be a more complex process, and you should work with a knowledgeable professional to make sure you cover all the bases. In the rest of this chapter we give you a general overview of key estate planning issues, including wills, trusts, and other planning tools.

The Simple Truth

Among the famous people who have died without a valid will are Presidents Abraham Lincoln, Andrew Johnson, and Ulysses S. Grant, as well as Howard Hughes and Pablo Picasso.

—Nolo.com

Creating Your Will

We've heard all sorts of excuses to avoid writing a will. "I'm too young." "I don't own enough to need a will." "Everyone knows who should get what I own." But the truth is, without a valid will, it's up to the probate court to determine how your assets are passed along after you die. Do you really want a judge to decide what your loved ones will inherit?

A will lets you specify who will inherit your property, who will be the guardian of your children, and who will be the *executor* in charge of winding up your affairs after you pass away. If you already have a will, great. But don't just file it away in the drawer and think that's that. It is very important that you and your spouse keep your wills up-to-date, so that they reflect changes in your circumstances and changes in the law. We've seen wills that provided for the care of children, when those kids were already grown with children of their own. We've seen wills that provide for the spouse, even though the divorce was final years ago. We've see wills that give a specific asset to an heir, but neither the asset nor the heir is still around.

To make sure that you have the proper wills and other estate planning documents in place, you can use Checklist 12.1.

A Penny Saved Is Millions Earned

Just before Benjamin Franklin died, he added a provision to his will leaving the cities of Boston and Philadelphia 1,000 pounds each, the equivalent of $4,444, to be placed in a fund that would gather interest over the next 200 years and be used for loans to young craftsmen to help them get established in their trades.

Boston focused on the long-term return on the money, while Philadelphia took to heart Franklin's wish that the money be loaned to individuals. Over the 200-year life of the trust, money from the Philadelphia fund was loaned to hundreds of individuals, mostly for home mortgages during the last 50 years. Boston, meanwhile, invested the bulk of the money in a trust fund, compounding the earnings.

By 1993, $2,256,952.05 had accumulated in Franklin's Philadelphia trust since his death in 1790. That seems like a lot of money, and it is. Until you consider that Franklin's Boston trust fund was then worth almost $5 million, more than twice the amount that had accumulated in the Philadelphia trust fund.

Boston ultimately used the money to fund the Franklin Institute of Boston, while Philadelphia's funds are now used to assist recent graduates of Philadelphia high schools who wish to pursue careers in trades, crafts, and applied sciences.

Ben Franklin's saying about a penny saved is well known. But by his legacy he proved the worth of another of his lesser known sayings: "The use of money is all the advantage there is in having it."

Checklist 12.1

Estate Planning

Date
Completed

1. Determine your wishes for the ultimate
   disposition of your estate, and discuss these
   issues with your spouse, adult children,
   and others who need to know.   _____

2. Estimate the amount of state and federal
   taxes your estate will have to pay. If your
   estate will not have enough ready cash,
   obtain life insurance to fund the estate's
   cash needs.   _____

3. Make sure that the title in which you hold
   property (single ownership, joint tenancy, etc.)
   is appropriate from an estate planning standpoint.
   If you have a living trust, be sure the assets are titled
   in the name of the trust.   _____

4. Make sure any gifts to relatives and
   charitable contributions are compatible
   with your financial condition and overall
   estate planning. Decide if you should make
   gifts to decrease the size of your estate (you
   can gift up to $11,000 a year to anyone tax free).   _____

5. If you own property in more than one state,
   consult with your attorney about actions
   you can take to minimize probate problems.   _____

6. If you own a business, decide who will run
   it after you die and make appropriate
   provisions. Fund any buy-sell agreements
   with insurance.   _____

7. Consult with your attorney about the use
   of revocable trusts, irrevocable trusts, or a
   combination of trusts as part of your estate plan.   _____

8. With your attorney, review existing wills
   and trusts to be sure they are consistent
   with your current wishes and circumstances.
   Name an appropriate executor and guardians
   for your children (and any disabled adults).   _____

Date
Completed

9. Have your attorney prepare health care directives, sometimes called living wills, detailing the type of care you want (or don't want) if you become incapacitated and specifying who you trust to make medical decisions on your behalf.   _____

10. Have your attorney prepare a springing durable power of attorney for financial matters. This document names a specific person to take care of your finances if you become physically or mentally incapacitated.   _____

11. Prepare a list of instructions for your loved ones, detailing your preferences regarding funeral and burial services and memorial tributes.   _____

12. Prepare a letter of instruction listing the items to be given to particular individuals, and be sure the letter is dated, signed, and clearly labeled as a letter of instruction. Your will should state that you intend to leave such a letter.   _____

13. Let your spouse and next of kin know where you've stored your wills, health care directives, letters of instruction, and other important documents. Destroy all copies of previous wills, trusts, and directives, so there isn't any confusion.   _____

Using Trusts to Protect Assets

Trusts can be fairly simple or incredibly complex. Here are the four categories of trusts that you may need.

Living Trusts

The most basic trust that you will probably need is also the simplest. It's called an *inter vivos* trust, more commonly known as a living trust. You create it while you are alive, rather than at death under the terms of your will. The big advantage of a living trust is that if you properly title your assets in the name of the trust, when you die they won't have to detour through probate court before they reach your heirs. Probate is expensive in terms of time as well as money: The process can drag on for months, with about 5 percent of the property eaten up by lawyer and court fees. Five percent may not sound like much, but if your home is worth $300,000, even though you have a big mortgage and few other assets, it still could cost $15,000 to get through the probate process. With a living trust, you can make any changes you want while you are still alive. For example, you can add or withdraw assets, or change beneficiaries.

A-B Trust

The A-B trust not only avoids probate, but also has tax savings features. Because current estate legislation allows for up to $1.5 million to be transferred to heirs free of estate taxes, increasing gradually over the next several years to $3.5 million in 2009, you might think these trusts are only necessary for wealthier individuals. But you could be a multimillionaire, if you count life insurance death benefits, retirement account values, and equity in your home. So even middle-income couples may be able to reap significant tax benefits through smart planning.

The A-B trust is primarily for married couples with children. It may also be referred to as a credit shelter trust, credit exemption trust, or marital bypass trust. Each spouse leaves property in trust to the other for life, and then the property passes to the children. The reason you would use a trust rather than a simple will is that with an A-B trust you can save hundreds of thousands of dollars in estate taxes, money that the surviving spouse can pass on to your children rather than their Uncle Sam. That's because the property left in this type of trust isn't subject to estate tax when the second spouse dies, because that spouse never legally owned it.

Testamentary Trusts

A testamentary trust is created by your will to become effective after your death. In your will, you name a trustee to undertake the management and distribution of the assets you leave in trust, according to detailed instructions. The testamentary trust isn't effective until after your death, at which point it becomes irrevocable and cannot be changed. You might provide for many kinds of testamentary trusts in your will, such as the creation of a trust to hold assets for minors or a trust to sprinkle assets and income among a group of beneficiaries based on their needs (for example, an educational fund for your grandchildren to be used for those who decide to go to college).

The testamentary trust is sophisticated yet uncomplicated, but it isn't as effective as a living trust. With a testamentary trust, the assets are first subject to probate before they flow into the trust. With a living trust, you can do everything you could do with a testamentary trust and also avoid probate. Nevertheless, some people want the simplicity of having only a will, and they don't want to spend the time and money it takes to create a living trust and title the assets properly, so they forgo the benefits of the living trust.

Irrevocable Trusts

An irrevocable trust is, well, irrevocable. That means you cannot make any changes to an irrevocable trust after transferring your assets, except as provided in the trust documentation regarding amendments, and you cannot terminate the agreement except under specific circumstances with the beneficiaries' consent. Irrevocable trusts can help you save significantly on federal income and estate taxes. That's because the assets you put into the trust belong to the trust, which is a separate taxable entity from you. That means the trust pays tax on any income it earns, and you don't. Also, if you transfer appreciating assets into an irrevocable trust, the growth in value belongs to the trust, not you, and so won't be a part of your estate when you die.

We had a client who was going to buy a large life insurance policy with herself as owner and her children as beneficiaries. Big mistake—the proceeds from the life insurance would be part of her taxable estate when she died, and her children would have owed nearly $500,000 in estate taxes. We showed her how to save taxes by buying the policy in the name of an irrevocable insurance trust set up expressly for that purpose. When she died, her kids got the money tax free.

The many types of irrevocable trusts include supplemental needs trusts to preserve a disabled beneficiary's right to governmental benefits, minors' trusts to provide for education and other needs of children under the age of majority, spendthrift trusts to reduce the beneficiary's estate and protect assets from creditors' claims, and charitable trusts.

The Simple Truth

⤳

When Brigham Young, a founder of the Mormon Church, died in 1877, he left behind an estate valued at about $2.5 million, a hefty sum in those days. He also left behind 18 wives and 48 children.

—Leonard J. Arrington, Brigham Young: American Moses
(University of Illinois Press, 1986)

You can do incredible things with trusts to protect your estate from taxes and control your assets for years after you are gone. But trusts can seem complicated and hard to understand. If you use trusts in your estate planning, make certain you are familiar with their provisions and your heirs understand the reasons you have constructed the trusts so they do not question or resent the trust arrangement after your death.

Planning for the Inevitable

If Death Is Imminent

As death approaches, planning no longer can be put off. One widow said sadly, "I knew my husband was dying, but I succumbed to magical thinking. I thought that if we didn't plan for his death, I was somehow bargaining for him to stay alive. He died anyway, of course, and I have often wished we had made plans for his death together."

When death seems imminent, here are some special steps to take in addition to contingency day planning to facilitate pragmatic issues and protect your assets:

- Locate and review wills, trusts, and other important papers.
- Execute a durable power of attorney to take effect upon your spouse's incapacitation. This will give you the legal right to make financial decisions on your spouse's behalf.
- Review beneficiary designations on life insurance and retirement programs, including IRAs, Veterans Administration life insurance, and other life insurance policies. Do not designate your estate as beneficiary, as that will subject your insurance proceeds to the expensive and time-consuming process of probate and administration costs.
- Consider a living will as well as organ and tissue donations.
- Transfer additional assets to living trusts, life insurance trusts, or joint ownership, and make gifts, where appropriate, to avoid probate and reduce estate taxes.
- Transfer vehicle titles to those who will live on, a transaction accomplished far more easily before death occurs.
- Remove important records, such as wills, deeds, and trust documents, from safe deposit boxes, and keep the records in a safe place at home. After death, the boxes may be legally sealed, and you may need access to the records to begin estate administration.
- Apply for credit cards in your own name, if you do not presently have any.
- Identify sources of cash to fund immediate needs, and make sure you will have access to adequate funds.
- Discuss funeral or memorial service arrangements, and contact clergy or other service providers.
- Notify close friends and relatives.

"Death ends a life, not a relationship."

JACK LEMMON

When Your Spouse Dies

The Simple Truth

In 2000, 45 percent of all women over age 65 were widows, and there were more than four times as many widows (8.5 million) as widowers (2.0 million).

—*Association on Aging*

Whether your husband's death is sudden and unexpected or whether he dies after a long debilitating illness, the impact of widowhood can be overwhelming. You must cope with numerous details under great emotional stress.

During the first few days after your husband's death, make sure that someone is in your home at all times. Unfortunately, your home is a prime target for any thief who knows of your bereavement. If you are not presently widowed, but your husband is ill, it is also important to have your house occupied or otherwise secured while you are at your husband's bedside during hospital stays.

When your husband dies, you must handle many urgent details. Immediately notify the family and close friends who will come to your aid and who you would like to have around you during the next few days. Ask them to notify more extended family, friends, and business colleagues who should be told the news in the first days following your husband's death.

Funeral Arrangements

When you visit the mortuary to make funeral arrangements, take someone with you who is calm and able to help you make practical decisions about costs and services. Don't be persuaded to spend more than you intended on a casket, a cremation urn, or other services. Get a written agreement that includes all expected charges.

The Simple Truth

A traditional funeral, including a casket and vault, costs about $6,000. Extras, such as flowers, obituary notices, acknowledgment cards, or limousines, can add thousands of dollars to the bottom line, and many funerals run well over $10,000.

—*U.S. Federal Trade Commission*

Death Notices

In many cities and towns, obituaries are published in the local newspaper. It may give you and your family comfort to write the obituary yourselves. If you choose not to do so, the funeral home will usually provide information to the obituary column of your local newspaper, including the date and place of funeral arrangements. You may also wish to compose an announcement to send to your acquaintances that tells of your husband's death, when and how he died, what services were held, and where memorial contributions may be made and condolences sent. Ask one of your close friends or a family member to compose the announcement for your review, unless you want to prepare it yourself.

Legal Proceedings

Let your attorney know immediately of your husband's death, so that he or she can start probate proceedings, if necessary, including the notification of death and filing the will. The attorney who drew up your husband's will can guide his estate through probate, if you feel comfortable with the attorney and the paralegal with whom you will probably be working.

When you have an important meeting with an attorney, financial advisor, trust officer, insurance agent, or accountant, take a close friend or family member with you. The friend can take important notes during the meeting and help provide you with clear, logical reasoning.

Social Security Benefits

If your husband was covered under the Social Security system, you will receive widow's benefits equal to his full benefits once you reach age 60, if you were married at least nine months (or zless if his death was accidental). The average monthly benefit for a widow in 2003 was $862. If your own earned benefits are greater, you will receive your benefits instead. If you have children under age 18, they will each receive 75 percent of your deceased husband's benefits. You may also be eligible for a 75 percent Mother's Benefit if you are not yet of retirement age. All these benefits are subject to a maximum family benefit ceiling. You can also collect a lump sum death benefit of $255.

Settling Up with the IRS

The estate tax return for your husband's estate is due nine months after his death, if his estate exceeded $1.5 million. Annual income tax returns for the estate will be due each April 15 until the estate is closed and its assets are distributed. For the year your husband died, you can file a joint income tax return, writing "deceased" and your husband's full name and date of death across the top of the tax return. You will report a full year of income and tax deductions for yourself, but your husband's income and deductions will stop at the date of his death. Sign the return at the bottom, and in the space for the second signature, write "filing as surviving spouse."

The Road to Financial Recovery

Once you have solved immediate problems, it's time to deal with the money, or lack of it. Take control of your financial life as soon as you are able. Beware of financial advisors who seem to put their own interests before yours, or who are eager to assure you about the safety of investments they cannot possibly guarantee. On the other hand, trusted financial advisors can be invaluable at this time, and creating a team of advisors who have your best interests at heart can assure that you will make the right decisions today to create future security for yourself and your family.

Financial issues aside, it is imperative that you allow yourself time to grieve. You will experience a wide range of emotions following your husband's death. Be patient with yourself, and to the greatest extent possible, rely on family and friends to help you through this difficult time.

"One often calms one's grief by recounting it."

PIERRE CORNEILLE

Small Steps to Becoming a Money Star

1. Schedule a contingency day with your spouse and adult children to discuss your current financial situation and the location of all important documents and records. This will enable everyone to be prepared in the event that you or your spouse is debilitated or suddenly passes away.

2. If you are widowed and you have trouble dealing with all of the paperwork involved, ask a friend or family member to go though things with you. Sort out what needs to be kept (for sentimental or financial reasons) and what you can let go. If you find that you can't take care of business alone, get help.

3. Create your own mourning rituals to help you work through this transition. Going through old photo albums to create a collage, visiting a special place the two of you enjoyed, or wearing a special piece of jewelry can help you to maintain your memories while moving on with the rest of your life.

4. Don't do anything drastic for a while. This might sound like an "inaction step" rather than an "action step," but there's a good reason for it. Your identity has undergone a tremendous shift, and it will take a while to sort out your future. Be sure to wait until the initial shock has settled and you have integrated widowhood into your life before you make any dramatic changes or big investments.

5. Modify your plans. After your husband passes away, you will need to make some changes to your estate and financial plan to suit your new situation. Consult your advisors on the best way to structure your financial life now that you are a widow.

CHAPTER 13

Taking a Chance on Love Again: Remarriage

> *Dear WIFE,*
>
> *After my divorce many years ago, I gave up on men and channeled my energy into my career. My single-mindedness paid off and I am now the vice president of a bank and financially secure. Last summer, I met a wonderful man. He recently asked me to marry him, and I love him, but I know the statistics. How can I protect my finances while creating a new union with this amazing man?*
>
> *Being Careful in LA*
>
> *Dear BC,*
>
> *Work for money, marry for love. Along with the ring and a license, WIFE suggests a prenuptial agreement to get your marriage off on the right foot. When broaching the subject, be sympathetic to your new partner's feelings, and assure him that you're in it for the long haul. If he is truly the man for you, he will appreciate that you're smart enough to safeguard your future!*

Financial Matters of the Heart

Love is even lovelier the second time around, and solid financial planning is even more important if you choose to remarry. This time, it is likely that both of you have accumulated more assets, possibly more debt, and more financial responsibilities than before your first marriage. If you are marrying for the second, third, or fourth time, you and your spouse will have the same issues as those marrying for the first: You will have to determine your goals and how you plan to achieve them, decide who is responsible for managing your daily finances, and discuss how investment decisions are made. In addition, you will need to take the necessary steps to protect yourself financially prior to that second walk down the aisle by keeping assets in your own name, maintaining your own credit, and having a separate retirement savings account.

Have you ever heard somebody say, "It was meant to be"? Ruth and Jerry married years ago. Initially Ruth had been attracted to Jerry's take-charge attitude, but as he became more controlling year after year, the marriage unraveled and they divorced. She had acquired a Ph.D. in social services and while at a conference ran into an old boyfriend from high school. Surprisingly, Richard and Ruth recognized each other after all those years, and the spark was still there. Over half of divorced women find love within five years after their divorce, and Ruth was no exception. Prior to her wedding to Richard, she came to us for advice before she tied the knot again. In this chapter you will learn what women need to know before they walk down the aisle once more.

"I love being married. It's so great to find that one special person you want to annoy for the rest of your life."

RITA RUDNER

Tying Up Loose Ends

Here are some tips for tying up loose ends before you begin again:

- If you are divorced, cut financial ties to your ex-spouse as soon as you can. That will clear the way for a less-encumbered relationship with your new husband.
- Whether you are widowed or divorced, review the title to real property and check your accounts (checking, savings, money market, and brokerage) to be sure they are all in your name. If you wait until you are remarried, you'll just complicate matters, as you deal with the issue of current spouse, former spouse, and your former single status.
- When dealing with your ex regarding money or family issues, be sensitive to his feelings about your remarriage. He may feel hurt, left out, resentful, or jealous. Those feelings are natural, so be understanding.
- To make the best of your new relationship, analyze carefully how your divorce or the death of your spouse has affected you. The emotional traumas you have experienced can leave lasting scars that inhibit you in your new partnership unless you make a conscious effort to overcome them.

Job Description for a Financial Partner

As you are getting into a new relationship, it is important to define roles. Each of you should have basic competencies when dealing with money. While one person may take more responsibility in one area, don't relegate all of your power and responsibilities to your partner. The beginning of the relationship is the perfect opportunity to start things out on the right foot.

Here are the financial functions each of you should be able to perform:

- maintaining good credit
- paying bills
- reconciling statements
- organizing and filing account statements
- dealing with creditors
- purchasing property
- reviewing retirement plans
- meeting with financial advisors
- comparison shopping
- saving money
- opening accounts
- buying insurance

If you or your partner need to brush up on your skills, you can help each other get up to speed.

"If you made a list of reasons why any couple got married, and another list of the reasons for their divorce, you'd have a lot of overlapping."

MIGNON MCLAUGHLIN

Tell It Like It Is

Marriage is about love and commitment, but it is also a legal and financial contract between you and your future husband. Regardless of how you plan to manage your financial affairs as a couple, you should both be frank with each other before you get married, so you each understand the full extent of your assets and obligations. We suggest you exchange credit reports before you exchange your vows.

In addition, you should share information with one another about:

- your annual income, including any retirement income you receive
- the financial support you provide for your ex-spouse, children, or other family members

- any commitment you have made to provide for your children's education
- your expectations to pay for a parent's care or have a parent move in with you some day
- any debts you are currently carrying and how you plan to pay them off
- regular financial gifts you make to family, church, or other charities

You are creating a stronger bond of trust by talking about these issues and disclosing to one another your assets and debts, your goals and your concerns.

The Simple Truth

In 1997, 43 percent of weddings were remarriages for at least one partner. Unfortunately, 60 percent of remarriages end in divorce.

—*U.S. Census*

Preparing a Prenup

A prenuptial agreement (or prenup) is often more important in a second marriage than in a first. Because of obligations to children, existing assets, and prior legal commitments, a written agreement assures that everyone's needs are clear and their financial interests protected. If your future spouse feels uncomfortable about the idea, reassure him that the agreement is intended to benefit and protect you both. The fact that you are revealing all of your assets prior to marriage should be taken as a sign of trust.

A properly drafted prenuptial agreement generally will cover the same topics that you have been discussing, except that it will formalize your discussions into a written agreement. That agreement should specify:

- how any premarital debts will be paid
- how jointly owned assets will be split in the event of a divorce or death
- how separate assets will be treated, regardless of the laws of the state in which you are living at the time you are married or divorced or die
- how your respective incomes are split during the marriage and upon divorce
- who is responsible for child care and education expenses during marriage and upon divorce

Prenups can protect your children's assets, providing for their inheritance in the event that you die or get divorced. Similarly, having a written agreement is critical if either you or your new husband owns a business. Prenups can also include language to protect your current interest and all future benefits that flow from a patent, trademark, or creative idea, whether it be a book manuscript, a computer software program, or a pharmaceutical patent.

Both you and your soon-to-be spouse should consult a family law or matrimonial lawyer to negotiate the terms of your premarital agreement and draft the final document. If you don't know of a suitable attorney, ask a trusted professional advisor for a referral. You can also contact the American Academy of Matrimonial Lawyers at www.aaml.org.

Do prenups hold up? Courts tend to honor premarital agreements as long as both parties to the contract are open and honest about their assets and liabilities and both have received advice from their own attorneys. Courts generally will not uphold premarital agreements that include false financial information or omit pertinent information about either partner's assets and liabilities or agreements that were signed under duress. Given this last consideration, it's generally wise to sign the agreement at least one month before the wedding, so there is little argument of coercion.

Postnuptial Agreements

If you did not sign a prenuptial agreement before marriage, you may want to use a postnuptial agreement to protect assets for yourself and your children, especially if you receive a sudden windfall or are expecting a large inheritance. Like a prenup, a postnuptial agreement specifies how assets and liabilities are to be divided during marriage, after divorce, or after one of you dies. Many couples use a postnuptial agreement to discuss one particular asset, such as an inheritance, business interest, or new home. Just as with the prenup, both of you should have separate legal counsel and provide full disclosure of all present and future assets to create a legally binding agreement.

Safeguarding Your Children's Interests After You Die

Another way to protect children from a first marriage is by creating a Qualified Terminable Interest Property (QTIP) trust, which will ensure that your solely owned assets are passed to your heirs after death. Your husband will receive the trust income during his lifetime, but after he dies, the principal goes to members of your family, not his. You can require that a QTIP trust be established by putting an appropriate clause in your will or living trust. For more information about wills and trusts, review Chapter 12.

The Simple Truth

☙

If you think Elizabeth Taylor was married lots of times, with eight marriages under her belt, think again. Former Baptist minister Glynn "Scotty" Wolfe of Blythe, Calif., first married in 1927. In 1998, he was separated from his 28th wife.

—*Guinness Book of Records*

Living Under One Roof

Love and marriage go together like a horse and carriage. Well, not necessarily: Welcome to the modern age. It's not uncommon for previously married couples to move in together without choosing to marry. In fact, for older individuals, it can be a smart financial decision to stay single.

The Pros and Cons of Cohabitation

Many women would lose their alimony if they chose to remarry. For others, the decision to stay unmarried makes estate planning easier because assets are kept separate for each person's heirs. To some it seems easier to live together than go through all the paperwork to meld two estates and create the necessary legal documents and trusts to ensure that property passes to the appropriate family members.

On the flip side, if you live together, you won't reap many of the legal and financial advantages that married couples enjoy. For example, if you are married and buy a house as a couple, both parties have a right to the property. But if you are living together and your name is not on the deed, you have no rights of ownership. Because you are not married, your partner's children will probably inherit the house after his death, unless he leaves it to you in his will. The same holds true for any other property your partner may own, such as a car or boat, if your name is not on the title.

Gifting is also easier for those who have tied the knot. Married couples can pass unlimited amounts of money to each other without any tax consequences, and they can inherit from one another tax-free after one of them dies. However, singles can only make gifts up to the standard threshold of $11,000 a year (in 2003) before getting hit with the federal gift tax. And each partner in an unmarried relationship can pass along no more than $1.5 million after his or her death before the federal estate tax kicks in.

Protecting Your Rights If You Cohabit

To ensure that you get—and keep—what is yours in the event that your partner dies or you split up, it's wise to draft a Living Together Agreement, or LTA. Similar to a prenuptial agreement, an LTA will specify:

- how you plan to divide the rent or mortgage payments
- how you intend to share living expenses
- whose debts belong to whom
- which assets each partner owns
- who will take title of assets you acquire while together
- how you will divide assets if you separate, including the home you own together
- who will provide for the personal and financial care of any children, whether from this relationship or a previous one, during the partnership and after separation

To further protect yourself, you should also avoid pooling assets and credit, which includes maintaining separate credit cards and store charge accounts. A joint checking account may be useful to pay for common household expenses, as long as you are both clear on how much each of you will contribute to the account and who will manage the bills. In addition, keep careful records of all major expenditures and purchases you and your partner make while you are living together.

Finally, to provide for the possibility that one of you might die, you need to do careful retirement and estate planning to ensure that each of your needs is met in your golden years. You can readily name your partner as the beneficiary of your IRA, SEP, or other retirement account, and vice versa. But you'll lose the benefits that are afforded a spouse, who can choose a lifetime distribution, rather than having to take the money out of the retirement account and pay tax on it in the first few years after death, as unmarried people are required to do.

To make sure that certain property goes to your partner and not to your children or other family members after you die, you will need a written will. Otherwise, the state will divvy up your assets during probate, and it is likely your partner will get nothing. Unfortunately, it's possible that your will could be contested, no matter how ironclad it is. A further safeguard is to establish a revocable living trust, as we discussed in Chapter 12, which lets you transfer the entire contents of the trust directly to your partner after your death.

The Simple Truth

&

___

Households made up of cohabitating senior couples rose 46 percent between 1996 and 2000, a bigger jump than that of their middle-aged counterparts.

—*U.S. Census Bureau's Current Population Survey*

___

___

Remarriage and Social Security

In the old days, widows were forced to live with their companions rather than get married, because if they married, they would lose their survivor Social Security benefits. But under current law women can keep their widow's benefits as long as they are at least 60 years old when they remarry.

But marriage still has an effect on how much Social Security you receive. Take the case of Bob and Carol and Ted and Alice. Bob and Carol were married for 14 years. They are now getting divorced. When Bob reaches 65, he will receive $750 per month in Social Security, based on his earnings.

At age 65, Carol is entitled to receive $250 per month in Social Security, based on her earnings. But since she was married to Bob for more than 10 years before they divorced, Carol can receive an amount equal to half of Bob's benefit, a benefit of $375 a month. This has no effect on Bob's monthly check. Since $375 is greater than $250, Carol will receive benefits based on Bob's earnings. (If Carol's earned benefits were $450 per month, she would likely choose to receive benefits based on her own earnings. Sorry—she can't have both.)

If Bob later marries Alice and they divorce after ten years, Alice also would be entitled to receive $375 per month based on Bob's earnings. (No matter how many women he marries, Bob still gets his $750 per month.)

If Carol remarries, to a man we'll call Ted, now Bob is out of the picture, and so are his Social Security benefits. Carol will be entitled to collect spousal benefits based on Ted's earnings history, not Bob's. But if Carol divorces Ted after being married to him for at least 10 years, guess what? She will be able to receive benefits based on the earning histories of either Bob or Ted or her own account, whichever is highest.

If Bob dies before Carol marries Ted, Carol will be entitled to widow's benefits, which approximate Bob's full Social Security benefit, as long as she doesn't remarry before age 60. How much will she get? She'll get Bob's full benefit at age 65, but she can opt to collect as early as age 60 if she'll settle for less.

And if Alice is still married to Bob when he dies, Alice will also receive full widow's benefits. And you were wondering why the Social Security system may go broke in 2032!

___

Small Steps to Becoming a Money Star

1. Don't get financially or legally entangled with someone you don't know very well. Plenty of starry-eyed lovers have signed documents without reading them, loaned money without collateral, or delivered unmarked packages for their lovers and found themselves in tremendous legal or financial trouble. Don't let this happen to you.

2. If you are planning to remarry, think about the dynamics of your previous marriage and what you would like to do differently this time around. Talk about your hopes, fears, and goals with your new partner, and ask him to share his feelings as well, so you know that you are both on the same wavelength.

3. When discussing money issues with your future spouse, remember that everyone has his own money style, as we discussed in Chapter 3. Be open-minded and express your differences frankly, so you can avoid misunderstandings and plan a prosperous future together.

4. Before you take another walk down the aisle, make sure you know the details of your soon-to-be-spouse's financial situation. You should each order a current copy of your credit report, and discuss your income, planned future expenses, and any outstanding debts, so there are no surprises when you return from your honeymoon.

5. At the same time you're planning your wedding, you should plan as a couple how to manage your household finances. Set aside some time with your sweetie to discuss budgeting issues and the division of responsibility for routine money matters, such as balancing the checkbook, researching investments, and paying monthly bills.

PART FOUR

The Joy of Money

CHAPTER 14

Countdown to Retirement

Dear WIFE,

My husband wants to retire in a few years, when he's 58. He says we'll have enough money, and he might be right. But frankly, I don't know what he'll do all day. I'm the one with hobbies, not him. And besides, he loves his job. What can we do to prepare?

Anxious in Atlanta

Dear Anxious,

WIFE's definition of retirement: Twice as much husband, half as much income. We recommend that before he decides to retire from his job, your husband should stay home a week and watch daytime television—maybe then he'll reconsider. Find out what is making him talk about early retirement. Maybe he's just suffering from "Vacation Deficit Disorder," brought on by too little time off. Both of you should take the quiz in this chapter to see if you are psychologically and socially ready for retirement. Perhaps slowing down rather than coming to a dead stop is the right answer. Studies have shown that combining work and leisure produces the most satisfaction. That's what the New Retirement is all about.

How Do You Feel About Retirement?

"I never did a day's work in my life. It was all fun."

THOMAS EDISON

Retirement planning is not about planning for a certain date but about preparing for the rest of your life. The concept of retirement at age 65 was to ease people's lives a bit in their last few years. But now, people are living into their eighties and beyond, and retirement at 65 or earlier seems a bit outmoded. For some of us, the span of our retirement may actually exceed our work years. The average age of retirement is now 57, with 30 years left to go. Why should you spend a full third of your life in idle days of golf and television?

The Simple Truth

The retirement age of 65 was originally set by the Social Security Administration in 1936. If the decision were made today and you adjusted for the change in average life expectancy, the current retirement age would be 79.

They say timing is everything. Older women who have put their careers on hold want to work, while older men who have worked for years and years want to retire. This isn't a problem unless they are married to each other. Take Hank, who had worked as an accountant for 35 years and looked forward to his last tax season, while his wife, Sharon, had taken time out to raise the children. After the kids were grown, Sharon went back to school and got a master's degree in environmental studies. At age 53, she had a new job she enjoyed a lot. It was challenging and exciting, and it gave her a social structure and sense of purpose. Hank wanted to retire to Florida, but Sharon didn't want to retire now that she was just getting started. How did they solve this dilemma? Sharon convinced Hank to stay put for another five years, while she got more experience so she could turn her employment into a consulting career she could do from anywhere. When they finally moved to Florida, she was able to continue working for her old company as a consultant and took on other clients as well.

More and more people are viewing retirement as an opportunity to explore interests they didn't previously have the time or resources to pursue. Rather than slowing down, today's retirees are speeding up and in many cases embarking on new careers or starting their own businesses.

Whatever path you choose in retirement, the last thing you want to face are concerns about your finances. Even if you continue to work, you may not keep a full-time schedule or have the same income level as before. And eventually, you may want to leave the workforce all together to pursue other interests, such as traveling, honing your hobby skills, or volunteering for charity. To make sure you have the financial means to support yourself in your senior years, it's imperative that you plan ahead.

Later in this chapter we will look into what it takes financially to retire, but right now it is time to explore the psychological aspects of retirement. How do you feel about the prospect of giving up your career? Are you prepared emotionally for the challenge of this major life change?

Quiz 14.1 is designed to help you clarify your feelings about retirement. It may raise issues you haven't considered. No matter what your decision regarding retirement—and you can change that decision next week or next year—take a moment to answer these questions. To complete the quiz, choose the one response that most closely represents your true feelings—not the answer you think is "right."

Quiz 14.1

Are You Ready to Retire?

How Do You Feel About Work?
1. When on the job, I
   a. get excited about new projects.
   b. feel fulfilled at the end of the day.
   c. count the hours until I can leave.
2. The best thing about my work is
   a. the variety of people I meet.
   b. the stimulation and the challenge of solving problems.
   c. the paycheck.
3. When I think about my job, I tell myself that
   a. I'd take on more responsibility as long as the projects were interesting.
   b. I would do this work even if I wasn't getting paid.
   c. I want to run away and never come back.

If you answered *As:* You like new challenges and flexibility. Your biggest task in retirement may be to keep yourself from getting bored, but that should not be difficult if you approach retirement with the same gusto that you bring to your work life.

If you answered *B*s: Your work is an important part of your life's purpose. You'll need to think about how you will continue to fulfill that purpose after you've stopped working. If you cling to your work identity too tightly, you could miss new opportunities.

If you answered *C*s: You seem to be unhappy in your job and you are in it only for financial security. It may be easier for you to walk away from work and enter retirement, but if you hold onto negative attitudes and bitterness, you may not enjoy your leisure time as much as you could.

How Is Your Support System?
4. At work, I
   a. am able to balance my professional and personal life.
   b. feel part of a team that rallies together when there's a crisis.
   c. get upset with someone nearly every week.
5. My associates and coworkers
   a. are nice people, but not my closest friends. I have a great group of friends and loved ones to support me.
   b. are almost my only social contacts.
   c. are people I would never see if I didn't have to work with them.
6. When I retire, I will
   a. spend more time with my family and friends.
   b. miss my coworkers.
   c. be alone most of the time.

If you answered *A*s: You have an excellent support network, which will ease your transition into retirement. Studies have shown that having support is as beneficial to your health as quitting smoking or losing weight.

If you answered *B*s: You have some close friends at work, and you will probably want to maintain these ties after retirement. Your coworkers may not have much time for you, since they'll still be working, so start now to make friends outside of the work arena with whom you can socialize.

If you answered *C*s: It is important that you make an effort to build your support networks inside and outside of work. Seek new social environments, such as a church or civic organization in your area.

What Do You Do in Your Leisure Time?
7. If I had more time off, I would
   a. take dance lessons. I've always wanted to do that!
   b. go for walks on the beach, play with the dog more often, and see more movies.
   c. sleep.

8. I'm looking forward to retirement because
   a. I'm ready for a new phase of life.
   b. I can do whatever I want, whenever I want.
   c. I deserve a break from this crummy job.
9. Retirement will give me time to
   a. travel and discover new facets of life.
   b. devote myself to the volunteer work I enjoy.
   c. sit and do nothing for a change.

If you answered *A*s: You have many plans and goals for your future that will ease your transition to retirement. Your energy and openness to new experiences will make your retirement a new adventure.

If you answered *B*s: You have hobbies and leisure activities you find enjoyable that you can continue in retirement. However, be sure to expand your horizons if you get bored.

If you answered *C*s: Your life has been so devoted to work that you didn't have any time to devote to yourself and your hobbies. Start developing new hobbies now to ease your transition.

Predicting What You'll Need in Retirement

What You Have vs. What You Need

These days, Americans have more options for saving for retirement than ever before. With the combination of Social Security, company retirement plans, IRAs, Keogh plans, and other saving vehicles, you'd think we'd be better prepared than we are. But women often fall far short of their retirement saving needs because they leave the workforce for long periods of time to raise a family or care for an elderly relative, thereby dramatically reducing their Social Security and pension benefits. Since women also live an average of seven years longer than men, it's imperative that you save as much as possible to meet your financial goals.

There are two crucial steps to determining how much you'll need for retirement: predicting your retirement expenses and predicting your retirement income. The closer you get to retirement, the more important these steps become.

Predict Your Retirement Expenses

Ask yourself these questions:

1. Do you plan to be active, traveling extensively, or will you settle into a retirement community and be content with the social and cultural life of your general area?
2. Where will you live? Will you own or rent your home, and what will your housing costs be?
3. What debts will you owe at retirement? Will your mortgage be paid off by the time you retire?
4. How much will your health care cost, including Medicare and any supplemental health insurance?
5. Do you have long-term care coverage to pay for the cost of nursing care if you become disabled?

Predict Your Retirement Income

To predict your retirement income, answer these questions:

1. When do you plan to retire, and how long do you expect to live in retirement?
2. Will you work part-time during retirement?
3. Are your investments increasing or decreasing in value each year?
4. How much will you receive from pension plans, Social Security, and other retirement plans? These amounts form the base upon which your retirement income will be built.
5. What assets will you liquidate for retirement? Do you intend to sell your house, releasing some of the equity? Do you have a business you will sell? Are there some assets you won't sell or liquidate, because you want to pass them on to your survivors?

Candy and Randy, a couple as much in sync as their names, came to us for retirement advice. They had calculated that when they retired in seven years, they'd have $5,000 a month in retirement income, which they thought would be more than enough for their needs. But when we reviewed their current spending with them, we found they were spending $7,500 a month! How could they cut their expenses to $5,000 a month when they retired? We sent them back to the drawing board to create a new retirement expense budget to make sure that $5,000 would be adequate. If they thought the budget was on target, we suggested they take it for a test run, practicing living on it to see how it felt.

They drew up the budget, as we suggested, and realized $5,000 a month just wouldn't work. But they could cut back to $6,500 a month now, and when their last child was through college, their expenses would fall even more. That gave them an extra $1,000 a month to sock away for retirement now, and they could save a little more in a few years. The increased savings would augment their retirement nest egg, providing additional funds to meet their more realistic income needs when they retire in seven years. It was fortunate they came in when they did, or they might have found out too late that they couldn't fund their full retirement on what they were saving.

"Waiting until everything is perfect before making a move is like waiting to start a trip until all the traffic lights are green."

KAREN IRELAND

The Social Security System

Many people believe that the Social Security system is meant to provide for full retirement, but that's not true. The system was intended to provide a basic floor on which Americans can build their retirement. Unfortunately, 26 percent of unmarried elderly women depend on Social Security as their only source of income. Without Social Security, the poverty rate for older women would be more than 50 percent.

Make sure that you plan ahead and save money through other investment vehicles for your retirement, so you can enter your golden years worry-free. You can find out what benefits you will be entitled to upon retirement by requesting an Estimate of Future Benefits at the Social Security Administration Web site at www.ssa.gov or calling (800) 772–1213.

"You can't help getting older, but you don't have to get old."

GEORGE BURNS

Countdown to Retirement

Whether you are going to work part time in retirement or you plan to quit work entirely, the closer you get to your retirement date, the more concentrated your planning must be. In the next few pages and in the table on pages 220–222, you will learn what steps to take in the last few years as you count down to retirement.

Five Years or More to Retirement

If you are five years or further from retirement, you have time to get your financial house in order and to plan carefully for your future. Your financial life may be complicated by kids in college and parents needing help. If so, plan your retirement carefully to take these expenses into account. As you prepare for retirement, create *two* budgets—one for today's expenses and a projected one for your retirement years. As you move toward retirement, your current expenses should dwindle to your projected retirement levels.

Many people think about saving for retirement, but at this point investing wisely is just as important as saving. Don't be too conservative with the money that you won't need for 10 years or longer, or you'll have difficulty outpacing inflation. You won't need all of the money on the day you retire, so even if retirement is just five years away, you are still a long-term investor.

Project your retirement income by talking to your employee benefits office at work. Find out what medical benefits you will receive, and then investigate the cost of additional medical insurance that you may need to make up the gap in Medicare coverage. This is a good time to look into long-term care insurance, which will protect you if you become disabled and need nursing care. The earlier you purchase long-term care insurance, the lower the monthly premiums you can expect to pay.

Check your Social Security benefits form to be sure that you have been credited with the proper earnings over the years. If any of the information is wrong—$0 wages reported in a year you were employed, for example—contact the Social Security Administration right way and correct your record.

Talk to your spouse about where you want to live in retirement. If you plan to move to a new community, begin now to create a social structure in that area. We know one couple who spent the last 10 years of their working lives in the new area to which they had decided to retire. In that way, they were able to use the social platform of work to create bonds to their community and those in it.

Two Years Before Retirement

Not much time is left, so financially, it's time to straighten up and fly right. If debts are a problem for you, reduce expenses so you can make extra payments to retire those debts. Make a two-year plan to become debt-free so you don't enter retirement with a slew of credit card debt hanging over your head. If you need to buy a new car or replace the carpet or appliances, do it now so that you can pay for the bulk of those items from your income before retirement.

Adjust your investments to reduce the risk on money that you will need in a few years. For example, you may decide that you need enough safe, liquid investments to support two or three years of expenses. Perhaps you'll want to move the money from more volatile stock investments into an intermediate-term bond fund and later into a series of CDs that will mature every six months, providing you with enough cash for the next six months' expenses.

Ask your employee benefits department to update the figures on how much your retirement stash will be worth when you retire, and decide whether you will take your pension in monthly installments or as a lump sum. Now is a good time to consult a financial planner or an accountant who is experienced in helping people make these decisions.

Check again on your Social Security record. If you found errors the last time you checked, make sure they have been corrected and that all new earnings have been posted to your account.

A projection of your retirement income is crucial at this stage. Recompute what you expect to receive from retirement plans and investments, to be sure they are enough to meet your projected retirement expenses. If you have a gap, how will you handle that? If you plan to fill the gap with continued employment, begin exploring your options in earnest. If you are thinking of a new part-time career that you've never tried before, explore it by actually working in the field on weekends or vacations, even if as an unpaid apprentice. If you will need additional education or skills, enroll in the course work now. Network with others in the field so that you will be able to connect with those who can use your services when the time comes.

We had a client who loved the camaraderie of the golf course, though he couldn't afford the initiation fees. In his last year before retirement, he took a course in golf club repair and started repairing clubs in his garage on the weekends. After retirement began, he geared up in earnest. His new venture was both a source of income and a source of pleasure, because he could hang out in the clubhouse, talking golf with the best of them. Another client has a part-time job as a starter at a public golf course, setting up foursomes and getting people started on the course each morning. He not only gets paid, but he gets reduced greens fees when he plays himself.

Three Months Before Retirement

Excited? You're almost there! Start thinking retired. No, we don't mean you should play tennis rather than going to work, but rather, you should move financially toward your new lifestyle. If you've been employed in an office, resist the temptation to update your fall wardrobe of suits and dresses. You won't need a huge wardrobe of those clothes in retirement. If you will be leaving work entirely or changing careers, don't renew your professional publications. If you plan to take courses at the local university or to travel, send off for the college catalogs and talk to a travel agent.

Begin the paperwork to finalize your retirement plans. If you will be receiving payments from your employer, be sure that you have completed the correct forms for the employee benefits office. If you will roll the money into an IRA, establish that IRA account in advance and talk to your financial advisor to decide how the funds will be invested when you receive them.

Review your Social Security earnings record one more time to ensure it is correct. If you expect to begin receiving benefits immediately, apply for your Social Security benefits now. Remember that if you intend to work more than minimally, your benefits will be reduced until age 65 (or older if you were born after 1937), so you might be better off delaying benefits.

Keep enough money in liquid investments (savings, CDs, and short-term bonds) to fund the income you will need for the next couple years or so.

If you are selling your home, it's time to get it ready to put on the market. If you are buying a new home or moving to a new location, scout out your new surroundings and begin the house-hunting process.

If your employer will continue to provide medical insurance to you as a retirement benefit, that's great. Otherwise it is time to decide on medical coverage and complete the application process.

By now your debts should be paid off. To reduce your expenses, if your mortgage is not large, consider paying it off from funds you have saved or will receive at retirement. See Table 14.1.

Table 14.1   Countdown to Retirement

Category	Five Years or More Before Retirement	Two Years Before Retirement	Three Months Before Retirement	In Retirement
Cash flow	Write out two budgets—one with current expenses, the other with expected expenses in retirement. Plan to pay off debts by retirement.	Update your current and future budgets. Get debts paid off as quickly as you can.	Consider paying off mortgage. Replace career expenses with any new retirement expenses.	Fine-tune your budget every year so that your spending stays in line with your income.
Investments	Project retirement needs and investment returns and discuss your goals and asset allocation with a financial planner.	Adjust the balance between growth and income investments to reduce your market risk.	Maintain at least half of your long-term portfolio in stocks to offset inflation. Increase liquid investments to pay for a few years' expenses.	Keep a portion of your long-term funds in stocks to offset inflation and provide growth.

Table 14.1 Countdown to Retirement (continued)

Category	Five Years or More Before Retirement	Two Years Before Retirement	Three Months Before Retirement	In Retirement
Defined benefit retirement plans	Ask your benefits office for a pension benefit projection, both monthly and lump-sum payments.	Decide whether to take your pension in a lump sum or monthly payments.	If you are taking a lump sum, make plans for a trustee-to-trustee rollover into an IRA.	Assess your investments within your IRA. Be sure to keep enough liquid to fund withdrawals.
401(k), IRA, SIMPLE, Keogh, and other defined contribution plans	Contribute the maximum to your plan. Wait as long as possible to tap the money so earnings grow tax-deferred.	Review your asset allocation to provide liquidity for planned withdrawals.	Decide whether you will roll over your plan to an IRA. At 59½, you may start penalty-free withdrawals.	At 70½, you have to begin taking minimum withdrawals from all tax-deferred retirement plans except Roth IRAs.
Social Security	Check your earnings statement regularly to be sure that your employers reported the correct amounts.	Double-check your account to be sure your earnings records are correct.	Decide when to begin receiving Social Security payments. Apply for benefits three months before you want to collect.	At age 65, there is no limit to the income you can earn without reducing your Social Security benefits.
Medical insurance	Ask your benefits office if you can continue medical insurance during retirement. Buy long-term care insurance.	If you need individual medical coverage, start shopping for it now.	Apply for medical coverage a month or two prior to retiring.	Medicare starts at age 65. Before then, shop for Medigap insurance.
Emergency fund	Put an amount equal to three month's expenses in a money market fund.	Set up a home equity line of credit that you can tap in case of emergency.	Maintain enough to cover a year or two of expenses in either cash or a home equity line of credit.	Review the level of your emergency fund periodically and make needed adjustments.

Table 14.1   Countdown to Retirement (continued)

Category	Five Years or More Before Retirement	Two Years Before Retirement	Three Months Before Retirement	In Retirement
House: sell vs. keep	Decide whether to keep your present house or sell it. If you plan to keep it and renovate, consider making the improvements now while you are still working and have the income to pay for them.	If you plan to move after retiring, visit potential locations during vacations. If you plan to stay put, pay for needed repairs and replacements now.	If you are selling, put your house on the market at least three months before retirement.	If you are selling your home, you and your spouse each can avoid paying tax on up to $250,000 of gains. This gives you the opportunity to scale down and capture money to fund your retirement.
Career	Decide if you are going to work in retirement. If so, begin preparing for your second career.	Establish your network, and check out potential jobs. To see if you like a new career, try it on weekends and vacations.	Set up a home office and begin your new career. Develop your business plan.	Continue networking to find new clients and referral sources.

The Simple Truth

By 2040, 25 percent of the U.S. population will be over the age of 65. The "old-old" population—those over 85—will triple by 2040.

—*Center for Strategic and International Studies*

Minimizing Your Tax Burden

If you think you don't need to worry about taxes in retirement, think again. Although your taxable income will probably be much lower than when you were in the workforce, you could still get hit with capital gains taxes on your investments, property taxes, and other expensive surprises if you don't plan ahead. Here are five simple tips for reducing your tax burden in retirement:

- **Avoid spikes in income.** If you take a lump-sum payment from an employer-sponsored retirement or pension plan, you could face a whopping tax bill. Consider rolling over the assets into an IRA and taking distributions on a regular basis rather than withdrawing all the money at once.
- **Don't roll employer stock into your IRA.** If your employer retirement account contains employer stock that has appreciated significantly, consider taking the shares of stock rather than rolling it over into an IRA. If you take the stock, you will owe tax on your original cost of the shares, which may be a fraction of their current worth. You won't owe taxes on the rest of the value until you sell the shares, and even then, you'll pay only 15 percent federal capital gains tax (only 5 percent if you are in the lower tax brackets). That's much better than rolling the stock into an IRA and owing ordinary income tax on all the funds you withdraw.
- **Save tax-deferred income for last.** If you have an IRA or other qualified retirement plan, spend your other funds first, so you take advantage of the tax deferral for as long as possible. The only exception is that if you are in a low tax bracket now and expect that your minimum distributions from your IRA at age 70½ will be large and thus taxed at a higher rate, you should begin taking distributions now to thin down your retirement funds. That is not true of money in a Roth IRA, which grows tax free, not just tax deferred. Since Roth IRAs do not require minimum distributions at age 70½, those funds should be the last money you withdraw, so you maximize the tax-free growth.
- **Time your capital gains.** If you sell stocks or mutual funds that have appreciated over time, sell the shares with the highest basis, to reduce the amount of taxable gain. If you have stocks or mutual funds that have decreased in value, sell some of them to realize losses that will offset your gains, thus reducing your tax bill.
- **Pick a tax-friendly state.** You can save a bundle by relocating to a state with low taxes. For example, Florida, Washington, and Texas are no-income-tax retirement meccas, while Delaware doesn't charge sales tax and has a low property tax rate. To see how different states stack up, visit www.kiplinger. com/links/retiremap. Even within the same state, certain towns are more tax-friendly than others, so be sure to shop around before putting down roots.

The Simple Truth

❧

Women are 8½ times more likely to reach 100 if a brother or sister lived to be that old, according to a 2002 study on aging. About 85 percent of centenarians are women.

—*Boston University Medical School*

The Triple Squeeze

Chances are, several hands are reaching into your wallet at this moment. If you feel caught in the middle, supporting generations on both sides of you at the same time as you are trying to save for retirement, welcome to the Sandwich Generation. As with all financial issues, you can manage this scenario with a combination of honest communication and advance planning. Here's what to do:

- Be realistic about what you can and cannot do. Develop a list of expenses, prioritize them, and compare with your income. Put your own retirement planning, if not *at* the top, at least near the top of the list.
- Hold a family meeting. Talk to your spouse about how you will provide for your children's education and your own retirement (see Chapter 9). Talk to your siblings and their spouses about how you will all provide for your parents' needs. If your parents are still in good health, you might all chip in to pay for long-term care insurance to protect against being hit with nursing care bills in the future.
- Look at ways to cut expenses and save tax dollars. If you support parents whose income is low, declare them as dependents and take a tax deduction. At work, use a flexible spending plan to pay for elder care with pretax dollars.
- Brainstorm creative ways to meet expenses. Can the children work? Can one of your parents supplement their income? If the children and grandparents get along well, perhaps an investment in real estate to house them both—like a duplex near the college—might make sense.

Women are born nurturers, and we have a tendency to overextend ourselves emotionally as well as financially when it comes to taking care of loved ones. If you're doing all the work—driving your elderly parent to and from the doctor's office, buying groceries, running errands, and visiting five times a week—ask for help. There is no reason you should be solely responsible for meeting everyone's needs.

The Simple Truth

༒

More than half of working women say taking care of aging parents affects their relationships with children, and 62 percent say caregiving has an impact on their relationships with significant others. Of women caring for an elder, a whopping 89 percent report an increase in stress and 37 percent report feeling exhausted.

—*National Association of Female Executives*

Small Steps to Becoming a Money Star

1. Be mindful of your health. It's easy to become sedentary in retirement, but staying in shape will not only help you feel better and live longer, but can also help reduce the cost of your premiums for medical insurance and long-term care coverage. Take this opportunity to improve your tennis game, schedule a weekly tee time, or sign up for nature walks to remain active even as you relax.
2. When planning your finances in retirement, be sure to budget for fun. In addition to counting the cost of regular living expenses, such as housing and car payments, groceries, and insurance coverage, earmark funds each year for special treats, like a European vacation or a trip to Disneyland with your grandchildren.
3. Turn a hobby into a cottage industry. For example, if you've always been good at crafts, consider selling some of your creations on consignment at a local shop or street fair. Or if you're an avid birdwatcher, you could offer guided tours in your area. Whatever interest you pursue, you'll stay busy during retirement, and the additional income can supplement your savings.
4. Check out retirement discounts. Many entertainment venues, tour companies, and other leisure providers offer a discount for retirees, some beginning at age fifty-five. If there isn't a discount posted, be sure to ask!
5. You have a lifetime of experience under your belt. Think about ways you can share your knowledge with others during your retirement. Contact your local community center, college, or university to find out how you can become a mentor in their mentoring program, or volunteer with your local church or school district.

CHAPTER 15

Doing Well and Doing Good

Dear WIFE,

Three months ago my sister and I each inherited $800,000 from a distant aunt. My sister is acting as if she won the lottery. She quit her job, bought a new car, and went on two trips to Hawaii. I, on the other hand, haven't done anything because I'm afraid to make a mistake. I am still working, and the money is just sitting in the bank. But now I'm thinking I'm a stick in the mud. Maybe I should be enjoying myself too. What do you think?

Rich & Reluctant in Massapequa

Dear R&R,

WIFE thinks a truly happy woman is one who really understands what gives her joy. Money can't buy happiness, but it can help you live your life more fully. Don't compare yourself to your sister. Be true to your own values. Remember, you are rich according to what you are, not what you have. Decide what you want from your life: Spend a little on luxuries, then invest the rest to help you realize your dreams.

What Does Money Mean to You?

"An object in possession seldom retains the same charm that it had in pursuit."

PLINY THE YOUNGER

What would you do if you won a gazillion dollars in the lottery? Never mind that your chances of winning are just slightly better than the chances of being abducted by aliens. Despite those odds, winning the lottery is a favorite daydream for a lot of us. So what would you do? The answer depends on your gender: Buy everything in the world, say most men (not exactly those words, but close). Use the money to take care of my family, say most women. Isn't it interesting that on the popular TV show *Survivor,* when the last two contestants were asked what they would do with the million dollars if they won, the man said he'd buy himself a new truck and a plasma TV and lots of other toys, whereas the woman said she'd use the money to pay off her mortgage, pay off her best friend's mortgage, and send her kids to college.

In many ways, a windfall molds itself to your personality and makes you more like you are. If you are immature and prone to overspending, that's what you'll do. If you are inclined to take care of others, you'll use your money in that direction. And if you are insecure about finances, you may be frozen in your tracks and live in constant fear of losing what you have.

Fortunately, more and more women are taking charge of their finances and using their money to pursue their passions, embark on new adventures, support causes they believe in, and live life to the fullest. They are starting businesses, exploring new careers, donating generously to charity, joining Money Clubs, and teaching the next generation of young girls the tools for financial success.

What's their secret? They know that wealth is a state of mind. The more comfortable you are with the idea of having money and the more knowledgeable you are about managing it wisely, the greater possibility that you will be prosperous all through your life. Throughout this book, we've discussed the myriad ways you can protect and increase your wealth and safeguard your financial future. But all these discussions are moot if you don't fully understand what you value in life and what you hope to accomplish. Ask yourself what money means to you and what you are looking for in life. How can money help you achieve it? Money is a tool to help you achieve what you want, not an end in itself.

Take a look inside yourself, no matter how much money you have. Is it possible to be too rich? Some women may think so. Equally challenging for many women is the process of becoming financially independent and feeling at ease with wealth.

The Simple Truth

❦

Among households with $600,000 or more in assets, 40 percent are now headed by women, and 23 percent of women outearn their husbands.

—*Faith Popcorn, Eveolution (Hyperion, 2000)*

How to Handle a Windfall

Sometimes the curve balls life throws us are positive, as in the case of receiving a large inheritance. But whether it's $25,000 or $2.5 million, a sudden windfall may feel like a mixed blessing if you're unprepared. Before you go on a whirlwind shopping spree or stick the lump sum in a savings account to earn a meager annual interest rate, take some time to review your options and your needs, so you can make the most of your money now and in the future. We already know that having wealth is an emotionally charged issue, so it's not surprising that the source of the money has a great deal to do with how women treat their windfall. Here is one woman's story.

Tamara had dreamed that one day she'd have wealth. One day she did, but it came as a nightmare rather than a dream, when a fiery plane crash killed her husband and two of her four children. For five long years she battled the airline at fault for the crash. Often she came close to abandoning her lawsuit: She had lost so much and the grief was overwhelming. But she persevered, cleaning houses to support her family during the tough times after the accident.

Finally, in 1993 she received a settlement of $2.2 million, a substantial sum of money but little consolation for what she had lost. With her sons in their early twenties and married with families of their own, Tamara, then 48, could live comfortably if she managed her money carefully.

We helped her structure her financial plan. But within a year, things were not going as planned. Her investments had performed better than expected, but Tamara had made additional withdrawals each time her sons needed money.

Down payments for new homes, furniture, cars, and private school tuition all came from mom's money. Emotions surrounding money are powerful, and with money Tamara tried to replace for her sons that which was irreplaceable. In all, Tamara had spent over $300,000 to support her sons' new lifestyles.

Soon the spending problem became worse. Her oldest son stopped working, and he wasn't paying his mortgage or taxes. With foreclosure looming, Tamara took over those payments too! This had to stop.

We met with her sons and their families and backed her up as she explained that they would need to support themselves starting right now. She still gives her sons and their families love and emotional support, but the financial faucet is turned off. As a result, her oldest son sold his house and moved to a home he can afford. He is working again, and the entire family is meeting regularly with a psychologist to deal with the buried emotions that surfaced as out-of-control spending.

As for Tamara, she has well over $1 million left. At her current spending level of $60,000 a year, she'll be just fine. She can live a long and happy life, and ultimately her sons will have a nice inheritance. She's back on track.

"Money may be the husk of many things, but not the kernel. It brings you food, but not appetite; medicine, but not health; acquaintances, but not friends; servants, but not faithfulness; days of joy, but not peace or happiness."

HENRIK IBSEN

In our seminar on Managing Inherited Wealth, we recommend these eight steps you can take to maximize the benefits of what you've received.

1. **Establish your financial team.** Even if you handle your own finances, receiving a large amount of money all at once is very, very different. Put together a team of trusted advisors, including an accountant, attorney, and financial planner. Don't just ask your friends; ask other professionals who they would recommend.

2. **Tackle taxes first.** An inheritance can take many forms, from a life insurance policy to a retirement fund, stock portfolio, house, or family business. Before you withdraw the money or take ownership of property, schedule a meeting with your financial advisors to discuss the tax ramifications and minimize your tax burden.

3. **Hurry up and wait.** If you received a lump sum of money, you may be tempted to spend or invest it right away. A smarter move is to stash your cash in treasury bills to keep your money safe and buy yourself some time while you assess your options. Remember, you get the chicken by hatching the egg, not by smashing it open.

4. **Tabulate your obligations.** If you have current outstanding debts or large bills on the horizon, such as college tuition expenses, you may want to earmark some or all of your inheritance to cover these costs.

5. **Invest according to your needs.** How you invest your inheritance will depend on your current and long-term financial needs. If you still have children living at home, you may want to set part of the money aside for their college education. On the other hand, if your kids are grown and you're nearing retirement, you might want to look at investments that can provide

a regular income stream in the years ahead. Whatever your priorities are, be sure you diversify your investments rather than putting all your money into one type of asset. A knowledgeable financial planner can help you determine the best allocation for your needs.

6. **Talk about the issues.** If you're married, tell your spouse how you honestly feel about the money you've received—elated or anxious or a combination of the two—and what you would like to do with it. Ask for his input and feedback as well, and decide together how the funds should best be managed. Although the money came to you separately, and you will likely want to keep it in your name alone, remember that marriage is a partnership and that you and your husband share common goals.

7. **Rank your priorities.** Before you start doling out the dollars you've earmarked as mad money, make a list of all the things you could spend it on, such as a luxury cruise, expensive jewelry, or a new wardrobe. Go through the list several times to decide which purchases are most important to you.

8. **Consider charitable giving.** Instead of spending part of your newfound wealth on material things, consider using the money to support a cause that you hold dear. Depending on the size of your inheritance, you may be able to establish a charitable trust, help pay for the construction of a building for your organization, or create a scholarship fund. Your financial advisor can help you explore different options.

"Be thankful for what you have; you'll end up having more. If you concentrate on what you don't have, you will never, ever have enough."

OPRAH WINFREY

Tailor an Inherited Portfolio

If you received a portfolio of investments as part of your inheritance, it's unlikely that your goals match those of the person from whom you inherited it, so you may need to adjust the portfolio to match your own objectives. For example, you may have inherited bonds from Great Aunt Sadie, who needed the income, but that current taxable income may just put you more in the hole at tax time. Instead, you may want those investments to fund your young children's education years from now.

Enlist the help of a financial advisor to examine each holding to see if it suits your needs. If you decide to sell it, you won't have to worry about capital gains prior to the time you took ownership of the assets. That's because the tax basis is "stepped up" to the value at the time the donor died.

The Simple Truth

❧

The largest wealth transfer in history is about to take place as baby boomers inherit from their parents. In turn, because women generally outlive their husbands, the family assets will become concentrated in the hands of boomer women. On average these women will be widowed at age 67 and will most likely survive their husbands by 15 to 18 years.

—*Dr. Nancy Dailey, When Baby Boom Women Retire (Greenwood Publishing Group, 2000)*

Giving to Charity

"You give but little when you give of your possessions. It is when you give of yourself that you truly give."

KAHLIL GIBRAN

Charity is twice blessed—it blesses the one who gives and the one who receives. Throughout history, women have demonstrated their philanthropic spirit. They have established schools, founded hospitals, and sheltered the homeless, never questioning their ability to make a difference in the world through their donations of time and talent.

What can you do to make a difference? When we began our quest sixteen years ago, we developed five guiding principles to make sure that we were using our time, talents, and money in the most effective way. We continue to use these principles today. And so can you. Use them as you search for a worthy cause, and periodically review them to make sure your efforts and resources enhance your life and the lives of others.

1. **Find your passion.** We knew that our passion was to use our skills to empower women, especially those in transition: divorcing, going through widowhood, or just experiencing tough times. What is important to you? What can you do to help others and make their lives better?
2. **Focus your gifts, rather than scattering them.** We knew who we wanted to reach, but how could we reach them? Our skills have always been helping people with finances. Put a hammer in our hands, and we'd end up with sore thumbs and not much accomplished. What are your gifts? Are you

good at organization, are you a people person, or are you really good at building things? Are you using your gifts to help others? You don't have to reach out to a lot of people: Helping one-on-one will make a huge difference in someone's life.

3. **Share your time and skills.** We didn't have a lot of time—we both had full-time jobs—so we wanted something we could do on the weekends. We both sat on numerous boards and foundations, but we found those to be passive, and we wanted to be actively involved helping others. How many hours a week do you have to give? Would you prefer to work alone or in a group? Do you want to work at your computer, talk to people on the telephone, or see people face-to-face?

"Service is what life is all about."

MARION WRIGHT EDELMAN

---

4. **Give money to the causes about which you are passionate.** We find that by donating our own money in addition to our time, we dramatically increase the number of people we help. If you have the financial resources, maybe it's not enough to just put in your time. What impact do your donations have? Do they support causes for which you really care? Would they be more effective if you gave them along with your time to a charitable cause about which you are passionate?

5. **Capture the power of the three *E*s: energize, engage, and enhance.** We truly wanted to make a difference, and we found that when we directed our energy, we engaged others who wanted to help, thus enhancing our cause. What activity can you do on a consistent basis to make an impact? Are there others you could engage to help?

"When I stand before God at the end of my life, I would hope that I would not have a single bit of talent left, and could say, 'I used everything you gave me.' "

ERMA BOMBECK

Our initial goal was to make a difference to the people in our local community. First we volunteered our time: teaching financial education classes in high schools, for women's groups, for senior citizens, anywhere we thought our talents could make a difference.

Then we found a special group of women who needed our help: women who were divorcing. We looked for programs to which we could donate our time and talents, but there weren't any that offered what these women needed on a consistent basis. We realized it was up to us, so we started the program Second Saturday: What Women Need to Know about Divorce. We engaged a local community college and asked attorneys, psychologists, and other professionals to volunteer their time to help us. They were thrilled to have a chance to make a difference.

The program provides comprehensive information about the legal, financial, and emotional aspects of divorce, but it does even more. It also provides scholarship money for women, often single mothers, who want to go back to school but could not otherwise afford to pay tuition and buy books. Is that energizing? You bet. And others are energized as well. We've received inquiries from people across the country to help them set up similar programs in their area.

Thousands of people have attended Second Saturday, and each has their own unique story. Over the past fifteen years, month after month, we've been privileged to make a significant difference in people's lives at a time when they needed help most.

You do what you can do, and then you find out there are more needs. We have been so energized by the difference we've made through Second Saturday that we began a similar program for widows called Suddenly Alone: What Women Need to Know about Widowhood. Other programs soon followed, such as The Capable Woman, and My Brilliant Career: Five Women Talk about Jobs They Love. Each program is unique, helping women in different situations find their own personal and financial paths.

"Whoever renders service to many puts himself in line for greatness—great wealth, great return, great satisfaction, great reputation, and great joy."

JIM ROHN

When the Internet came along in the mid-nineties, we jumped right on. As a nonprofit charity run completely by unpaid volunteers, we saw that the Internet would help WIFE reach women all over the world. Soon, even without advertising, WIFE.org became a trusted source for millions of women seeking financial knowledge. But it's funny how one thing leads to the next. The information was there, but something still was missing: the support, camaraderie, and connection to help women get themselves on the right track financially. Women were looking for simple things they could do themselves and ways they could help their friends and support each other. Once again, we learned by listening to what people wanted and needed. Here's a letter we received from Carol O., similar to many we've received over the years:

Dear WIFE,

For many years I've had a dream of starting up an investment type of club, helping women and also educating myself in the process on financial issues. I've been reading a lot of books on money management, but I'm not sure on where to start or how. I first thought of inviting a few lady friends over and discussing a budget. In fact, I've sent out a few invitations to some of my friends to attend my first meeting. Is there any advice you could offer me? I live in Johannesburg and have had a very hard upbringing. I want to change all of that to everything that is positive in life! Life is beautiful and should be enjoyed, if only we know how. I'd like to stop making stupid mistakes that I could have avoided if only I'd known which decisions were the right ones.

Over the years, we had recommended that women like Carol start or join investment clubs. But investment clubs aren't the answer for the issues she raised. After years of searching and thinking, the solution dawned on us: Money Clubs! We could teach women how to start their own groups to help each other learn more about the financial issues important to them, just as Carol O. had begun to do. That was the genesis of the Money Clubs (www.moneyclubs.com).

Women in groups can change their world. And that's where you fit in: You may not want to start your own nonprofit organization as we did, but you *can* gather together a few of your friends to help each other. Money Clubs provide a supportive environment to empower women financially, and there is no cost to start or join a Money Club. Best of all, you'll find that amazing things happen in Money Clubs.

At WIFE, we continue to dream big dreams and set ambitious goals. We realize that truly making a difference in the world requires a positive vision. We've come so far, and yet there is a lot to be done. Do we think big? You bet. We're a lot like the little train who said, "I think I can, I think I can."

Here are our visions for how we can make a difference in the future:

- We visualize *a million women* actively involved in Money Clubs across the country. That's what it will take to make an impact in the fabric of women's lives and the lives of their children and families. Together, we will make a significant difference, a few women at a time.
- We visualize a Second Saturday network of programs across every state so that women everywhere will have access to the information they need to empower themselves as they face the difficult process of divorce.
- We visualize major corporations helping us to promote financial literacy to their employees and their customers through programs like ours.
- We visualize exploring other avenues to spread the word about how women can help each other learn the simple truths about money and the role it plays in their lives, empowering themselves and others to grow and learn.

Here is another of the letters that keeps us going and growing. It's a letter we received from Kay W. in North Carolina, after she attended her first Money Club meeting:

Dear Money Clubs,

Money has always been my least favorite subject! Every time I would think about it, I would get anxious. However, a good friend asked me to attend a Money Club meeting with her. I went dragging my feet and complaining the whole way . . . Was I surprised! The evening was one of the most empowering experiences. We talked about how money was handled in our family while we were growing up. Everyone told their own story. It was the first time I realized that I was, after all these years, STILL handling money as I was trained by my father when I began working in high school. I endorsed my paychecks over to my father while he gave me "pin money" and took care of everything else. He did not feel I was capable of managing my own money . . . a mere girl who was supposed to be taken care of by a man. And I have believed him all these years.

But now, hearing everyone else's story gave me a new insight and COURAGE to begin changing my relationship with money. Since the meeting, I have a sense that I have a RIGHT to my money, and it has not slipped from my hands. But the strangest of all . . . money has begun coming to me from the oddest sources . . . like pennies from heaven. I am beginning to think that there is a definite connection. It's not affirmations . . . those don't work for me. It is, in fact, a different way of perceiving myself in relation to money.

I could never have arrived at this awareness by myself, through a book, or via the Internet. I needed the GROUP and their stories to bring my experience into a new awareness. There is really a MAGIC about women coming together to support and empower each other. Out next meeting is coming up soon. I can hardly wait to see what else I learn about myself and money! Thank you so much for your wonderful idea . . . THE MONEY CLUBS!

What Will You Do Today?

Think of your philanthropy as your investment in the future of our world. When you are making a difference in people's lives, it gives you the energy and courage to continue on to see how much further you can go. That's the power of charity—it returns to you far more than you can ever give. We are enthusiastically moving ahead, step by step, and you can too. So think about it: What will you do today?

Thousands of worthy causes could benefit from a donation of your time or money. In fact, there are more than 800,000 charities in the United States alone.

So how do you decide which organizations to support? Think about two or three areas or causes you want to assist, and make this your philanthropic mission. Not only will your gifts have more impact, but you will find your giving more satisfying.

Once you have chosen a cause to which you'd like to commit, it's time to start researching organizations dedicated to that issue. Here are a few of the key matters you should address:

The Charity's Mission   For example, if you're thinking of supporting an AIDS organization, find out the focus of its work. Does the organization help fund research for a cure, finance educational programs to foster prevention, or provide a service to people who suffer from AIDS, such as home meal delivery? Be sure the organization's priorities are in line with your own.

How the Money Is Spent   Ask for documentation that shows how donations are being used. Note what percentage of funds are allocated to overhead and operating expenses for the organization, compared to the percentage that directly supports the stated mission. Ideally, at least 70 percent of the funds should be allocated toward program services. The American Institute of Philanthropy (www. charitywatch.org) acts as a watchdog group, each year grading hundreds of organizations on their use of funding.

Whether Gifts Are Tax-deductible   If you want an itemized tax deduction for your gift, it must be made to a qualified tax-exempt charity, usually one that qualifies under tax code Section 501(c)(3). If the charity is not well known, you can find out whether a charity qualifies by asking for a copy of the organization's "exemption letter."

The Simple Truth

Women are more likely to volunteer than men. In 1998, 62 percent of women donated their time for a good cause, compared to 49 percent of men.

—*Independent Sector, a Washington D.C.-based research organization*

Follow in Their Footsteps
As if doing good by helping others wasn't reason enough to donate to charity, you may be inspired by the philanthropic work of others. Women, in particular, are becoming

more philanthropic and are making a greater impact on charitable programs than ever before. The leading ladies among today's most active philanthropists include:

- Catherine B. Reynolds, a successful businesswoman, who pledged $38 million to the National Museum of American History and $1 million to Ford's Theatre.
- Meg Whitman, chief executive of eBay, who gave $30 million to Princeton University.
- Talk show host Oprah Winfrey, who has donated millions of dollars to support the empowerment and education of women, children, and families worldwide through The Oprah Winfrey Foundation.
- Sara Lee Schupf, the namesake of the famous frozen desserts, who used much of her inheritance to start a family foundation with a multimillion dollar endowment to encourage women in science.
- Author Sallie Bingham, who gave $10 million to the Kentucky Foundation for Women.
- Catherine Muther, former executive at 3Com and Cisco Systems, who used $5 million in earnings from her lucrative stock options to create a fund that supports women's initiatives, from girls' sports programs to female entrepreneurs.
- Joan Kroc, widow of McDonald's founder Ray Kroc, who gave $80 million to San Diego's Salvation Army.

Money Lessons for the Next Generation

What better legacy can you create than to have your children carry on your values? That's why it is so important to talk to your children about money and the role money plays in a person's life. What's more, giving your kids the tools to manage their own money wisely can instill in them the same sense of accomplishment and self-confidence that you experienced by learning about smart financial planning. They will also be better prepared to deal with the challenges of the workplace, the lure of credit card offers, and the nervous excitement of starting a family, buying a house, or even launching their own business.

Of course, teaching your children about money goes beyond practicing their math skills with your change purse. Your children can learn about money and how it works in their lives in ten basic areas.

> "To bring up a child in the way he should go, travel that way yourself once in a while."
>
> JOSH BILLINGS

Teaching Children Responsibility

- Model good behavior, since your children will do as you do and not just as you say.
- Let your own word be your bond: It's better to promise something small or not at all than to promise something wonderful and not deliver.
- Encourage independence. Allow your children to handle as much responsibility as will challenge and motivate them.

Teaching Children Good Work Habits

- Teach time management. Show your kids how to break projects down into smaller pieces that can be accomplished step by step.
- Make work a social activity. Teach them to enjoy doing the things necessary to keep themselves clean, healthy, financially secure, and learning.
- Don't take over if your children shirk their responsibility. If your children take on household chores and are unwilling or unable to perform, teach them the consequences of their inaction.

Teaching Children Enterprise

- Develop your children's computer literacy. Give them a project to research on the Internet, such as a large purchase or a family vacation, and allow plenty of time to complete it.
- Help your children create their own business. A baby sitting, lawn care, or pet care service can teach children a lot about finding customers, collecting pay, and keeping records.
- Read and tell stories about people who have achieved big dreams, pushed the limits of the known world, or transformed the economic structure of our lives.

Teaching Children Charity

- Encourage your children to volunteer. Your children can work with animals, volunteer at the hospital or a nursing home, or contact a business where they'd like to work and offer to be a nonpaid intern.
- Teach charity by example. Make charity a regular family ritual, whether it's Thanksgiving Day at the homeless center or a regular trip for Meals on Wheels.
- Teach your children to give the gift of love. Nonmonetary gifts are appreciated, especially by family, so encourage your children to make relatives a gift or provide a service.

Teaching Children Objectivity

- Discuss politics and economics openly in your home. Have a debate on a candidate's position or a ballot initiative.
- Keep your children focused on what's important and teach them not to be too impressed with status. Wealth is not about wearing someone else's name on your clothing or owning the coolest gadget.
- Reverse roles with your children. The next time they want the latest toy, ask them to assume your role. Would they buy the toy for you? What else could they do with the money?

Teaching Children Cooperation

- Make your family money meetings exciting. Make popcorn, display a flipchart of family financial goals, or pay out interest on your younger children's savings at this time. Money can be a game, not a chore.
- Teach your children to think "win-win." When conflicts arise, ask them, how can we settle this dispute in a way that satisfies all of us? What do we each really want?
- Make your children aware of the portion of the family budget that applies to them. Rather than telling a child "We can't afford that," it might be better to say, "We've allocated $50 to that category and we've already spent that this month."

Teaching Children Basic Money Skills

- Teach young children the basics of money. Make sure your elementary age children know the difference between the denominations of money and know how to count their change when they buy something.
- Talk to your children while shopping. Explain how discounts work, let your children see how coupons will save money, and teach your children to comparison-shop.
- Let your children observe the negotiation process. Next time you buy a car, ask their opinion of the value, what tactics to use, and how to get the best deal.

"No one has yet realized the wealth of sympathy, the kindness and generosity hidden in the soul of a child. The effort of every true education should be to unlock that treasure."

EMMA GOLDMAN

Teaching Children Wise Saving and Spending

- Put savings first. Once your children have determined how much money to save from their allowance, make sure they set the money aside first and only spend what's left.
- Help your children make lists. Together you can make a shopping list for the school supplies they need, or the holiday gifts they need to buy.
- Let your children make mistakes. If they run out of money, don't bail them out. If you bail them out now, they'll expect much bigger handouts from you when they become adults.

Teaching Children Personal Finance and Investing

- Look for personal finance classes at your children's school. These classes can greatly help children improve their understanding of money and the role it plays.
- Make the concept of taxes real. Explain the hidden costs that taxes add to the economic system. Show your child how much the gasoline tax adds to the cost of gas and how much sales tax adds to the cost of the toy. Where does the money go?
- If you are an investor, share your knowledge with your children. Teach your children how to read the stock quotes in the newspaper or how to look them up on the Internet.

Teaching Children Financial Decision Making

- Start allowances early, around age five or six. Don't let your children get in the habit of asking you for cash rather than choosing responsibly how to save and spend their own money.
- Teach children how credit cards work. If children know how the cards work before they get one, they may be able to handle the responsibility better than teens who get a card and know nothing about them.
- Start a family Money Club. Your older teens may benefit from being included in a Money Club where they can report to other family members about money issues and help make group decisions.

"Don't be afraid to give your best to what seemingly are small jobs.
Every time you conquer one it makes you that much stronger.
If you do the little jobs well, the big ones will tend to take care of
themselves."

DALE CARNEGIE

Small Steps to Becoming a Money Star

1. Money has a natural ebb and flow. Spend ten minutes focusing on the ebb and flow of money in your life. Sometimes there is more than you need, and other times there is less than you want. This exercise will help give you perspective the next time your money seems to have "deserted" you. It will be back soon with the next flow tide.

2. Before you can teach your children about money, you must understand how you learned yourself. Revisit the section in Chapter 3 about your money style, and consider how the lessons you learned about money growing up affect your priorities as an adult. Do your spending and saving habits reflect your true values, or are they reflexive behaviors you inherited from your parents? Which values and beliefs do you want to pass on to your children?

3. Make a list of ten money thoughts you have had in the past two weeks. Were they positive or negative? How could you treat yourself better? How can you send a message of respect and love to yourself with your money?

4. Make a plan for giving back. Create a list of the causes and organizations you believe in, and brainstorm ways you can best offer support. Find your passion, and focus your gifts. Once you've decided where to direct your energy, write down your pledge, whether it's to donate time or money or both. Post it someplace you will see it often, to remind yourself of your commitment.

5. Form a support group. Do you know other women who could use financial guidance? Invite them for a casual gathering at your home, and talk about the money issues that concern you. Odds are, some members of the group will be able to offer support and advice to others facing similar issues. If there is interest among your friends and peers, you could hold regular meetings and start a Money Club of your own!

Four Easy Steps to Starting a Money Club

When you start a Money Club, you are starting a personal adventure in financial freedom. Money Clubs are an incredibly successful way for women to get together to achieve their money dreams and support each other on their journey to prosperity. It's a great opportunity to make new friends and meet old ones while you learn from others and motivate each other every step of the way. Starting a Money Club is a fun, easy way to resolve financial issues that always seem to get in your way. Onward!

1. Before You Begin

Before you start a Money Club, take a few minutes to ask yourself these questions:

Who Will I Invite to Join the Money Club?

You can invite friends, family members, or acquaintances to join the Money Club. Coworkers, business associates, and neighbors are perfect candidates. If you belong to any kind of group—a hobby club, investment club, book club, or simply a group of friends—you can bring the group together to improve each member's financial life.

How Often Will the Club Meet?

Money Clubs seem to work best when meeting every other week, but you can set any schedule you like. Some Clubs meet once a month, while others meet as often as once a week.

When Will the Club Meet?

The Money Club can meet at any time—as a brown bag lunch meeting at work, during the evening, during the weekend, or during the day—whatever works best for members. Most meetings last about an hour.

How Many People Will Be in the Club, and Where Will We Meet?

Most clubs have between four and ten members. Before you determine how many members your club will have, decide where the Money Club will meet. If meetings are in your home, you might want to keep it to eight or fewer members. Ideally, no one member will have to host every meeting of the Club. Members are usually eager to host a meeting of the Club at their houses. If your library, church, community center, YMCA, or a local restaurant or bookstore has a meeting room available, this can also work well. Any place that's clean and dry will work just fine.

Now that you have a clear vision of what you want for your Money Club, you can find others who are motivated to improve their financial lives.

2. Choosing Members

You can find eager Money Club members among your friends, business associates, neighbors, or even online. Anyone who is interested in improving her financial life is a good candidate for the Money Club. When choosing new members, keep the following in mind:

- *Invite motivated people.* Choose people who truly want to make changes in their financial lives and are willing to make an effort to learn and grow.
- *Choose positive, supportive people.* Don't invite people who say, "It can't be done." Choose people who will support others' dreams and goals. Avoid naysayers and negative people.
- *Leave junior high behind.* Avoid factions and politicking. Choose people who want to work together toward financial independence, not gossips or backstabbers.
- *Spread the word.* Anyone can benefit from being in a Money Club. Although the concept was intended for women helping other women, men can form their own clubs or join coeducational clubs. With adult supervision, teens also can benefit from joining a Money Club. You may find that more people want to join your Club than can comfortably fit in your meeting area. Perhaps you can help them start their own Club at another location or time.

3. Ready, Set, Go!

Your group will need to complete some basic tasks to get ready for the financial journey ahead. First, be sure to share all members' addresses, phone numbers, and e-mail addresses. One member can gather this information and type it up in an e-mail for the group or make copies to distribute at the next meeting. Also ask each member to sign the Money Club Pledges that appear at the end of this section.

Name your club. Your club should choose a name that suits your personalities, something like Money Bags, Girls Just Wanna Have Funds, Hot Money Mamas, Super Savers, or simply The Financials. Find inspiration in movie names, clever sayings, popular songs, and plays on words.

In most Money Clubs, group leadership rotates from meeting to meeting, giving each member a chance to direct the group. If your group prefers that you lead every week, be a steward of the group and ensure that everyone gets a chance to hear and be heard.

At the first meeting, welcome the members and prospective members and make them feel comfortable in the group. Here are some tips to help the group come together:

- *Provide refreshments.* Food is always a good way to break the ice. Just remember, you don't have to be a French pastry chef to buy a box of cookies and provide coffee, tea, soda, or water. If you want to make a light meal, go for it.
- *Make sure the room is comfortable.* Adjust the lighting, the seating, and so forth to make sure everyone can see and hear everyone else and no one is leaning over the edge of her chair, trying to figure out what's going on.
- *Introduce everyone.* Ask each group member to share a bit about herself and why she decided to join the Money Club.
- *Don't dominate.* Allow everyone to speak without dominating the conversation. There are no wrong or silly questions. It is up to all members to make sure that everyone feels comfortable and included. Don't try to steal the limelight. Provide an opportunity for every member of the group to be heard.
- *Be a friend.* Support your fellow Money Club members in their financial journey. Encourage their dreams, goals, and the whole "educational process"—you know, that stuff we're here for!
- *Have a blast.* While you're learning about money, don't forget to have fun!

Emphasize the importance of attendance and participation. If members attend and participate, their money skills naturally will improve. No elaborate preparation or study is required. Just trust in the process of learning. Money Clubs are not like instant pudding: Don't expect results in 10 minutes or less.

4. Enter the Zone

Money Zones are the heart of the Money Club concept. Each Money Zone helps you figure out (or at least try to!) a specific financial subject, such as credit card debt, savings, or financial goals. You can review the full list of Money Zones in the Money Truths and Dreams Questionnaire in Chapter 1. You'll find the module for each Money Zone on the Internet at www.moneyclubs.com. Each Money Zone module has these parts to cover in your meeting:

Icebreakers

Icebreakers are short exercises that help you learn more about each other. These are fun (and often very funny) games and questions. Geared to your chosen subject, they will get you laughing and talking in the Zone.

Things to Talk About

These are discussion topics for the Zone that will help your group brainstorm ideas and exchange information. This is where you learn, explore, and find out how to change your life. Dig into each Zone, and amazing things will happen!

Catch Yourself Doing Something Right

Share your recent money triumphs with your fellow group members, and give yourself a pat on the back for all of your hard work!

What Will You Do Today?

Decide how you will take action toward your financial dreams. What Small Steps are you going to take before the next meeting to move your life forward? In other words, What Will You Do Today?

Money Magic

Set an affirmation that will help you stay on track until the next meeting. You can use this affirmation to help focus your mind if you start to drift into negative territory.

Just for You

This part of the Money Zone is a private exercise you can do by yourself, before the next meeting, to learn more about this financial area. No one will see your answers to this section. This is for you and you alone!

Additional Meetings in the Zone

You may find that your group has a lot to talk about in this Zone, so if you like, schedule the next meeting to continue your discussion, using this same format. You can also delve deeper by having members review the suggested readings, and then go through the discussion points at your next meeting. Or invite an expert to talk to your group about the Zone.

That's it, ladies! Follow these simple rules at each meeting, and you will see amazing results. Your Money Club is yours to develop and grow in any way you want. As you shape your club, you will be shaping your financial life. As you help yourself, you will be helping others.

The Money Club concept works. It is founded on years of research, and we know that if you participate to your fullest, you will grow and prosper. As you move forward, let us know what you discover in your club, suggest new Money Zones for us to develop, and tell us about your successes. With your permission, we'll include your comments on the Money Club web site at www.moneyclubs.com. Go to the web site to get up-to-date information and ideas.

In the Money Club, money grows in groups. Share your success with others. Encourage your friends to form Money Clubs of their own. Together, we can make a huge difference, as we take personal responsibility and help each other move ahead.

We are here for you and want to make a lasting difference in your life. We are your Money Guides. Please e-mail guides@moneyclubs.com.

The Money Club™ Confidentiality Agreement

All information disclosed during Money Club meetings is to be kept private among the members of the Money Club.

I promise not to disclose, in whole or in part, in any form or by any means, verbal or written, the information told to me in confidence by fellow Money Club members.

I understand that violation of this confidentiality pledge is grounds for expulsion from the Money Club.

Signed _____   Date _____

The Money Club™ No Selling Agreement

Money Clubs are designed for educational purposes only, and may not be used in connection with any commercial endeavors.

Organizations, companies, and/or businesses may not become members of Money Clubs.

Individuals may not use the Money Club to sell any product or service or for any other commercial purpose.

Illegal and/or unauthorized uses of Money Clubs will be investigated, and appropriate legal action will be taken, including without limitation, civil, criminal, and injunctive redress.

Signed _____   Date _____

Helpful Resources

The following books, organizations, and web sites offer general information about financial planning and managing life transitions to help you get started on your path to financial success.

Books

ABCs of Divorce for Women, Carol Ann Wilson and Ginita Wall (Quantum Publishing, 2003)

Best Intentions: Ensuring Your Estate Plan Delivers Both Wealth and Wisdom, Colleen Barney and Victoria Collins (Dearborn Trade Publishing, 2002)

Conscious Spending for Couples: Seven Skills for Financial Harmony, Deborah Knuckey (John Wiley & Sons, 2002)

Divorce and Money: How to Make the Best Financial Decisions During Divorce, Violet Woodhouse, Dale Fetherling, Victoria F. Collins, and M. C. Blakeman (Nolo Press, 2002)

Finding Your Way After Your Spouse Dies, Marta Felber (Ave Maria Press, 2000)

Get a Financial Life: Personal Finance in Your Twenties and Thirties, Beth Kobliner (Fireside, 2000)

Girl, Get Your Money Straight! Glinda Bridgforth (Broadway Books, 2002)

If Success Is a Game, These Are the Rules, Cherie Carter-Scott (Bantam Doubleday Dell, 2000)

The Laws of Money, The Lessons of Life: Keep What You Have and Create What You Deserve, Suze Orman and Linda Mead (Free Press, 2003)

Mind, Body, Soul & Money: Putting Your Life in Balance, Carolle Jean-Murat, MD (Mosley Publishing Group, 2002)

Money Shy to Money Sure: A Woman's Road Map to Financial Well-Being, Olivia Mellan and Sherry Christie (Walker & Co., 2001)

The Motley Fool's Guide to Couples and Cash: How to Handle Money with Your Honey, Dayana Yochim and David Gardner (Motley Fool, 2003)

One Up on Wall Street: How to Use What You Already Know to Make Money in the Market, Peter Lynch and John Rothchild (Fireside, 2000)

Prenups for Lovers: A Romantic Guide to Prenuptial Agreements, Arlene G. Dubin (Villard Books, 2001)

The Retirement Savings Time Bomb . . . And How to Diffuse It, Ed Slott (Viking Press, 2003)

Rich Dad, Poor Dad: What the Rich Teach Their Kids About Money—That the Poor and Middle Class Do Not! Robert Kiyosaki (Warner Books, 2000)

Secrets of Six-Figure Women: Surprising Strategies to Up Your Earnings and Change Your Life, Barbara Stanny (HarperCollins, 2002)

She Wins, You Win: A Guidebook for Making Women More Powerful, Gail Evans (Gotham Books, 2003)

Smart Couples Finish Rich: 9 Steps to Creating a Rich Future for You and Your Partner, David Bach (Broadway Books, 2002)

Stepwives: Ten Steps to Help Ex-Wives and Step-Mothers End the Struggle and Put the Kids First, Louise Oxhorn, Lynne Oxhorn-Ringwood, and Marjorie Krausz (Fireside, 2002)

Talking Money: Everything You Need to Know about Your Finances and Your Future, Jean Sherman Chatzky (Warner Books, 2002)

Taming the Tuition Tiger: Getting the Money to Graduate—with 529 Plans, Scholarships, Financial Aid, and More, Kathy Kristof (Bloomberg Press, 2003)

Unmarried to Each Other: The Essential Guide to Living Together as an Unmarried Couple, Dorian Solot and Marshall Miller (Marlowe & Co., 2002)

Use the News: How to Separate the Noise from the Investment Nuggets and Make Money in Any Economy, Maria Bartiromo (HarperBusiness, 2002)

The Wealthy Spirit: Daily Affirmations for Financial Stress Reduction, Chellie Campbell (Sourcebooks Trade, 2002)

What's Your Net Worth? Click Your Way to Wealth, Jennifer Openshaw (Perseus Publishing, 2001)

The Wise Inheritor: A Guide to Managing, Investing, and Enjoying Your Inheritance, Ann Perry (Broadway Books, 2003)

Your Money or Your Life, Joe Dominguez and Vicki Robin (Penguin USA, 1999)

Web Sites

Women's Institute for Financial Education (www.wife.org) is the oldest nonprofit organization dedicated to providing financial education to women in their quest for financial independence. It was started by the authors in 1988.

Money Clubs (www.moneyclubs.com) is the source for information about the Money Clubs, an incredibly successful way for women to get together to achieve their money dreams and support each other on their journey to prosperity.

GE Center for Financial Learning (www.financiallearning.com) provides an easy-to-use, objective, comprehensive web site under the guidance of an unpaid board of experts. Ginita Wall has served on this advisory board since its inception.

PracticalMoneySkills.com is a free web site sponsored by VISA designed to help educators, parents, and students practice better money management for life.

America Saves (www.americasaves.org) is a nationwide campaign to help individuals and families save and build wealth, offering information, advice, and encouragement.

Equality in Marriage Institute (www.equalityinmarriage.org) is dedicated to educating women and men about the importance of equality in marriage and divorce.

At www.bankrate.com, you can find out current rates for CDs, mortgages, and more. This site also offers good articles on various financial topics.

The Small Business Administration site (www.sba.gov) has heaps of information about starting and running a small business, including sections on financing your venture, managing employees, and networking to expand your company's reach.

The Online Women's Business Center (www.onlinewbc.gov), a program sponsored by the Small Business Administration's Office of Women's Business Ownership, offers lots of information on business basics, as well as grants and other funding opportunities for women entrepreneurs, mentoring programs, links to local services, and more.

SOHO Online (www.soho.org) is an excellent resource for small office home office entrepreneurs, offering advice on marketing, finance, legal issues, technology, recommended books, and other topics.

The Dollar Stretcher–Living Better for Less (www.stretcher.com) is your weekly resource for simple living. Gary Foreman, editor of *The Dollar Stretcher*, is also a columnist for WIFE's web site.

LowerMyBills.com lets you automatically research, compare, and lower all your recurring monthly bills, including telephone, cable, Internet service, credit cards, insurance, and other common expenses. Just type in the information you're seeking, and you'll be presented with a list of the rates for each available service provider.

Fantasy Stock Market (www.fantasystockmarket.com) is free, fun, and educational. Test and enhance your investment skills without using your own money. Features include a Personal Portfolio Tracker, Stock Quotes, Charting, Research, Most Requested Stocks, and Prizes.

Investopedia (www.investopedia.com) is a handy online dictionary for investing and financial information.

The Social Security Administration (www.ssa.gov) lets you go online to request your Personal Earnings and Benefits Statement and find out your estimated Social Security income in retirement.

Women's Institute for a Secure Retirement (www.wiser.heinz.org), created in 1996 by the Heinz Family Foundation, is an independent nonprofit organization devoted to educating women about retirement issues.

SavingforCollege.com is the Internet guide to 529 plans, where you can shop for and manage accounts with descriptions and links to all the state plans, performance results, and recent federal developments.

Money Life (www.ivillage.com/money) is iVillage's comprehensive financial resource center. Our very own Ginita Wall serves as an expert at the site.

mPower Café (www.mpowercafe.com) provides a comfortable place for you to learn about retirement planning and investing.

Consumer Credit Counseling Services (www.credit.org) is dedicated to helping people out of financial trouble. These services can consolidate bills into one easy monthly payment, lower interest charges, and teach you how to pay with cash and live on a sensible budget.

College for Divorce Specialists (www.cdsCollege.com) is a great source to find a Certified Divorce Specialist who has completed specialized training in the financial issues of divorce.

WomansWallStreet.com has articles and columns about investing and careers.

Stepfamily Association of America (www.saafamilies.org) is a national, nonprofit membership organization that provides educational information and resources about stepfamilies.

Divorce Magazine (www.divorcemagazine.com) offers hundreds of articles, expert advice, links to other divorce related web sites, and much more, to help you not only survive but thrive through the process of divorce.

Making Lemonade–The Single Parents' Network (www.makinglemonade.com) is chock full of articles and resources for single parents. Editor Jody Seidler is also a columnist for WIFE's web site.

Nolo.com has articles and information about almost every aspect of everyday law, from divorce to estate planning to dog law.

AARP (www.aarp.org) is the nation's largest organization of mid-life and older persons. This site offers loads of information about financial, social, and health issues. It also offers a program for dealing with grief and loss (www.aarp.org/griefandloss).

SmartMoney.com (www.smartmoney.com/retirement) has a special retirement section, with loads of informative articles, stock and fund quotes, worksheets, calculators, and special sections on IRAs, 401(k)s, and other retirement planning vehicles.

The American Institute of Philanthropy (www.charitywatch.org) is a nationally prominent charity watchdog service whose purpose is to help donors make informed giving decisions.

Index

About the Authors

Candace Bahr, CEA, CDS, is one of the top 10 financial advisors in the United States according to *Registered Rep,* a leading industry magazine for investment professionals. She is a successful entrepreneur and wealth manager with more than 20 years of experience. As a managing partner of Bahr Investment Group, she specializes in portfolio design and implementation for high net worth individuals, with a focus on the needs of women in transition.

In addition to being a full-time financial advisor, Candace is a highly regarded educator and cofounder of the Women's Institute for Financial Education (WIFE.org). She is listed in the International Register's Who's Who in Executives for 2003.

An accomplished and dynamic speaker, Candace has motivated a variety of audiences to take charge of their financial lives. In addition to her public speaking engagements, millions of people have watched Candace's weekly financial reports over the last seven years on KDCI/CNN Headline News. She has appeared on MSNBC, CNBC, PBS, and several network stations throughout the country.

Candace is also the regular "Money Matters" columnist for *Décor & Style* magazine and has been recently featured along with WIFE in many nationally known publications, including *Fortune, Bloomberg, Money Magazine, Kiplinger's,* and *The New York Times.*

Ginita Wall, CPA, CFP®, CDS, is a nationally recognized expert on the subject of women and money. Quoted in *The Wall Street Journal, USA Today, Newsweek, Money, Good Housekeeping, Redbook, Family Circle,* and other publications, she has appeared on the *NBC Nightly News, MSNBC, CNNfn, National Public Radio, CBS This Morning,* and the Discovery Channel's *Home Matters.* She is a regular guest on numerous other radio and television broadcasts.

Ginita specializes in guiding people through life transitions, including divorce and widowhood. Cofounder of WIFE and originator of the acclaimed Second Saturday program (What Women Need to Know about Divorce), Ginita Wall is a well-known specialist in the financial complexities of divorce. Author of eight books, including the recent *ABCs of Divorce for Women,* she's been named one of the 250 top financial advisors in the country by *Worth Magazine* eight years in a row. She is also listed in *Who's Who in Finance.*

Ginita writes extensively for a number of publications and web sites, including iVillage.com and Cox Interactive Media. She also serves as an advisor for the General Electric Center for Financial Learning and *Divorce Magazine,* and she has been an advisor to the American Academy of Matrimonial Lawyers.

Ginita is a frequent speaker for women's groups, conventions, professional groups, and philanthropic organizations.

How to Reach Us

If you would like more information about the Money Clubs or the nonprofit Women's Institute for Financial Education, you can contact us at the web sites www.wife.org or www.MoneyClubs.com, or write to us at P.O. Box 910014, San Diego, CA 92191 (phone 760-736-1660).

Contact us if you would like information on:

Donations: your contributions to WIFE are tax deductible

Educational programs, such as Second Saturday (divorce), Suddenly Single (widowhood), or My Brilliant Career (career)

Keynote speeches

Customized content for your web site or publication

Scheduling the Money Club seminar "It's More Than Money—It's Your Life!" for your organization or conference

How your corporation or organization can join with us to make a difference in women's lives